Cyberspace and Cybersecurity

Second Edition

George Kostopoulos

CRC Press
Taylor & Francis Group
Boca Raton London New York

CRC Press is an imprint of the
Taylor & Francis Group, an **informa** business

AN AUERBACH BOOK

CRC Press
Taylor & Francis Group
6000 Broken Sound Parkway NW, Suite 300
Boca Raton, FL 33487-2742

First issued in paperback 2020

ISBN 13: 978-0-367-65755-0 (pbk)
ISBN 13: 978-1-138-05771-5 (hbk)

Library of Congress Cataloging-in-Publication Data

Names: Kostopoulos, George K., 1939- author.
Title: Cyberspace and cybersecurity / George Kostopoulos.
Description: Second edition. | Boca Raton, Florida : CRC Press, [2017] |
Includes bibliographical references and index.
Identifiers: LCCN 2017018342| ISBN 9781138057715 (hardback : acid-free paper)
| ISBN 9781315116488 (e-book) | ISBN 9781351653077 (e-book) | ISBN 9781351651653
(e-book) | ISBN 9781351641937 (e-book)
Subjects: LCSH: Computer networks--Security measures. | Cyberspace--Security
measures. | Computer crimes--Prevention.
Classification: LCC TK5105.59 .K6787 2017 | DDC 005.8--dc23
LC record available at https://lccn.loc.gov/2017018342

Visit the Taylor & Francis Web site at
http://www.taylorandfrancis.com

and the CRC Press Web site at
http://www.crcpress.com

Contents

Foreword

2017 and the years that will follow bring continued changes to the cybersecurity universe. The "silver bullet" point solution is passé. Integrated and orchestrated cyber solutions are now in vogue. Automated security responses, which frankly this security community needs to collaborate on more diligently, is the direction in which we need to head. Changes must be made as current detection and protection models are completely overwhelmed. Next generation firewalls can't arrive soon enough to help cope with advanced attacks, data breaches, ransomware or even unusual user behavior. The future of cybersecurity resides in the combined approach of machine learning and threat intelligence, as we can no longer worry about false-positives. Emphasis needs to be placed on "how" to solve the security problem versus the predominant industry mindset focused on "what" the problem is. This is where "out of the box," non-traditional thinking for an integrated, interoperable solution is paramount—one, which will enable closing the security gap between the relentless attacker and the response time needed from the tireless defender.

Saying all this, it's still evident to me that we operate today with mostly 20th-century tools with an 18th-century mindset all while trying to address a serious 21st-century problem. This remains our *cyberspace* challenge. We have a threat landscape that is enormous, connecting digitally and growing quickly. Today 10 billion devices are connected to the Internet with predictions that in just 3 years, by 2020, this number will jump to 50 billion devices. That's a million new devices per hour! Yes, we need to be VERY concerned. It is my belief that the Internet, however, is not broken. It's what we put on the Internet that's broken. The first step forward to solving any problem is to understand it. This is where Dr. George Kostopoulos' second edition of *Cyberspace and Cybersecurity* captures key contributing elements to both the risks and vulnerabilities found within this man-made cyber domain.

Next, the demand for information security professionals continues to rise dramatically. Even with the severe cybersecurity workforce shortage, we can add another 100,000+ job openings by year-end. The time is now to be fearless and to take a personal interest, as this is an industry with negative unemployment. As the complexity and attack numbers increase, coupled with the growing Internet of Things (IoT), increased regulatory and compliance scrutiny, and pressures from industry boards, companies have found it necessary to reevaluate their security risk posture. Furthermore, employees today compound the bring your own device (BYOD) issue by carrying their personal IoT devices across physical and asymmetric security boundaries. The demand for fresh cybersecurity thinking will therefore continue to expand, unfortunately very much leading the supply. This problem will continue to grow for the foreseeable future. In addition, cybercrime damages will continue to rise (costing the world $6 trillion annually by 2021), up from $3 trillion last year. Malware, such as ransomware, will be the fastest growing threat in terms of new attacks and costs. Finally, globally and over the next 5 years from 2017–2021, spending on cybersecurity products and services will exceed $1 trillion cumulatively. Saying our environment has a great deal to contend with is merely an understatement.

From a futures perspective, data bandwidth is increasing, making it harder to inspect traffic inside our networks and data-centers. This problem is compounded when more and more traffic becomes encrypted, a seemingly good thing, except when it comes to security inspection. One can only imagine if all malware one day soon used SSL to send out commands to its command & control (C2) center.

Bottom line, if we're not great at protecting devices today, we will really be in trouble when we get to 50 billion (plus) devices. We therefore need to understand the cyberspace domain much better, and we certainly need to be much more responsive.

Looking ahead, there will be major clashes between privacy and security, as advances are made on both fronts from various legislative actions. We will also likely see the U.S. weigh tougher response options to such activities, not limited to cyber tactics, but also including diplomatic, law enforcement, economic, and other policy means. The future must therefore summon smart ways to automate security and this includes leveraging non-traditional means, to include via the Cloud.

In summary, George's second edition remains a timely read… especially with its updated chapters on industry vulnerabilities. This book continues to cover a great deal of ground and is a trusted "go to" tutorial providing a comprehensive checklist, shared in an understandable and educational manner. Dr. Kostopoulos reinforces his awareness to the industry's critical attributes, their capabilities, and capacities found within *"Cyberspace and Cybersecurity."* Each chapter deals with an important and realistic aspect of cybersecurity together with the vulnerabilities and the risks. Together, the chapters provide an excellent overview of this exceedingly complex topic, a perspective that has equally horizontal as well as vertical implications, and will keep the reader cognizant of the interrelationships among the disparate disciplines making up cyberspace. The author's use of current examples is in effect a complementary way of doing our work for us. Readers will be taught not only where to invest their time in wisely understanding the critical facets but also shown the awareness of how to maintain solid security hygiene. In retrospect, this updated second edition really is an invaluable resource.

Beyond the numerous recommendations shared throughout this book, Dr. Kostopoulos' knowledge of what it takes to survive in this man-made domain is amplified in his desire to extend a typically one-way street of cybersecurity awareness through the underlying theme of helpfulness to remain more secure. In the end, this is probably what I admire most about the approach this author has taken. Again, this second edition easily takes a difficult subject area with all its dynamics and elects to provide the reader with the value of having established guidelines for building a secure organization—right from the start.

Riley Repko
CEO, Trusted Cyber Solutions LLC

Preface

There is an expression that is repeatedly heard: *every business is a technology business*. Today, we can safely rephrase it to *every business is a cyber business*. Indeed, practically every human activity has a cyber dimension. At work, we are in touch with our professional environment with our eyes glued to the screen and our hand glued to the mouse; at home we are similarly reaching friends. On the road, we use our Web-powered mobile phone to stay in touch, and, tired at home, we search the Web to view a nice movie and relax.

Besides our physical dimension, we all now have a cyber dimension. In addition to being citizens of X or Y country, we are also citizens of cyberspace. There is no need for a physical passport in order to travel in, within, and out. Actually, it is needed and we do have one—it is our IP address—and it imprints itself in hundreds of places as our requests and replies travel in cyberspace. This is a virtual "country" with everything one may find in the physical world, except cyber police.

The Modern World

The continuous technological developments of the twentieth century in telecommunications and computing, supported by the advances in semiconductor chemistry and physics, progressively led to the feasibility of inexpensive networks and associated devices. A major end-product of this century-long, continuous, interdisciplinary, and intensive technological race has been the Internet, also referred to as the World Wide Web, WWW, or the Web. The Internet serves as our global, as well as local, communications infrastructure through which practically all human interactions pass. Consequently, it has become the virtual oxygen of the planet, and its failure will lead the planet to suffocation.

Prior to the Internet there were, indeed, global networks, but they were serving specific sectors—banking, telecommunications, military, or news services. While the Internet's technological development has been rather evolutionary, its impact in the world has been absolutely revolutionary. It only took the first decade of the twenty-first century for the Internet to wrap the world in its web, from which it is impossible to get out.

Over time, and parallel to the term *Web*, a new term has entered all languages. This is *cyberspace*, which refers to a collection of networks, activities, and new human attitudes. Beyond this definition, *cyberspace* can be described as the habitat of a *cybersociety*, with a multitude of sectors that run parallel to those of the traditional society.

Cyberspace has given the world unprecedented power, as well as unprecedented dependence, and, unfortunately, a loss of privacy. With the Internet's ubiquitous presence, many new products and services have been created, all absolutely counting on the availability of the Internet. In today's world, cyberspace is an integral part of any enterprise. As a consequence, cybersecurity is an absolute prerequisite. Cybersecurity must safeguard the following four principles that are absolutely needed for any trusted cyberspace engagement.

- *Confidentiality*. Data transmitted or stored are *private*, to be viewed only by authorized persons.
- *Integrity*. Data transmitted or stored are *authentic*—free of errors made in storage or in transit.
- *Availability*. Data transmitted or stored are *accessible* to all authorized.
- *Non-Repudiation*. Data transmitted or stored are of *indisputable authenticity*, especially when supported by acceptable digital certificates, digital signatures, or other explicit identifiers.

Cybersecurity measures must support the above four principles. Cybersecurity measures are expected to confirm, beyond reasonable doubt, the identity of users for the purpose of *authentication*; and to attest the validity of the *authorization* parameters presented by a user. In addition to the above, Cybersecurity measures must also be able to provide *accountability* through an electronic audit trail. Such a trail should be able to attribute each and every activity, taken place in the information system, to an action initiated by an identifiable network terminal, which will lead to a person.

Today, all communication and computation technologies have merged, creating a seamless medium where digitized data, text, sound, images, and video travel at electronic speeds from one end of the world to the other. Such activities implement functions and operations that cannot be realized in any other way. Cyberspace has engulfed all aspects of life, and each and every aspect of life has some direct or indirect dependence on it. Consequently, the uninterrupted, unobstructed, and secure availability of cyberspace constitutes a prerequisite to the efficient performance of practically all sectors of society.

Purpose and Audience

The purpose of this book is dual. The first purpose is to offer the readers an educated awareness of the issues that affect cyberspace and cybersecurity, as they stand today, and the second one is to provide the necessary infrastructure on which the readers can build their own cyberspace and cybersecurity expertise in a lifelong learning mode. As for the addressed audience, it is again dual. The first audience is the non-cybersecurity techies who want to tip-toe into cyberspace and cybersecurity and get a flavor of the wide spectrum of related issues before they dedicate themselves to cyber defense. The second audience is non-techies concerned with cyberspace and cybersecurity who want to get a head start on this very important aspect of modern life.

The Book

Cyberspace and cybersecurity are two wagons of a fast-moving train, and this book aims to help the reader pick up speed and hop on the train. Once on it and with the acquired background, the reader will be able to follow the technological advances and eventually contribute to making the train safer. Toward that end, the book has been arranged into twelve chapters.

Chapter 1. *Vulnerabilities in Information Systems.* In this chapter quantifying and measuring vulnerability are discussed, along with ways to avoid it through secure coding. Also, the Security Content Automation Protocol developed by the National Institute for Standards and Technology is reviewed, which is extensively used in measuring vulnerability in software systems.

Chapter 2. *Vulnerabilities in the Organization.* Here, organization-related vulnerabilities are reviewed. They include access authorization and user authentication, as well as human factors in information security and ways to minimize risk. Also covered are the wireless networks—Bluetooth, Wi-Fi, and WiMAX—and measures to increase their security. Cloud computing is examined, along with its advantages and disadvantages.

Chapter 3. *Risks in Information Systems Infrastructure.* Examined here are the risks inherent in the various information system components, namely, hardware, software, and people, as well as in cyberspace at large. Also reviewed are available cyberspace insurance programs and the offered coverage.

Chapter 4. *Secure Information Systems.* In this chapter the need for an information security strategy is emphasized, pointing out asset identification as a cornerstone to such strategy. Also discussed are communication issues between assets and between users, focusing on email security. The chapter concludes with coverage of information security management, identifying and discussing the related issues.

Chapter 5. *Cybersecurity and the CIO.* Presented in this chapter are the traits a Chief Information Officer (CIO) needs to have to successfully address the cybersecurity challenges. Included are the personality characteristics, the needed education and experience, and the responsibilities that come with the position. Also examined is the changing role of the CIO from a super techie to a corporate strategic planner.

Chapter 6. *Building a Secure Organization.* Here, the prime concern is the business aspects of the organization and the continuity of these businesses should an adverse incident take place. Such an incident may not necessarily be a hostile intrusion, but possibly an act of nature. Also reviewed in this chapter is the need for a flexible corporate policy on data security and Internet use, and the compliance requirements that are posed by the cognizant authorities.

Chapter 7. *Cyberspace Intrusions.* In cybersecurity, the intrusion detection and prevention systems (IDPS) comprise the first line of protection. Here, the IDPS are discussed, focusing on configurations, capabilities, selection, management, and deployment. Also covered are the application-based software versus the appliance-based software, which now constitute the trend.

Chapter 8. *Cyberspace Defense.* This chapter focuses on the defense of the personal computer while in cyberspace against attacks and malware. Discussed are defense principles, techniques, and, most importantly, security tools. The tools reviewed include security analyzers, firewalls, antivirus software, file shredding, file encryption, and antiloggers. Here, the emphasis is that file security is in the hands of the user, and files can be totally safe if proper defense measures are applied.

Chapter 9. *Cyberspace and the Law.* Reviewed here are the various international and US federal laws and legal initiatives aiming at providing a legal infrastructure for what transpires over the Internet. Covered is the role the United Nations may play in establishing an international cyber order that will address intellectual property and cybercrime issues. Numerous US data and information-related laws are being reviewed, with ten prominent ones elaborated on.

Chapter 10. *Cyber Warfare and Homeland Security.* This chapter has three parts. The first is on cyber warfare, where cyber terrorism and cyber espionage are discussed, along with the hope of a possible cyber weapons treaty, a treaty that will curtail sovereign states from open cyber hostilities. The second part is on the US Department of Homeland Security and its role in the country's cyber preparedness. The third part views the Internet as a cyber ecosystem where its defense has to be in a worldwide distributed fashion. Also covered in this chapter is cyber training and its components.

Chapter 11. *Digital Currencies.* This chapter elaborates on the new concepts of cyber crypto currencies and their association to cybercrime. Thus, introducing the reader to the fast developing cyber currencies and their worldwide applications.

Chapter 12. *Transformation of Traditional Crimes into Cybercrimes.* This chapter has been authored by General Emmanuel Sfakianakis of the Greek Police Force. Gen. Sfakianakis's senior career has been in cyber forensics and cybercrime investigations and criminals prosecution. In his chapter, he illustrates how traditional crimes—from treason and espionage to human trafficking and draft evasion—have used electronic and cyber technologies, becoming difficult to discover and even more difficult to prosecute.

Each chapter has carefully designed exercises that will help the instructor lead students into their own research on chapter-related topics.

Acknowledgments

The author acknowledges and greatly appreciates the support of the Taylor & Francis editorial team, General Emmanuel Sfakianakis's contribution of Chapter Twelve, "The Evolution of Traditional Crime into Cybercrime," and Mr. Georges Raad's artistic design of the book's cover.

Author

Dr. George Kostopoulos was born in Athens, Greece, and pursued his university education in the United States, having earned a Bachelor of Science degree in electronics engineering, a Master's and PhD in electrical and computer engineering, and a Master's degree in international economics. His career started as a design engineer in the US defense industry. Later, in 1975, he joined academia, teaching and conducting research.

Dr. Kostopoulos is the author of numerous engineering papers, with his latest one challenging the effectiveness of the extensively used RSA Security Algorithm. He has written two engineering books titled, *Digital Engineering* and *Cyberspace and Cybersecurity*, with the latter also being published in Chinese. He is also the author of *Greece and the European Community*, analyzing the Treaty of Rome based on which the Community was formed.

Throughout his long academic career, Dr. Kostopoulos has been mostly in the United States with overseas professorial posts in China, Algeria, Saudi Arabia, the United Arab Emirates, Kuwait, Mexico, Germany and Greece. In Greece, he was a visiting professor at the Ioannina National University where he participated in the establishment of the Computer Science Department. He also taught *Principles of Taxation* at the Athens campus of the American LaVerne University.

In addition, he served as a consultant in European Union educational programs.

Presently based in Athens, Greece, Dr. Kostopoulos is a Professor of Cybersecurity at the University of Maryland University College in the university's online graduate program and also serves as a PhD advisor at the Al-Farabi Kazakh National University.

1

VULNERABILITIES IN INFORMATION SYSTEMS

Cyberspace: From terra incognita to terra nullius.

Introduction

Vulnerability in any system is the result of an intentional or unintentional omission or of an inadvertent design mistake that directly or indirectly leads to a compromise in the system's availability, integrity, or confidentiality. In information assurance, vulnerabilities may hide in each level of security, be it information access security, computer and storage security, communications security, or operational and physical security. In the case of information systems, the major components are people, hardware, and software. Therefore, the presence of vulnerabilities must be sought in each of these three areas. Figure 1.1 illustrates the factors that contribute to a secure cyberspace and the expectations out of cybersecurity.

Over half a century ago, designers, engineers, and scientists successfully quantified the concept of reliability for the design and maintenance of hardware and of software to a lesser extent. Today, efforts are being made to quantify the abstract concept of vulnerability as it applies to the security of information systems. The aim is to express the perceived level of security in a way that is measurable, standardized, and understood and to improve "… *the measurability of security through enumerating baseline security data, providing standardized languages as means for accurately communicating the information, and encouraging the sharing of the information with users by developing repositories*" [1].

Vulnerabilities can be hidden in data, code, and most often in processes that inadvertently allow unauthorized access. Intrusions, however, can occur not only in the Internet, but also in the intranets,

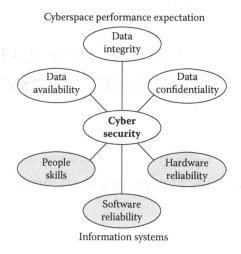

Figure 1.1   Cybersecurity serving as the infrastructure of cyberspace.

where most often security is not as strong. Security can be strengthened through intelligent mechanisms of authentication applied at both ends—the user side as well as the server side.

At the user side, authentication can be greatly fortified with the introduction of additional mechanisms, such as one-time passwords (OTP), provided via intra- or extra-Internet channels [2]. Such channels can be biometrics, questionnaires, or additional transparent parameters related to the user device identification numbers, such as manufacturer's serial number, Media Access Control (MAC), or International Mobile Equipment Identity (IMEI).

MAC, also referred to as *Physical Address*, is a 48-bit number, expressed as 12 hexadecimal digits, that uniquely identifies the network interface of the computer. The network interface circuit may be an insertable network card or may be embedded in the computer's motherboard. Figure 1.2 shows how the MAC address of a personal computer can be identified.

IMEI similarly uniquely identifies devices that utilize mobile telephony and is a number, usually 13 to 15 digits long. Mobile telephony providers assign a telephone number to devices linking them to their IMEI identification. Figure 1.3 illustrates the IMEI numbers available inside mobile phones.

In addition to the available MAC and IMEI numbers, device serial numbers and network parameters can also be used for authentication,

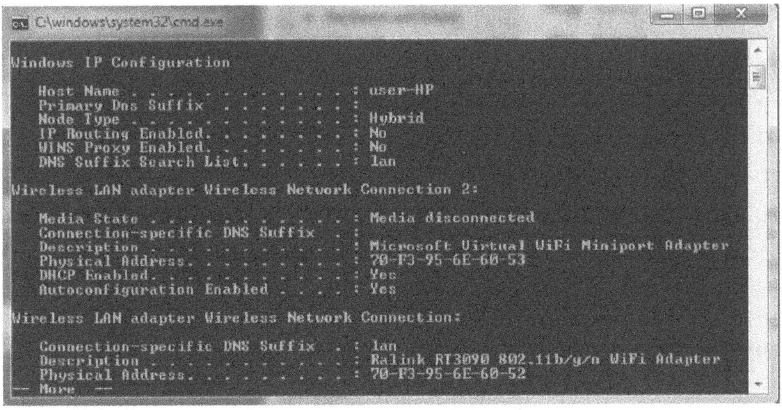

Figure 1.2   MAC address in a personal computer, 70-F3-95-6E-60-52.

Figure 1.3   Mobile phone IMEI numbers.

such as intranet and Internet addresses. The above apply to client authentication toward the server.

At the server side, the use of certificates, IP restrictions, and data encapsulations can greatly enhance authentication and security. While in transit, data can be protected by hash codes, such as the *cyclic redundancy code* (CRC), and by the private key/public key encryption mechanisms.

Vulnerabilities in information systems can originate in a very wide variety of causes, ranging from firewall penetrations and Trojan horse attacks to decentralization and static resource allocation. Most frequently, vulnerabilities are introduced while systems are being upgraded or adapted to new operational environments.

Causes of Vulnerability

In the context of cybersecurity, vulnerability is a deficiency that can result in a performance degradation or system failure. Such deficiency may be in the application itself, or it may be in the hosting computer, in the network, or even in the user's training deficiencies.

That's why applications need to be continuously reviewed. Applications' parameters, besides the software code itself, include the interfaces with the hosting system as well as interfaces with the users. Thus, the code must be replaced with the updated one, the hosting system's new characteristics must be taken into account, and the user skills should be enhanced.

Patches provided by the developer must be immediately applied. Plus, applications designed for a certain version of an operating system may not necessarily operate with another, prior or later.

While an application in itself may be secure, its remote accessibility may be of weak controls, such as passwords or other authentication mechanisms, thus creating a system vulnerability.

Often an organization's network is loaded with applications that inadvertently, and unintentionally, allow cross-accessing. That is, legitimate entry into one application allows backdoor entry into another. In this case, network segmentation is needed to eliminate such vulnerability. For example, the financial operations network and access points should be physically separated from the users' access to products' information.

It must be realized that protection, let it be for a country, for a house or for a database, has numerous parameters, each coming with a price tag. So, each shield of protection needs to pass a cost-effectiveness analysis, in order to optimize the organization's resource allocation.

Vulnerabilities can be created from inside the organization. This is what we call *insider threat*. Such threat is not necessarily of malicious intent. Mostly, such vulnerabilities are results of the following two major categories:

- Lack of personnel cybersecurity training
- Immature judgment, especially in the application of cyber-security measures

In-house cybersecurity training for all accessing the Web is similar to obtaining a driver's license, with the difference that cybersecurity training needs to be updated as cyber threats evolve.

Measuring Vulnerability

The US National Institute of Standards and Technology (NIST) has developed a protocol for the standardized classification and assessment of the security content in a software system in order to "standardize the way security vulnerability and configuration information is iden-tified and catalogued" [3]. The protocol is named Security Content Automation Protocol (S'CAP, pronounced "es-cap") and consists of the following six components.

1. **Common Vulnerabilities and Exposures (CVE).*** This is a depository of registered known information security vul-nerabilities, where each occurrence has its own unique iden-tification number. Initially, such occurrence is defined as a candidate vulnerability, and if accepted it becomes an *entry* registered in the MITRE CVE List [4] and is eventually reg-istered in the National Vulnerability Database (NVD) [5]. As of late summer 2010, the NVD contained 43,163 CVE Vulnerabilities, increasing at a rate of 11 vulnerabilities per day. In that database, one will find security weaknesses of

---

* Common Vulnerabilities and Exposures (CVE) is "international in scope and free for public use. CVE is a dictionary of publicly known information security vulner-abilities and exposures." http://cve.mitre.org/.

numerous software, including well-known operating systems and Internet browsers.

2. **Common Configuration Enumerator (CCE).*** This is a similar depository, but contains security vulnerabilities and interfacing inconsistencies found in system configurations. Such information can help in regulatory compliance, in determining proper interoperability, as well as with audit checks. The provided information is in narrative form identifying existing problems and usually recommending solutions [6].

3. **Common Platform Enumerator (CPE).**† This component of the protocol is concerned with the proper naming of the software and offers a hierarchical structure. This way, the software is defined explicitly, greatly facilitating software inventory management [7].

4. **Common Vulnerability Scoring System (CVSS).**‡ This is an algorithm that takes into account parameters related to the development and use of the subject software and provides a score expressing the level of calculated security [8]. The provided algorithm is available for use at no cost, and it enjoys widespread use by system designers and security analysts performing risk analysis and system planning. A CVSS calculator available online implements the developed algorithm [9].

---

* Common Configuration Enumerator (CCE) "provides unique identifiers to system configuration issues in order to facilitate fast and accurate correlation of configuration data across multiple information sources and tools." http://cce.mitre.org/.

† Common Platform Enumerator (CPE) "is a structured naming scheme for information technology systems, platforms, and packages. Based upon the generic syntax for Uniform Resource Identifiers (URI), CPE includes a formal name format, a language for describing complex platforms, a method for checking names against a system, and a description format for binding text and tests to a name." http://cpe.mitre.org/.

‡ Common Vulnerability Scoring System (CVSS) "provides an open framework for communicating the characteristics and impacts of IT vulnerabilities. Its quantitative model ensures repeatable accurate measurement while enabling users to see the underlying vulnerability characteristics that were used to generate the scores." http://nvd.nist.gov/cvss.cfm?version=2.

5. **Extensible Configuration Checklist Description Format (XCCDF).*** This is an XML template that facilitates the preparation of standardized security guidance documents that present vulnerabilities or security concerns about software at large or about specific configurations or uses of addressed software, in a normalized "configuration content through automated security tools" [10].

6. **Open Vulnerability and Assessment Language (OVAL).**† This serves as a common thread "across the entire spectrum of information security tools and services... (and)... standardizes the three main steps of the assessment process," namely, the representation of system information, the expression of the specific machine states, and finally the assessment reporting, all in a language that is common in the information systems security community. Enterprises are using OVAL in a wide variety of critical functions, including vulnerability assessment, configuration management, patch management, policy compliance, benchmark documentation, and security content automation [11].

"The Security Content Automation Protocol (S'CAP) is a synthesis of interoperable specifications derived from community ideas."‡ Figure 1.4 illustrates the components that comprise the protocol.

Outside of the S'CAP, other initiatives provide standardization in additional areas, as illustrated in Figure 1.5. Among them are the

---

* Extensible Configuration Checklist Description Format (XCCDF) "is a specification language for writing security checklists, benchmarks, and related kinds of documents. An XCCDF document represents a structured collection of security configuration rules for some set of target systems. The specification is designed to support information interchange, document generation, organizational and situational tailoring, automated compliance testing, and compliance scoring." http://S'CAP.nist.gov/specifications/xccdf/.

† Open Vulnerability and Assessment Language (OVAL) "is international in scope and free for public use, OVAL is an information security community effort to standardize how to assess and report upon the machine state of computer systems. OVAL includes a language to encode system details, and an assortment of content repositories held throughout the community." http://oval.mitre.org/.

‡ The Security Content Automation Protocol (S'CAP) "is a synthesis of interoperable specifications derived from community ideas ... [and it] continually evolve(s) to meet the ever changing needs of the community." http://S'CAP.nist.gov/.

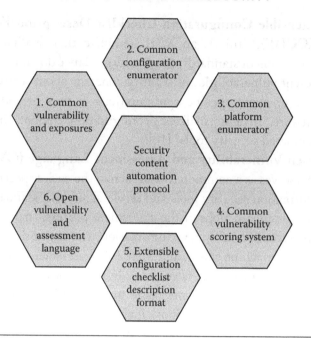

Figure 1.4   Components of S'CAP. http://scap.nist.gov/.

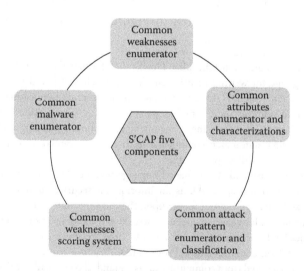

Figure 1.5   S'CAP five additional areas of standardization.

Common Weaknesses Enumerator (CWE),* the Common Malware Enumerator (CME),† the Common Weaknesses Scoring System (CWSS),‡ the Malware Attribute Enumeration and Characterization (MAEC),§ and the Common Attack Pattern Enumeration and Classification (CAPEC).¶

Collectively, the above standards comprise a very powerful infrastructure for information systems vulnerability assessment and reporting. Thus, vulnerabilities, weaknesses, and malware can be described in an accurate, standardized, quantitative, and explicit way. Using the S'CAP technology, information systems can be classified as to their level of security in a way that is standard and eventually industry-wide acceptable.

Avoiding Vulnerabilities through Secure Coding

In the software development culture, not too long ago, the design objective used to be the development of effective programs with a minimum number of lines of code or to be executable in a minimum amount of time or some combination of both. Reflecting the high cost

---

* Common Weakness Enumerator (CWE) "provides a unified, measurable set of software weaknesses that is enabling more effective discussion, description, selection, and use of software security tools and services that can find these weaknesses in source code and operational systems as well as better understanding and management of software weaknesses related to architecture and design." http://cwe.mitre.org/.

† Common Malware Enumerator (CME) "was created to provide single, common identifiers to new virus threats and to the most prevalent virus threats in the wild to reduce public confusion during malware incidents." http://cme.mitre.org/.

‡ Common Weakness Scoring System (CWSS), like the CVSS above, is similarly based on a comprehensive weaknesses algorithm that takes into account numerous factors that "can contribute to a vulnerability within that software." http://cwe.mitre.org/cwss/index.html.

§ Malware Attribute Enumeration and Characterization (MAEC) "is a standardized language for encoding and communicating high-fidelity information about malware based upon attributes such as behaviors, artifacts, and attack patterns." http://maec.mitre.org/.

¶ Common Attack Pattern Enumeration and Classification (CAPEC) "is sponsored by the Department of Homeland Security as part of the Software Assurance strategic initiative of the National Cyber Security Division. The objective of this effort is to provide a publicly available catalog of attack patterns along with a comprehensive schema and classification taxonomy." http://capec.mitre.org/.

of memory and the low speed of the processors, the valuable commodities were memory space and execution speed. Fault tolerance for data integrity was often entering the mind of the designers, but extra code for security never, since all systems were stand-alone and physically isolated from each other.

In major software designs, vulnerabilities can be minimized by segmenting the code and the data into *resident* and *transient* sections, following the principles of operating system design. That is, when an application is called, routines and data access are brought in as the immediate need calls for, rather than bringing in the entire inventory of the application. This way, should there be a malware intrusion, the damage will be contained to the downloaded (memory loaded) part of the application.

Today, generally speaking, neither memory space nor processing speed seem to be programming constraints any more. That era is irreversibly gone, being replaced by a world of high-speed total interconnectivity. The Internet offers such a high level of utility that every connectible piece of equipment, from cell phones to supercomputers, seeks to be connected. The provided level of this advanced utility and convenience results in enhanced productivity that often overshadows the accompanying security risk. Experts openly say: "The Internet is a hostile environment, so you must... [be able to] withstand attack[s to survive]" [12], and it is often referred to as the Wild Wild Web, WWW.

Consequently, the code that will be used on the Web has to be designed with the possibility of hostile attacks in mind, in exactly the same way that a building has to be designed and built to withstand earthquakes. The criterion as to what constitutes good code has now changed, from minimal code to minimally vulnerable [13].

There is a Greek popular proverb that advises, "It is better to spend your time securing your donkey onto a tree than spending it searching for the lost donkey." This directly applies to the design of Internet-exposed software. It is better to spend our time designing secure software rather than facing the consequences of intrusions—costly development of patches, bad publicity, etc. In other words, today, the concepts of software quality and software security are embedded within each other. Thus, if the software specifications call for protection, a corresponding security mechanism has to be in place. An increasing trend is for Web applications to come with their own firewalls rather than exclusively relying on those of the hosting system.

The cost of fixing a vulnerability is usually very high if one considers the intangible damage that is being produced. During the fixing, resources will have to be taken away from other assignments to attend to this matter in a very urgent way. In monetary terms, the cost of fixing a vulnerability is a five- to seven-digit dollar figure, depending on how deep in the design the vulnerability exists. The necessary procedure to rectify a vulnerability typically takes the following steps, also illustrated in Figure 1.6.

1. Location of the origin of the vulnerability
2. Design of a patch that will strengthen the code and eliminate the vulnerability
3. Application and testing of the patch
4. Confirmation that there are no side effects
5. Drafting of patch documentation
6. Preparation of a patch distribution plan to all affected clients
7. Patch installation
8. Confirmation of the effectiveness of the patch; public relations campaign to offset prior negative publicity

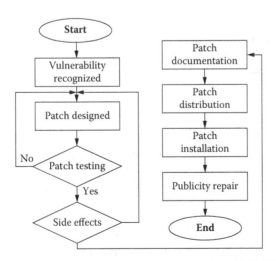

Figure 1.6 Steps necessary to rectify a software vulnerability.

Unless the origin of the vulnerability is explicitly identified, any patch may cover a problem without eliminating the root of the vulnerability. The most frequent vulnerabilities caused by insecure code are

- **Buffer overflow.** Program activities, especially inputs, allocate a certain amount of finite space for the new, created data to be stored. Excessive amount of data fills up the buffer, and the program will crash, unless the program has preventive measures [14].
- **Arithmetic overflow.** This usually occurs when there is an accumulation, and the accumulator's maximum number is exceeded. The next amount to be added *rolls over* the accumulator, creating a false result unless, again, preventive measures are incorporated [15].
- **Format string attacks.** Insecure code allows user-provided input to be treated as a command when it can only be data. If permitted, attackers can install their own executable code [16].
- **Command injection.** Lack of input validation will permit disallowed commands from being accepted and executed [17].
- **Cross-site scripting (XSS).** This is injection of malicious code into a client software, usually to bypass access controls [18].
- **SQL injections.** This is an SQL code that misleads an application into executing it [19].
- **Insecure direct object reference.** This applies to a webpage retrieval. Rather than being referenced by its HTML file name, it is referenced by the direct object definition that the page has in a database. This reveals the identity of the database, and an attacker may use it to retrieve other files [20].
- **Insecure storage.** This is storage of critical files without encryption or read/write protection. Poor examples of steganography fall in this category [21].
- **Weak cryptography.** This is file encryption that can be easily deciphered [22].
- **Race conditions.** This occurs when one resource is granted to a second user before the first has finished [23].

Software security must originate in the product specifications. It is not a step in the software development, but it is a solution that has to be interweaved with the functional design and code writing. That is, the software designer's mindset must have two parallel tracks—functionality and security—with security being a mechanism that reveals and subsequently blocks intrusions. Such security mechanism should be robust and well designed and should never be replaced by some data *obscurity scheme* that attempts to *outsmart* the attacker.

Besides thinking of the possible attacker, the designer must also think of the user convenience and provide a security mechanism that poses no hindrance to the normal operations, being as transparent to the user as possible.

Mistakes Can Be Good

No matter where, mistakes are always viewed negatively and are identified as moments of failure. This is a wrong attitude. When Thomas Edison was told that he failed one hundred times before perfecting the incandescent lamp, his response was that, since he learned something new from each of the one hundred times, his success process simply took one hundred steps. Of course, making the same mistake again and again is not a sign of wisdom. The point to make here is that there should be no fear of making mistakes, as long as they are made in good faith, do not lead to catastrophes, and have, hopefully, added some new knowledge.

It would be a mistake to extend an application, or a user for that matter, more security privileges than needed to perform an assigned task. When applications are being installed, all needed resources must be listed with the required privileges, such as read, write, create, delete. This way, should a malware install itself in the application, the potential damage will be minimal, and the malware will not be able to roam inside the system.

Similarly, when a computer is a single user, it should not necessarily operate in the *administrator mode*, but in the *user mode*. This way, should a malware manifest itself in the *user mode*, it will not propagate into the *administrator mode* privileged areas. By having privileged layers—*user, super-user, admin, super-admin*—malware is contained to a certain extent.

Threats Classification

Basically, there are three types of threats, namely, illegal data change, illegal data access, and illegal obstruction to data access, as illustrated in Figure 1.7.

The information security researchers at Microsoft broadly classified all threats in six categories, the acronym of which conveniently make up the word STRIDE (spoofing, tampering, repudiation, information disclosure, denial of service, elevation of privilege) [24]. Table 1.1 lists the six threat categories and the associated characteristics.

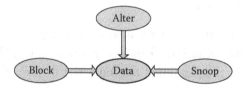

Figure 1.7   Three major types of threats to data.

Table 1.1   Information Systems Threats

CATEGORIES OF THREATS	DEFINITION OF THREAT	AFFECTED SECURITY PROPERTY	POSSIBLE SOLUTION: ENHANCED MECHANISM FOR…
Spoofing	Presentation of false identity	Authentication user identity confirmation	User recognition
Tampering	Modification of content (code, data, or process)	Code, data, or process integrity	User access
Repudiation	Denying performance of documented past action	Absolute verification of past action	Activities fogging
Information disclosure	Unauthorized access to content (code, data, or process)	Data confidentiality	Data fencing
Denial of service	Partial or total incapacitation of a resource	System accessibility and availability	Packet filtering
Elevation of privilege	Unauthorized upgrading to a higher level of access	Allocation of access authorization	Level recognition

Threat Modeling Process

In information systems, threats—potential attacks that may capitalize on a system's vulnerabilities—originate in a variety of sources and
bear various levels of gravity. There is a need for a structured approach
toward defining and dealing with threats. Below is a sequence of steps
that can serve as a mechanism for that purpose.

1. Define what constitutes the information system in question.
   That is, determine the functional and geographical borders of
   what we refer to as being our system. Beyond what point is it
   not our responsibility or liability?
2. Now that we have quantified our system, we attempt to identify what we consider as being the threats that are based on
   internal or external vulnerabilities. The STRIDE categories,
   mentioned previously, can serve as a starting point to threats
   classification.
3. Recognize which of the threats, in your context of operations,
   constitute absolute danger that may lead to a catastrophic
   impact on the system. Define the modes under which such
   threats can become successful attacks.
4. Develop defense options for each and every recognized threat,
   and rank the considered defense mechanisms based on effectiveness and demand of resources.
5. Select optimum approaches to threat eliminations, balancing effectiveness, probability of occurrence, severity of occurrence, and solution development cost.

This is an iterative process requiring the participation of all who
are associated with the secure performance of the system, namely,
analysts, designers, programmers, users, trainers, sales, and evalua-
tors, as illustrated in Figure 1.8. This process needs to be reviewed
at certain time intervals or when new threats are known to have
surfaced.

Security Starts at Home

Of course, home is the creative phases of the Software Development
Life Cycle (SDLC), especially the program design and coding stages.

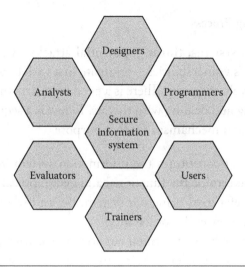

Figure 1.8   Participants in the development of a secure information system.

SDLC is often described as consisting of seven basic transitional stages. Namely,

1. From abstract needs to formal requirements—Analysis
2. From formal requirements to overall design—Design
3. From overall design to program code
4. From all of the above to documentation drafting
5. From all of the above to system testing
6. From system testing to system utilization (or to a previous step)
7. From system utilization to needs enhancement (Step 1)

During the analysis phase the *security requirements* are being defined, while in the design phase the *security mechanisms* are being developed. Later, in the testing the vulnerabilities are hopefully discovered and eliminated.

Vulnerabilities elimination usually takes one of two forms. One is removal of the causes of the vulnerability, and the other is removal of the effects of the vulnerability. Depending on the prevailing rationale, normally one of the two solutions is implemented.

It is now standard practice and a legal requirement in all major construction sites to have safety engineers overseeing all activities for the workers' safety. Similarly, in information systems development, software security professionals must oversee the development process from a to z and perform the following [25]:

- Identify common programming errors that lead to vulnerabilities.
- Establish standard secure coding practices.
- Educate software developers (/designers).

Furthermore, intra-organizational software development initiatives may include

- Programmers certification in secure coding
- Software certification as to secure coding
- Utilization of software analysis tools

Software tools are very important in the development of secure and well-documented code and can be classified in the following four categories [26]:

- *Code Coverage*—Keeps track of the code and data locations that have been created, read, or modified.
- *Instruction Trace*—Records the execution of each instruction, making it available for subsequent step-by-step analysis.
- *Memory Analysis*—Keeps track of the memory space utilization, looking for possible violations.
- *Performance Analysis*—Based on the user's criteria, software are analyzed and fine-tuned for performance optimization.

This way, information system applications will be secure as well as reliable. The Software Engineering Institute at the Carnegie Mellon University is leading in the development of standards, tools, and training aiming at the design of reliable and secure information systems [27–30].

The major problem with software development is their life cycle economics and logistics, where very often the pre-release investment does not match the post-release revenues. Often, the idea-to-product-release-time is minimized, frequently resulting in the release of non-secure software.

To the rescue of fast software development have come the object-oriented languages and the structured programming concepts that underlie the design of modern information systems. Yet, *secure software by design* still constitutes a new principle preaching that security must be an integral part of functionality.

Security in Applications

Vulnerabilities also come with insecure applications. Microsoft Word 2003 is a typical example. Its defect is that, upon requesting a *save*, the previously deleted text, though not appearing in the final document anymore, still remains part of the file. When the Word file is opened in the Notepad, deleted text can be clearly seen, while in the Word document it is not part of the final visible text.

This vulnerability violates the user's privacy, and implied confidentiality, without offering any added functionality. In this case, the only solution is, at the end of the document preparation, to *select all*, *copy* it, and *paste* it in a brand new document.

However, the average users neither suspect the existence of vulnerabilities, especially with big name products, nor do they have the technical skills to discover and rectify software design defects. It is the responsibility of the organization's information security officers to be knowledgeable of the existence of defects in software that they approve for use and to advise users accordingly.

The United States Department of Homeland Security (US-DHS) maintains an extensive Computer Emergency Readiness Team (US-CERT) that warns the public of the existence of vulnerabilities in software that are widely used and that maintains online a *Vulnerability Notes Database* [31].

Vulnerability Note VU#446012, for example, identifies and describes a "Microsoft Word object pointer memory corruption vulnerability" [32]. The Note points to Microsoft's own Security Bulletin that states: "When a user opens a specially crafted Word document using a malformed object pointer, it may corrupt system memory in such a way that an attacker could execute arbitrary [malware] code" [33]. The Note continues that "Office documents can contain embedded objects" (that may contain malware).

It is, therefore, advisable prior to using an application to visit this database and become aware of the presence of any vulnerabilities of interest. Sorting the above-mentioned database [34] by *Severity Metric*, one may recognize that appearing on the top are vulnerabilities that are caused by buffer overflow. It is consequently imperative that buffers be of dynamic size, as well as self-cleaning of the obsolete data.

A most common gateway to malware attacks is the Web browser. On one hand, it has to be open and powerful to facilitate the display of data; on the other hand, it has to be configured to protect the host computer. Security experts believe that "Many web browsers are configured to provide increased functionality at the cost of decreased security." An excellent guide to *Securing Your Web Browser* is available online that can benefit novices as well as experts [35].

Introducing Countermeasures

A cybersecurity countermeasure is an action that aims to block or minimize the impact of a cyber attack against a Web-connected asset of ours. Such action may be the utilization of a certain process, of a certain device, of a certain technology, or of a certain system. By asset, we include every Web-connected unit of ours, such as a computer, a smartphone, a device, or a server.

While vulnerabilities may not be eliminated altogether, countermeasures can be applied that will minimize the significance of the threat. Defenses against external threats can be of various forms, such as:

- Screening the URL of online system access attempts against a list of pre-approved ones.
- Minimizing the intrusion risk by reducing access privileges wherever they are not absolutely necessary. Or, extend them and retreat them as the need calls for.
- Minimizing the online availability of sensitive data, thus reducing the exposure to possible intrusion.
- Having passwords that are immune to "dictionary" attacks by including letters of foreign languages.
- Using multi-factor authentication, such as receiving additional access parameters via mobile telephony.
- Designing for high volume traffic, so that "flooding" attempts to the interface ports will not succeed.
- Developing the ability to recognize Distributed Denial of Service, DDoS, attacks, through dynamic metrics, that continuously observe the resources utilization.

Table 1.2   Foreign Government Cybersecurity Agencies

COUNTRY	AGENCY NAME AND URL
Australia	The Australian Government Computer Emergency Readiness Team http://www.ag.gov.au/www/agd/agd.nsf/page/GovCERT
Canada	The Canadian Cyber Incident Response Centre (CCIRC) https://www.publicsafety.gc.ca/cnt/ntnl-scrt/cbr-scrt/ccirc-ccric-en.aspx
European Union	The European Network and Information Security Agency (ENISA) http://www.enisa.europa.eu/
France	French Networks and Information Security Agency (FNISA) http://www.ssi.gouv.fr
Germany	German Federal Network Agency, the Bundesnetzagentur (BnetzA) http://www.bundesnetzagentur.de
New Zealand	The Centre for Critical Infrastructure Protection (CCIP) https://www.ncsc.govt.nz/
United Kingdom	The Centre for the Protection of National Infrastructure (CPNI) http://www.cpni.gov.uk/

- Use of firewall, anti-virus software, and updating of the software (updates and patches) of Web-connected devices.
- Log and report intrusion attempts and suspicious Web requests.
- Disconnect or deactivate Web-accessible assets not being used at that moment.
- Conduct a frequent (daily or weekly) audit. Be aware of the type of applications that reside in your system.

International Awareness

Similar to the US-CERT, other countries concerned with the safety of cyberspace have established similar government agencies for that purpose. Table 1.2 provides a partial list of foreign government agencies with cybersecurity responsibilities.

Exercises

1. Review paper "Common Control System Vulnerability" at http://www.us-cert.gov/control_systems/pdf/csvul1105.pdf (7 pp.), and present your summary in a two-page report.
2. Review paper "Vulnerability Analysis of Certificate Validation Systems" at http://66.135.41.137/about/library/whitepapers

/w06-02v1-vulnerability_analysis_of_validation_systems
.pdf, and present your summary in a two-page report.

3. Review paper "System Vulnerability Mitigation" at http://
www.sans.org/reading_room/whitepapers/awareness/system
-vulnerability-mitigation_1339 (19 pp.), and present your
summary in a two-page report.

4. Open 2003 MS Word and create a file with only the words
"Good morning." Delete everything and write "Good night."
Save the file under the name Good.doc. Open the file using
the Notepad. View the lower part of the code. You will see
the deleted words "Good morning." What conclusions do
you draw? Visit the following United Nations report to see
how a vulnerability created a diplomatic incident. http://www
.aquol.com/archives/2005/10/redactions_on_h.php

5. In a two-page report, explain the buffer overflow vulnerability. Cite five references—news releases—where this has been
identified as the cause of denial of service.

6. Visit the websites of Table 1.2, and research toward finding
more such agencies and their policies.

7. Identify the preferred performance of residential alarm systems, and develop the formal (quantified) requirements.

8. Select two Web browsers and make a comparative study of
their security features.

9. Research the use of the terms *administrator* and *super
administrator*.

10. Research the use of the terms *user* and *super user*.

2

VULNERABILITIES IN THE ORGANIZATION

Cyberspace is the infrastructure of the modern world, and Cybersecurity is the infrastructure of Cyberspace.

Introduction

Internet presence has become a prerequisite for the operation of any organization, whether it is a government agency, a business activity, or an academic institution. Every organization needs an *open door* to the public, with the ability to serve its constituency online and the capacity to securely hold data. The Internet presents unprecedented opportunities for practically every organization. However, along come unprecedented dangers that may lead to costly, often irreversible, damage.

Let us consider the cost of the *one penny intrusion*. The story goes that in a certain bank the online system was compromised, and one penny was removed from an account. Let us see how much that penny will cost the bank. Following the discovery of the account compromise, an emergency meeting of twenty executives was called which lasted for four hours. A decision was made to reconcile all of the bank's 250,000 accounts based on the previous day's records. This activity would require two full days of the bank's five-member IT department. A public relations campaign was authorized, via several media, to hopefully offset any negative publicity. Undoubtedly, the cost of the *one penny intrusion* ended up as far more than the one penny loss.

Organizational operations are not physically performed and monitored anymore, but are done electronically via shared databases and via intranets, extranets, and the Internet. That is, we operate based on the perception of reality and not with reality itself. A bank manager looks at the screen to see the financial standing of the bank and does not count the bills and the coins that are in the hundreds of the bank's locations.

While the convenience, efficiency, and effectiveness provided by the information systems are of unprecedented magnitude, similarly are the accompanying dangers. As a result, it is imperative that organizational security measures must match the ever-increasing threats. In the case of a security breach in an information system, the most important security measure is the real-time detection, notification, and instant countermeasure.

A certain white paper states: "The business... needs to detect attacks or vulnerabilities instantaneously and provide effective solutions."* Therefore, incident detection is the cornerstone in any security plan— a plan that is supported by the design of a secure system that provides an incident analysis and a vulnerability repair procedure.

Common Organizational Vulnerabilities

In the definition of an organizational information system, each and every functional requirement needs to have an accompanying security component addressing external as well as internal possible attacks. According to statistics, the most successful cyber attacks are of the *hybrid* nature. An insider, knowledgeable of a vulnerability, helps an outsider to successfully bypass the system security and access the organization's resources.

In information system design and implementation, besides the expected nominal performance, security functions need be added that will prevent the creation of vulnerabilities. Most vulnerabilities arise from one or more of the following:

Data Backup: Backing up data in intervals that are incompatible with systems operations speed. It is the CIO's decision whether data be backed up every hour, minute, second, or millisecond. The frequency of moving data from the soft backup storage to the hard archival media has to be carefully selected. Also, decisions need to be made as to the permanency of data and their accessing policy. Deletion of unnecessary data can

---

* Internet Security and Business, Part One, http://www.backupdirect.net/internet -security-and-business-part-one.

be very important because it may be under compliance regulations. The dependence of postintrusion analyses on backed-up data is absolute, because the access trail of archived data* can provide valuable information.

Operational Buffer Overflow: Every piece of data entry or entry request is temporarily stored in a buffer while being serviced. Easy software design calls for a fixed-size buffer of a guesstimated size. Whatever the size, the buffer may fill, making the particular function inoperable or inaccessible. Security-minded software design calls for a dynamic size buffer that may endlessly extend itself into the vast available disk storage. Attackers would overflow targeted buffers, usually resulting in data or code overwriting. It is possible that attackers may install malware that a *naive* buffer may pass for executable code with disastrous consequences.

Operational Speed Saturation: Endless and persistent requests, though simple, may exceed the computational limits of the system and virtually incapacitate external communications with bona fide users. Again, security-minded software design calls for provisions to ignore or block persistent requests of common origin.

Access Authorization and Authentication

Authorization codes and processes are often vulnerable for a variety of reasons. The most common are

- System allows the user endless password entry attempts. In this case, the attacker automates the attack, using a password generator that in a matter of time discovers the correct password.
- System does not allow the user many password entry attempts, and the user writes the password in possibly vulnerable places.
- System demands password change at frequent intervals, creating inconvenience to the user, and user makes minimal changes, with each change adding vulnerability.

---

* Archived Data: Data that are not being used anymore at the operational level of the organization, but contain valuable information that may assist in postintrusion analyses.

Present authentication technologies include the following four *factors*, also illustrated in Figure 2.1A–D:

- Something the user knows (e.g., password, PIN)
- Something the user has (e.g., ATM card, smart card, USB device)
- Something the user is (e.g., biometric characteristic, such as a fingerprint) [1]
- Something the user receives, e.g., one-time passwords (OTP) received via mobile telephony (such as short message service, SMS) or via the Internet (such as email or other personally accessible application)

"User names and passwords no longer provide adequate security" [2]. A successful solution to the password problem has been the use of

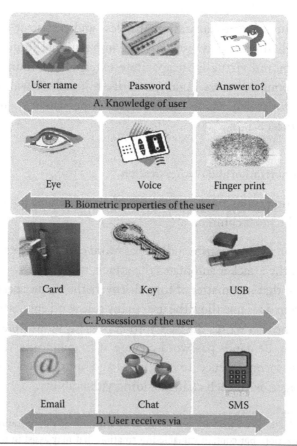

Figure 2.1   Authorization criteria.

OTP [3], where the authorization server, via an alternate channel, sends the user an OTP each time the user needs to access the system. Such passwords can be valid for a short period of time, with the possible alternate channels being

- Mobile telephony, where the authorization server sends the OTP to the user's cell phone via SMS or even machine spoken
- The Internet, where the authorization server sends the OTP to the user via chat, Skype, MSN, or as an email [3]

This solution falls in the category of the so-called *Two Factor Authentication* (TFA).* TFA implies the application of two authorization modes to best authenticate the user. The first factor is a conventional one, such as *user name* and *password*, and the second factor is an unconventional mode, such as the answer to a certain question or a biometric parameter, or a *parabiometric*† parameter.

The "two-factor authentication solution leverages an everyday tool—the [mobile] phone—[that is very close to the person] to secure [authentication for] account logins and transactions" [2]. This type of authentication falls in the parabiometric category.

The participation of the mobile phone in the authentication process can be as simple as receiving an OTP or even speaking back a certain passphrase for voice print authentication. Furthermore, even if an attacker enters the correct user name and password, the authorized user will receive an immediate call informing them of the access. If the access is an intrusion attempt, the legitimate user "can immediately block the account and notify the company's fraud department, [that] can instantly take appropriate action" [2].

Multifactor (multimode) authentication procedures are on the rise and are being progressively deployed in high-security applications. An OTP example is illustrated in Figure 2.2, where the password is sent to the user via mobile telephony as an SMS.

---

* Two Factor Authentication: Access is provided when two independent modes of secret parameters are presented to the access control authority.
† Parabiometric Parameter: A parameter that is closely identified with an individual, but it is not a physical property of that person. Examples are a user's mobile phone number, laptop's MAC address, or the IMEI of a mobile device used in the access authorization process.

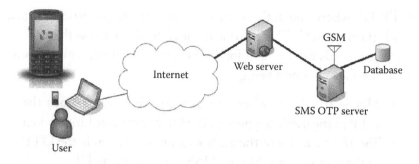

Figure 2.2 Authentication technology using an OTP delivered as an SMS to the user. (Courtesy of Nordic Edge, http://www.nordicedge.se.)

An OTP can be combined with biometrics, as shown in Figure 2.3, where the fingerprint reading and an OTP is sent to the server for resource access.

A network illustrating the biometric OTP technology appears in Figure 2.4.

Figure 2.3 Biometric fingerprint reading in USB form. (Courtesy of http://www.yubico.com.)

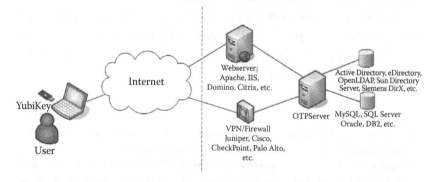

Figure 2.4 Authentication technology network using biometrics (fingerprint) and OTP. (Courtesy of Nordic Edge, http://www.nordicedge.se.)

Human Factors

An unclassified US government report has revealed that "The great majority of past compromises have involved insider, cleared persons with authorized access who could circumvent physical security barrier, [and] not outsiders breaking into secure areas" [4].

Personnel, whose activities involve the Internet or other modes of data handling, constitute a critical organizational asset, which may turn into a weak link. Their activities may be writing code, programming databases, using a USB storage device, or merely sending emails. Each and every such activity needs to be performed in a security-minded way and in accordance to policies. "Technology alone is not the answer" [5].

The establishment as well as the enforcement of policies, as to how organizational data are to be entered, modified, read, or deleted, constitutes the backbone of data security in any enterprise. Equally important is the audit trailing capability within the information system, so that data changes can be traced to their origin.* There are numerous ways of notifying data owners that their data is being accessed.† Depending on the criticality of the data, appropriate measures can be taken, ranging from receiving an email to receiving an SMS message on a mobile phone.

While technology can reasonably protect the electronic assets of an organization, it cannot, with the same ease, protect against insider threats.‡ Overwhelming statistics point out that most attacks on databases are internal or external with internal help. The expression goes: You cannot protect yourself from your bodyguard, your cook, or your doctor. It is difficult to set barriers between the organizational data and those who have a bona fide need to use them. Neither can an organization treat its members as potential criminals. However, security

---

* Audit Trail: Audit trail is the process that reveals the chronological sequence of actions that have resulted in the completion or attempt of a transaction or data change.
† Data Owner: The data owner is the entity that controls the access of certain data and is also responsible for the security of the data—integrity, confidentiality, and availability.
‡ Insider Threat: Insider threat is the potential risk that entrusted members of an organization will abuse their designated access to organizational data to the detriment of the organization.

mechanisms need be in place so that no member in the organization can single-handedly cause major damage. Equally important is that no member in the organization can affect data access or changes without leaving a trace [6].

> Case studies and survey research indicate that there is a subset of information technology specialists who are especially vulnerable to emotional distress, disappointment, disgruntlement and consequent failures of judgment which can lead to an increased risk of damaging acts or vulnerability to recruitment or manipulation [6].

The same way *level of vulnerability* is being assigned to software, processes, or procedures, it should also be assigned to personnel handling critical organizational data. This is a very sensitive matter that, if not administered with extreme professionalism, may lead to the creation of alienation within the organization.

The CIO, together with the HR head, bears the responsibility of assessing the presence and level of a potential vulnerability in each and every member of the organization who handles critical data. In that respect, all members of an organization need to receive specific training and security guidelines. For the federal sector, an explicit document is provided by the National Institute for Standards and Technology (NIST) [7]. The guidelines are meant for government agencies, but equally apply to the civilian sector, with the emphasis being on awareness of the possible adverse consequences should there be an information security compromise.

Security Services

Security services may be provided by in-house talent, by external data security organizations, or by a combination of the two. Either way, the in-house Chief Information Security Officer (CISO or CSO) is the ultimately responsible person and ultimate authority in the information system definition, design, and implementation and in subsequent operations and security management.

Significant benefits can be derived from the use of external security organizations with experience and expertise that exceed that of the internal talent. However, in principle, the organizational vulnerability

Table 2.1 Security Consultancy Services

Security audit	Intrusion tests	Network monitoring
Security architecture	Performance tests	Data migration
Security design	Off-site data archiving	Resource acquisition
Antivirus service	Off-site data backup	Security training

will increase when external security consultants enter an organization. Table 2.1 lists most services typically offered by security consultancy organizations.

External Technologies

The concept of *Enterprise Information Architecture* often goes beyond data, databases, intranet, and cyberspace and includes external technologies and resources. One such case is the use of the Global Positioning System (GPS) offered and maintained by the US Department of Defense [8]. The GPS, a twenty-four satellite system, provides the location information in the form of longitude, latitude, altitude, direction, and time. Figure 2.5 illustrates the GPS and its twenty-four satellite constellation.

This technology finds application in numerous industries, "such as emergency response services, law enforcement, cargo security, nuclear materials transport, aircraft navigation, and critical time and synchronization standards for utilities, telecommunications, and computer networks" [9].

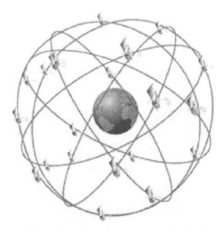

Figure 2.5 GPS and its 24 satellite constellations.

While the system is highly accurate and reliable, and free of vulnerabilities, the system's "GPS signals are not secure" [9]. The radio reception of the provided data can be jammed by attackers and, even worse, can be *spoofed*, fabricated to mislead the user. Thus, erroneous data will mislead the user as to the exact location of the tracked asset.

Fortunately, there are certain countermeasures that, although they do not restore the correct signals, give an indication of foul play. In the case of signal jamming, the GPS receiver receives a relatively strong radio signal but produces no data, leading to the conclusion that the signal is being jammed. As for spoofing, one may confirm the data produced by the received signals through conventional means, for example, verifying the direction of travel using a compass or comparing the received time using a clock. Also, the spoofed signal will be stronger than the expected one, "1×10^{-16} watts" [9].

Therefore, although the GPS signals originate from a very credible source, awareness of possible hacking should be included in the organizational data security equation.

Vulnerabilities in Networks

Networks are the most sensitive and critical component in any organization, and this is where we need to effectively prevent, detect, and respond to security incidents. The networks' cyber defense requires the coordinated engagement of a comprehensive portfolio of security tools that work well together in an intelligent and automated manner.

Not too long ago, all of an organization's data, although networked, were inside the organization's physical limits. Today, the availability of cost-effective external data-storage, through Storage-as-a-Service (SaaS) providers, commonly called *cloud*, has created new vulnerabilities. Such data storage options are the best of unknown security measures. This means that whatever data an organization stores, at least outside its absolute supervision, must be reliably encrypted.

The trend for external IT support, which has now reached the point where available, is Infrastructure as a Service (IaaS). That is, an organization only needs computers with Web browsers and Web access. Undoubtedly, IaaS can provide extensive economical benefits to an organization, but the level of vulnerability is unknown.

Networks are the main entry point for cyber criminals, and therefore maximum defense must be applied at the organization's cyber entry points. The practice has been to employ tools and techniques to apprehend such intrusion attempts.

Such attempts must be recognized and blocked. For this purpose, there are commercially available tools, identified as Network Intrusion Prevention Systems (NIPS or IPS), normally installed at an organization's Web entry point. The NIPS serve as the entry-exit cyber policeman, examining each and every packet of data going in or out of the organization's network, and decides, based on policies, whether to block or to allow passage to the packets.

IPS software may play an active role, as described above, or a passive role, only recording the entry–exit point activity and developing statistics that can be analyzed and can create intelligence.

Wireless Networks

An organizational network and the associated assets are also threatened by vulnerabilities in the wireless internal or external communications. While the three standardized wireless technologies—Bluetooth, Wi-Fi, and WiMAX—do have secure communications features, vulnerabilities do exist and need to be known and properly addressed by the users. By virtue of being wireless and operating in the radio frequency (RF) spectrum, such networks are exposed to some threats that are difficult to defend against. These are

- **Eavesdropping.** The availability of traffic analyzers enables the reception and capture of exchanged data very easily. Subsequently, data, though encrypted, can be collected and possibly deciphered at a later time.
- **Noise injection.** This is the intermittent injection of RF noise bursts aiming at the corruption of normal communications.
- **Jamming.** A powerful RF source transmitting in the vicinity of the organization's units and in the spectra of operations can incapacitate the network. Of course, the source location can be easily identified unless the source is mobile.
- **Man-in-the-middle.** This is a case where an adversary with a similar wireless capability is posing as a legitimate base station, mobile station, or subscriber station.

The most commonly used standardized wireless networks are Bluetooth (BT), Wireless Fidelity (Wi-Fi), and Worldwide Interoperability Microwave Access (WiMAX).

Bluetooth

Bluetooth (BT) is the commercial name of a data communications protocol certified by the IEEE (Institute of Electrical and Electronics Engineers) and technically known as the IEEE 802.15.1—1Mbps WPAN (Wireless Personal Area Network) Protocol. The protocol's aim is to provide "standards for low-complexity and low-power consumption wireless connectivity" [10].

Despite the extensive security precautions that have been entered into the BT specifications, it appears that the BT operating system design has inadvertently left several vulnerabilities. However, the fact that most BT code is in firmware makes BT wireless technology resistant to "*malicious code*" [11]. Figure 2.6 illustrates a BT WPAN, serving as a cable replacement for an up to 30-feet, 10-meter, range.

Figure 2.6 PAN employing BT technology.

To be vulnerable to intrusion risks, a BT-equipped device—mobile phone or personal computer—must have its BT feature activated. That is, the device must be in the *Discoverable Mode*. Furthermore, in all BT communications—bona fide or malicious—the devices— victim and attacker—must be within a 10-meter proximity to each other for communication to take place. However, the availability of highly sensitive receivers makes BT eavesdropping possible from much longer distances. Vulnerabilities in the BT-equipped devices can be considered as passive or active. In the passive ones intruders spy or create inconvenience, while in the active ones intruders inflict casualties on the victim's device databases.

Passive Vulnerabilities

The presence of the targeted device can be recognized through pinging. Repeated pinging can render the BT features of the victim-device inoperable. While a BT-equipped device is commu- nicating, an intruder may determine the device's address and use it to communicate with it, thus disabling it from properly com- municating with other devices. Improvements in BT specifications would eventually eliminate the penetration of devices in the non- discoverable mode.

The BT wireless technology operates in an unlicensed band where numerous other applications find it equally convenient to operate. The Wi-Fi wireless LAN technology is there, using the very same band, as do microwave ovens and many cordless phones. Consequently, BT-equipped equipment found within the radiation terrain of one such product may be unintentionally inoperable [12].

Active Vulnerabilities

Via BT communication, an intruder may take full control of victim- device commands—namely, the AT Commands that control the mobile phone—without, in any way, attracting the attention of the victim- device owner. In this vulnerability, intruders can use the victim-device as if it were in the palm of their hand. Data can be altered, calls and messages can be sent and received, the Internet can be accessed, and even conversations can be listened to via the intruder's phone [13].

With specialized software, intruders not only may access all data in a victim-device, but they may even read the phone's unique hardware identification, the so-called International Mobile Equipment Identity (IMEI) [14].

Precautions

In the BT protocol specifications, a variety of security mechanisms have been embedded. However, in addition to establishing security policies, enterprises may also deploy BT software that scan the environment and monitor the BT band to

- Identify the various types of active BT devices
- Provide all retrievable attributes of the identified devices (class, name, and manufacturer)
- Provide connection information (pairing)
- Identify available services (fax, printer)

The level of the risk associated with the use of the BT wireless technology is directly related more to the specific application and less to the inherent BT architecture. Taking into account the numerous limitations under which BT technology operates—low RF power, distance, bandwidth—no highly sensitive or critical application will turn to the BT for support. For what it offers, namely, cable replacement, and for as long as basic precautions are adhered to, the BT wireless technology will be as secure as was intended to be, namely, for minimal-security intra-office applications [15].

Wireless Fidelity

Wireless Fidelity (Wi-Fi) is the commercial name of a data communications protocol certified by the IEEE, technically known as the IEEE 802.11—Multi-Rate DSSS* [16]. Wi-Fi is the wireless equivalent of IEEE 802.3 wired Ethernet protocol [17].

---

* DSSS (Direct Sequence Spread Spectrum): This is a telecommunications modulation technique where the original signal is multiplied by a *known noise* to cover the entire given bandwidth, and it is then transmitted. At the destination, a counterpart demodulation technique retrieves the original signal.

Major technology developers and OEM companies have formed the Wireless Ethernet Compatibility Alliance (WECA) to support certification of Wi-Fi equipment. WECA was established by the industry's network and microchip giants including 3Com, Cisco, Sony, Intel, Motorola, Nokia, and Toshiba, and it is now serving as a Wi-Fi equipment clearinghouse with a present membership of over 250 manufacturers [18]. The 802.11 protocol provides a universal wireless LAN (WLAN) infrastructure standard, through which interoperability among "Wi-Fi certified products" is guaranteed [19]. Prior to the establishment of the WLAN standard, and for decades, the WLAN applications stagnated because each major telecommunications manufacturer had its own designs. With the establishment of the Wi-Fi standard, WLANs became a standard intranet facility.

Wi-Fi security features were originally established by the WEP,* followed by the WPA,† and are currently defined by the WPA2,‡ with the next generation of access protection covered by 802.11w.

There are presently three versions of the Wi-Fi standard, namely, the 802.11a, 802.11b, and 802.11g. Versions "a" and "g" offer a data rate of 54 Mbps, using a 5 GHz and a 2.4 GHz band, respectively. Version "b," the oldest standard, has an 11 Mbps data rate operating at a 2.4 GHz band [20]. Being unlicensed, the 5.0 GHz band is a very busy one. However, application of the 802.11h standard, which supports Dynamic Frequency Selection and Transmit Power Control, ensures "coexistence between Wi-Fi and other types of radio frequency devices" such as the BT [21].

The next Wi-Fi version is the 802.11n. The "n" standard not only quadruples the data throughput, bringing it to the 200–600 Mbps range, but is also backward compatible with legacy versions "a," "b," and "g." The "n" version capitalizes on the availability of a sufficient bandwidth, and through "multiple antennas, [and] cleverer encoding...

---

* WEP (Wired Equivalent Privacy) is a Wi-Fi optional encryption standard. When activated, WEP encrypts the data that are wirelessly communicated. WEP provides a 40- or 64-bit encryption key based on which secure communication takes place between a radio NIC and its respective access point. NIC: Network Interface Card connects a computer to a network wired or wirelessly.

† WPA (Wi-Fi Protected Access): This is a 128-bit key WEP.

‡ WPA2 (802.11i) (Wi-Fi Protected Access 2) is a 128-bit key WEP, which has provisions for PKI authentication.

Table 2.2   802.11 Wireless LAN Basic Characteristics [20,21]

IEEE WLAN STANDARD	OVER-THE-AIR DATA RATE	MEDIA ACCESS CONTROL LAYER DATA RATE	OPERATING FREQUENCY
802.11b	11 Mbps	5 Mbps	2.4 GHz
802.11g	54 Mbps	25 Mbps	2.4 GHz
802.11a	54 Mbps	25 Mbps	5 GHz
802.11n	200–540 Mbps	100–200 Mbps	2.4 or 5 GHz

[aims] to achieve raw data rates up to 600 Mbps" [22]. Table 2.2 displays the basic specifications of the four 802.11 versions [21,22].

In a wireless Wi-Fi system, excluding the software, there are two physical components: the access point (AP),* and the wireless interface unit, which is an insertable card, an embedded circuit, or a USB device. The system's central component is the AP, which interfaces the "wireless" world with the wired one—referred to as the infrastructure.

Thus, the AP, on one side, communicates with the organization's network, the so-called *infrastructure*, and on the other side, communicates with its wireless clients and serves as a router meeting the networking needs of the wireless stations, as shown in Figure 2.7. The AP provides shared LAN/Internet access using Network Address Translation (NAT).

In a non-protected Wi-Fi environment, a *wardriver* (WD)† can use a victim's bandwidth to access whatever is accessible. As a minimum, the WD can access the Internet or the victim's intranet, and as a maximum, the WD can access all files in the victim's computer and penetrate into any other place that is accessible by the victim's computer. In other words, in a non-protected Wi-Fi environment, a WD can take full control of the victim's computer.

Worth mentioning is that any visit to the Internet by the WD will bear the victim's router identity, which may implicate the victim beyond easy proof of Wi-Fi hijacking. There are numerous cases of Wi-Fi hijacking covered in the media, most too sad to mention.

---

* AP (Access Point) interfaces the wired network infrastructure to the wireless one. Contains radio interface, logic and router.
† WD (Wardriver) is an intruder who drives by Wi-Fi areas with a laptop trying to access the Internet for free and/or to snoop on Wi-Fi clients' sensitive data.

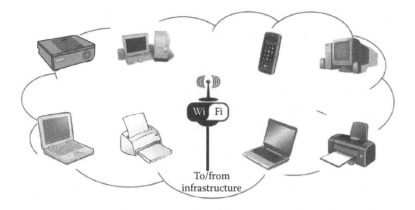

Figure 2.7 Typical WLAN where diverse types of equipment communicate with each other and with the infrastructure, all via Wi-Fi.

Wi-Fi Precautions at Home

Below is a list of precautionary measures that must be followed while using Wi-Fi in a home environment.

One: Turn Off the IBSS* Mode. In this mode the mobile unit is open to communication without any restriction. Hackers may link and silently access sensitive information. Such risks can be eliminated if the IBSS is disabled. Also, turn off the Wi-Fi access connection as soon as it is not needed anymore.

Two: Turn On the Infrastructure Mode. The infrastructure mode enables Wi-Fi clients to access resources on the other side of the access point (printers, servers, etc.).

Three: Turn Off SSID† Broadcasting. Since in the home environment one does not anticipate unexpected Wi-Fi devices, it is not necessary for the access point to broadcast its SSID identity to the world. Usually, this ID is entered manually, and only once, during laptop login and is remembered afterwards.

---

* IBSS (Independent Basic Service Set) mode, commonly known as ad-hoc mode. In this mode, Wi-Fi clients can connect to each other directly without the need for an access point. This can be useful in a secure environment, like a conference room, where participants can set up an "ad-hoc" network to communicate with each other.

† SSID (Service Set Identification): This is the Wi-Fi network identifier—a secret key—established by the network's administrator. The SSID is included in the header of all communicated packets.

Four: Change Router's Access. The router, located in the AP, is accessible via a name and a password. They are set at the initial installation, but can be reconfigured at any time. These two parameters should be changed at intervals. Also, the default fictitious local, intranet, IP address, which may have come as 192.168.1.1, can be changed to any other, as long as the numbers in the four fields range from 0 to 224, without leading zeros. Also, "there is no need to keep the default router name." To the contrary, any change from the default values will contribute to a better security posture. Typically, the default values are the same for all access points of a given manufacturer and are usually known to intruders [23].

Five: Turn On the Encryption. The Wi-Fi specification includes the so-called Wired Equivalent Protection (WEP). The encryption algorithm comes in 40 and 64 bits. A later version, the WPA2, comes in 128 bits. Each time a mobile unit logs on to a Wi-Fi access point, the unit's login name and password can be easily captured by a "sniffer." One way to prevent that is to use PKI,* where each side knows the other side's public key, and a "passkey" can be established under encryption without exposing any non-encrypted information. The latest version of the Wi-Fi security protocol, WPA2, does provide PKI. It needs to be pointed out that the encryption *dissolves* once the data reach their destination. That is, WPA2 is for the air-transit only. Furthermore, "the underlying [encryption] algorithm is flawed and subject to relatively easy cracking." There are even websites that provide the steps to crack a WEP [24].

Six: Turn On the MAC† Address Filtering. Usually, Wi-Fi access points contain a gateway that has Media Access Control (MAC) filtering capabilities. One may allow the filter to pass traffic only from devices of known MAC addresses. These devices may be in the infrastructure (that is, on the wired side

---

* PKI (Public Key Infrastructure): An encryption scheme based on digital certificates.
† MAC (Media Access Control) is the 32-bit address of a unit's Network Interface Card (NIC). An intelligent access point allows access to clients of authorized MAC addresses.

of the access point), they may be printers or other computers, or they may be in the wireless space—the Wi-Fi card of
the laptop, a Wi-Fi PDA, and the like. If in a wireless network, the SSID is known, then "without MAC address filtering, any wireless client can join" [25]. However, this will not
deter the advanced hacker who knows how to capture packets
and extract the SSID and MAC addresses from them.

Seven: Scout the Airwaves. Using specialized software, like
the packet sniffer freeware *Ethereal*, one must frequently
scout the airwaves for unexpected Wi-Fi access points or
Wi-Fi clients. Such tools, like the *Ethereal*, can capture data
"off-the-wire from live network connections... can read captured files... decompress them on the fly... [and can currently
dissect]... 759 protocols" [26].

Wi-Fi Precautions at the Hotspot

For the convenience of clients, public hotspots do not use any of the
possible security features of the Wi-Fi (WEP or WPA encryption) or
networking (MAC filtering). To facilitate clients' connections, Wi-Fi
access points actually broadcast their SSID. In a hotspot, clients start
by turning on their Wi-Fi option, connect to the access point, submit
a valid credit card number, and the link is established. For a mobile
unit to communicate with the access point, knowledge of the SSID of
the access point is necessary.

For a Wi-Fi client to be hacked it is not necessary that the mobile
unit be in communication with any access point. The mere fact that
the Wi-Fi feature is on is sufficient to establish vulnerability. Wi-Fi
clients in, either public or corporate, hotspots need to take several
precautions to maximize the defense of their sensitive information
from intruders. Below are some precautions that need be taken while
at a hotspot.

One: Hotspot Legitimacy. Hackers often set up a fake access
point in the vicinity of a legitimate public hotspot and attempt
to lure connection seekers. Through such connections, hackers
would capture sensitive information (user names, passwords,
credit card numbers, etc.), making subsequent illegal use.

Wi-Fi clients need to absolutely ascertain that the hotspot they attempt to connect to is a legitimate one. Usually, the facility associated with the hotspot service (waiting rooms, coffee shops, etc.) would have appropriate signs posted. There are several websites that list known legitimate hotspots worldwide [27].

Two: File Encryption. Files including emails should be encrypted prior to transmission. There are numerous encryption options using dedicated software or using features embedded in applications such as word processors and email clients. One may install an encryption application that "automatically encrypts all... inbound and outbound Internet traffic" [28].

Three: File Sharing. While in a hotspot, keep the file sharing option off to prevent unwanted file transfer.

Four: Turn the VPN* on. This way, intercepted data are rendered useless because of encryption.

Five: Firewall Use. A hotspot, most probably, uses a single static IP address to possibly serve 200 clients. That is, all clients are in the same subnet, making it easier for a client-intruder to snoop on other clients. That problem can be minimized with the use of a "personal firewall." One may purchase a firewall or may use the one provided by the Windows XP. Through the firewall one may restrict traffic and block or permit "communications that might... be dangerous" [29].

Six: Rules of Thumb. Regardless if one is accessing the outside world wired or wirelessly, certain additional precautions also apply: use of the latest antivirus software, use of the most updated version of the operating system, use of Web-based secure (https) email, individual password protection for

---

* VPN (Virtual Private Network) is a security concept using IPSec.

IPSec (Internet Protocol Security): This protocol provides encrypted tunneling with header and payload encryption and transport with payload encryption only. It also provides advanced authentication features.

Tunneling: Tunneling is a security concept where data are first encapsulated in a private protocol (such as IPSec) and afterwards are encapsulated again in a public protocol for transportation via any standard networks (Internet, intranet, etc.).

sensitive files, and last but not least have a computer password mechanism that locks the computer if there is no keyboard or mouse activity for x minutes.

Wi-Fi Precautions at the Enterprise

Corporate Wi-Fi security demands a much more serious tackling of the Wi-Fi vulnerabilities. For such cases advanced protocols and VPNs are in order. In the enterprise environment the Wi-Fi security precautions may include all the above described, as well as the ones below.

One: Perimetric Fencing. Solutions are currently available where positioning of RF sensors can geometrically determine if a client is within the authorized physical area. Such technologies, which need onsite *terrain training* and *fine tuning*, have offered 100% security in testing. Using perimetric fencing, "Wi-Fi environments can be protected in a 3-D air space [to an accuracy of]... about 5 feet" [30].

Two: Advanced Authentication. Rather than relying on the nominal security features of the Wi-Fi, an enterprise may use advanced authorization/authentication protocols, such as DIAMETER.*

Wi-Fi has by now become a cornerstone technology in local wireless communications. Its major vulnerabilities—session hijacking, man-in-the-middle, and denial-of-service—are being continuously mitigated through advances in security technologies and through increased security awareness on the users' side. With the increase in the effective data rates to exceed 200 Mbps, there will be plenty of bandwidth for advanced encryption techniques and for sophisticated authorization/authentication protocols. It is expected that security standard 802.11w, with the *per packet encryption key* and additional powerful features, will significantly enhance Wi-Fi security and will reduce successful intruder attacks [31].

---

* DIAMETER is an advanced communications protocol providing increased wireless security. It is the successor of the RADIUS (Remote Authentication Dial In User Service) protocol.

Worldwide Interoperability Microwave Access

The Worldwide Interoperability Microwave Access (WiMAX) is the IEEE Wireless Networking Standard 802.16 and was released in 2004. Its specifications are continuously enhanced with amendments that aim at making it a viable wireless replacement of cable, ADSL,* and T1[†] wired technologies. WiMAX serving as fixed or mobile LAN[‡] or Metropolitan Area Networks (MAN) uses licensed and unlicensed frequency bands for high- and low-power transmissions, respectively, to provide Broadband Wireless Access (BWA).

WiMAX Features

The unlicensed bands in the 2–10 GHz spectrum limit the range to that of the Wi-Fi, which is about 10 to 50 meters, where transmitted power is usually limited to 200 mW. The licensed bands in the 10–66 GHz line-of-sight spectrum, where transmitted power can reach 20 watts, can offer a radius range of 50 km from a single base station. Furthermore, the standard WiMAX data rate is 70 Mb/s. Figure 2.8 shows a WiMAX control window and a USB WiMAX adapter.

Several laptop vendors offer "WiMAX ready" units [32], and WiMAX USB adapters are available, as well [33]. WiMAX technology is also being utilized for long-distance point-to-point connections via repeaters using directional antennas. WiMAX features include

- Roaming—offers client mobility (802.16e)
- Forward error correction—uses fault-tolerance algorithms
- Adaptive modulation—trades range for bandwidth
- User and device authentication
- Confidentiality of transmitted data messages

---

* ADSL (Asymmetric Digital Subscriber Line) is a wired telephony technology where a data channel is frequency multiplexed with the regular voice communications, and it is demultiplexed at the user's site using a splitter that provides a voice outlet to be connected to a standard telephone and a data outlet to be connected to a data terminal. The first facilitates traditional telephony, while the latter usually provides Internet access.
† T1 is a wired telecommunications standard indicating a data speed of 1.544 Mb/s (1,544,000 bits per second).
‡ LAN (Local (intra-building) Area Networks): MAN (Metropolitan (intra-city) Area Networks).

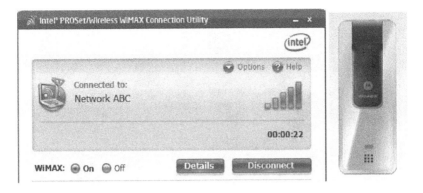

Figure 2.8 WiMAX control window and a USB WiMAX adapter. (From Intel, http://-download.intel .com/support/wireless/wmax/5350_5150/S6/intelrproset wirelesswimax userguide.pdf.)

- High data throughput—reaches 75 Mb/s
- Triple-DES* encryption—for authentication and transmission
- AAS†—uses advanced antenna techniques (802.16e)
- Speeds up to 1 Gbps and 100 Mbps for fixed and mobile operations, respectively (802.16m)

Figure 2.9 illustrates a possible WiMAX environment where Internet service is provided in a 50-km radius to the entire population. In this scenario, Internet is provided to a single user with a mobile phone, a laptop, or a desktop, as well as to multi-user organizations such as office buildings, residential compounds, or industrial parks.

Contrary to WiMAX products and services vendors, researchers allege that there are several vulnerabilities in the WiMAX technology. With the 802.16e specifications in place, most of the alleged vulnerabilities have been removed. However, the following vulnerabilities remain, as pointed out in a NIST report [34].

- End-to-end (i.e., device-to-device) security is not possible without applying additional security controls not specified by the IEEE standards.

---

* DES (Data Encryption Standard): This is an encryption cipher believed to be breakable through bruteforce. Triple application makes code breaking impractical with today's computational power.

† AAS (Advanced Antenna Systems) are smart antenna technologies that enhance gain, directivity, and data throughput.

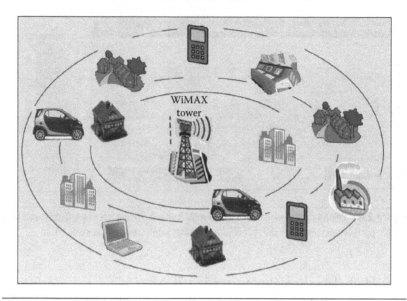

Figure 2.9 Typical WiMAX network where Internet access can be wirelessly provided to a metropolitan area.

- Data SAs (Security Associations) cannot be applied to management messages, which are never encrypted.*
- Lack of mutual authentication may allow a rogue BS (Base Station) to impersonate a legitimate BS, thereby rendering the SS/MS (Subscriber Station/Mobile Station) unable to verify the authenticity of protocol messages received from the BS.

Therefore, for the confidentiality of management messages, WiMAX users need to improvise their own security scheme. In this case, the Diffie–Hellman Key Agreement Standard, which is often used in cases where confidential communications need to start without any prior keys exchanged, can also be used. A list of countermeasures that can reduce risks in wireless networks are described in documents prepared by the NIST† [34–38].

---

* SA (Security Association): This term refers to parameters used to provide secure communication between two or more entities. Such parameters include special identifiers and encryption keys, types, and ciphers.
† NIST (National Institute of Standards and Technology) is a US government agency responsible for providing the country with standards and guidelines in technology and science issues.

Cloud Computing

The increasingly low cost of computer and telecommunications hardware coupled with the standardization of software has resulted in *cloud computing*. The term *cloud computing* refers to a new concept in the acquisition of computing power as a service. This service is provided out of pooled resources, where the user has no knowledge of the physical origin of such service. Figure 2.10 illustrates the concept of cloud computing where users need only Internet access.

Providers of such services may even share resources, creating a service that can be paralleled to the distribution of electrical power. In this context, computing power includes software, virtual hardware, data storage, and data access. In a way, it is similar to the concept of time-sharing of the 1970s, but it is much more powerful and accessible via the Internet, rather than via telephone modems. Today, with cloud computing an organization needs no computer center, because all computational needs are realized and provided as a service via the Internet. Cloud computing falls in the four basic definitions listed in Table 2.3.

Cloud computing providers offer *Infrastructure*, *Platform*, and *Software* as a *Service* (abbreviated as IaaS, PaaS, and SaaS, respectively). Users subscribe to such services and configure their own virtual computer center with servers and databases as if they were to purchase physical equipment for that purpose. In such an operating mode, an organization may reconfigure and scale the computational

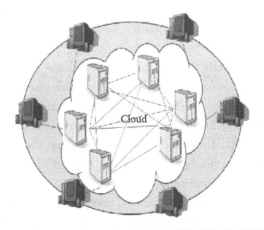

Figure 2.10 Cloud computing. The only user requirement is Internet access.

Table 2.3   Cloud Computing Option

Public cloud	A commercial center of vast computing resources that are provided to the public on an on-demand basis in a metered fashion.
Private cloud	A privately owned center of shared computing resources that are provided to the community's members on an on-demand basis in a metered fashion. The security and privacy measures are customized to the owners' needs.
Community cloud	A community-owned center of vast computing resources that are provided to the community's members on an on-demand basis in a metered fashion. The security and privacy measures are customized to the community' needs.
Hybrid cloud	A combination of the above options.

needs at any time and be charged on a pay-per-use basis. The motto of this new industry is "buy exactly the capacity you need, when you need it, by the hour or by monthly subscription" [39].

Users' applications and data, delivered through shared data centers, may reside in geographically diverse locations and may even change locations transparently to the user. Yet, everything is Web accessible via the same logical addresses. With screen sharing as well as application sharing now possible on the cloud, cloud computing has become even more attractive for over-the-Web interactions. Cloud computing has been receiving increasing support as a practical solution to building a corporate data center all in a virtualized manner and without allocating physical space. Table 2.4 provides a list of the most acclaimed advantages of cloud computing.

There is no doubt that cloud computing is a very strong irreversible trend, but along with it come security and privacy challenges that translate into vulnerabilities which need to be carefully weighed before walking into this rose garden.

"The security challenges cloud computing presents, however, are formidable, especially for public clouds whose infrastructure and computational resources are owned by an outside party that sells those services to the general public" [40]. The above statement, coming from a very authoritative body like the NIST, can make CIOs and CSOs stop in their tracks. There is a strong concern that the outsourced custody of the physical storage of sensitive organizational data constitutes in itself a major vulnerability.

To many, and by definition, cloud computing is a nonsecure environment. But to a growing number, cloud computing is the way to go and is here to stay. As for security and privacy, additional measures

Table 2.4   Cloud Computing—Advantages

1. Reconfiguration	Users can redesign their computational infrastructure at the click of a mouse, selecting and removing resources (servers, storage, applications, networks, and services) as the need arises.
2. API support	Application Programming Interface is possible for cloud software interaction with machines or humans.
3. Reduced cost	Cloud computing reduces barriers-to-entry by facilitating the creation of organizational data centers out of metered resources through a pay-as-you-need business model.
4. Reduced skills	Necessary skills to set up and maintain a virtualized data center in a cloud are far less demanding than those of maintaining a physical one.
5. Connectivity	Cloud connectivity services include Internet as well as mobile phone access.
6. Reliability	Use of multiple redundant sites can secure business continuity and disaster recovery.
7. Scalability	Cloud computing provides on-demand scalability in a self-service mode allowing system reconfiguration for an increased or decreased size or use of resources.
8. Security	Security features are provided, normally too expensive for individual users to afford.
9. Maintenance	Cloud computing providers install the latest in software versions and antimalware protection.

can be taken to bring this new mode to par with the traditional in-house data centers, in that respect.

Before embarking to transitioning into cloud computing, verifiable assurances must be obtained that organizational security and privacy requirements are fully satisfied. Cloud computing providers often offer nonnegotiable service agreements. However, this is not absolute, and negotiated ones can be obtained.

It has to be emphasized that the cloud computing system does include the client software and their access software and devices, and security and privacy policies must be safeguarded on this side as well.

Whenever necessary, a cloud computing provider should be able to demonstrate the effectiveness of the offered services, especially those related to security and privacy. Often, third-party auditors are brought in to attest as to the validity of the claimed services. Cloud computing falls in the general category of outsourcing, with all associated risks. Therefore, a thorough risk analysis is called for before engaging in any such agreements. The major perceived disadvantages in subscribing to a cloud computing environment are listed in Table 2.5.

Table 2.5   Cloud Computing—Disadvantages

• System complexity	• Cloud computing platforms, especially the public ones, because of their size and increased functionality, are open to errors and vulnerabilities.
• Multi-tenancy	• Concerns are that in a multi-tenant environment of shared resources, lack of strong compartmentalization may result in security or privacy issues.
• Internet vs. intranet	• Cloud computing is Web accessible and by definition less secure than an isolated organizational intranet.
• Personnel	• Personnel of public cloud computing may not have the required level of security clearance.
• Forensics	• In a cloud environment, depending on the level of internal auditing, it may not be possible to link performed services with associated hardware. Furthermore, past strings of computer- and human-generated activities can be difficult to trace and document to a court-acceptable level and can be impossible to duplicate.
• Cloud policies	• Cloud computing providers' security and privacy policies and practices may or may not comply with those of demanding private or government tenants.
• Account hijacking	• While examples are not available, strong concern exists in the possibility of credentials hacking and subsequent website compromise.
• Service outage	• There are numerous examples where causes beyond the control of the cloud providers have resulted in outages of several hours at the least expected times. This is an issue that can be well worded in a service agreement, but lightning will not read it before striking.
• Incident response	• Such an event will require a coordinated effort of the service subscriber and service provider in the formidable task of audit trailing that may involve the prior use of shared hardware.

While "the transition to an outsourced, public cloud computing environment is in many ways an exercise in risk management" [40], cloud computing, now in its infancy, will eventually become the mainstream data center hosting due to its cost-effectiveness that will be improving over time.

Internet of Things

The first era of cyberspace was when its only *inhabitants* were computers. It was a great accomplishment to have a single network—the Internet—covering the entire globe, and to be able to send and receive text, audio and video in real time. The second era of cyberspace was when the smartphones flooded it, far outnumbering the number of connected computers. We have now entered the third era of cyberspace, where it will be flooded with *things*, making it an Internet of Things (IoT). It is expected that by the year 2020, there will be 24 billion IoT devices serving the world in practically every aspect of life.* With the influx of the IoT devices, the capacity of the IPv4 protocol, which accommodates up to 4.3×10^9 IP addresses, will need to be upgraded to the Ipv6 protocol, which will accommodate more than 340×10^{36} IP addresses—an astronomical 39-digit number.[†] However, it is believed that the IPv4 protocol will be sufficient for the immediate future.

These *things* are standardized Web accessible devices with the ability to interface with sensors and actuators, enabling us to interact in real time within practically any environment. In brief, via the Web or using Bluetooth, IoT devices *sense, communicate, analyze* and *act*, without constraints. IoT devices can serve as autonomous intelligent agents, improving operations to increase effectiveness, safety and efficiency. The level of innovation will reach unprecedented heights. What we expect to see, at large, is as follows:

* Uninhibited and ubiquitous connectivity
* Cost Reduction in Products and Services
* Miniaturization
* Advances in Data Analytics
* Increase in Cloud Computing
* Reduction in Energy Consumption though intelligent lighting and temperature control
* Enhanced Health Care with Silent 24/7 Monitoring
* Productivity Increases
* Unthinkable Product and Services

Indeed, with the use of IoT devices, there will be extensive benefits to society. Specific IoT applications include the following examples:

* The tracking of livestock, making sure that each and every one is properly fed.
* The tracking of trees, making sure that there is no illegal deforestation activity.

---

* http://www.intel.com/IoT
† http://www.internetsociety.org/what-we-do/internet-technology-matters/ipv6

- The sensing of soil moisture for optimal irrigation to land plots as the need calls for.
- The use of health monitoring devices to monitor values of health parameters, such as breathing, heartbeat, temperature, blood pressure, etc., while being instantly alerted on deviations from expected values.
- The remote recording of electricity consumption, which formerly required a person to read each and every electric meter in town, rain or shine.
- The auto crash detector and emergency help dispatcher.
- Parking spot reporter, whereby a website displays the location of available parking.
- Tracking parameters of fleet vehicles, such as location, speed, fuel level, engine temperature, etc.

Considering that IoT devices utilize microcontrollers—single chip computers—of limited computational power and storage capacity, parallel to the above rosy expectations come a lot of concerns, similar to those raised when smartphones were introduced, such as the following:

- What constitutes a *good design* practice?
- What is the level of fault tolerance?
- Is there redundancy?
- Are malfunctions detectable and correctable?
- Are there sufficient educational resources to produce this large number of IoT engineers?
- Are collected data properly time stamped?
- How is the performance being monitored?
- How are the security risks assessed and quantified?
- How are data confidentiality, authentication and access control safeguarded?
- How will field-upgrading take place?
- How long will it take before IoT device industry standards are established?
- How long will it take before IoT legal infrastructure is established?
- How will security or performance faults be handled?
- Should IoT devices have an enforced expiration, disabling them at a certain point in time?

With so many eyes and ears around the world, it is only natural that privacy issues will be raised. In many cases, it will be unannounced invasion of privacy without consent or even awareness. A sample of already raised privacy issues regarding the IoT devices is as follows:

- Data collection: mode, use and disposal.
- Privacy preference: expression, enforcement, transparency.
- De-personalization of "statistical" data collected via IoT devices.
- Balance between privacy and security.
- Privacy by design.
- Liability and trust issues.

It is true that, if there are sensors all over, the work of the law enforcement agencies will be easier. For example, cameras in public areas can, hopefully, deter crime, and an IoT device in every car will facilitate recovery, if stolen, but such applications, if abused, cause serious civil liberties violations. Regardless of the use or potential abuse, IoT devices should be designed so that

- The level of built-in security is proportionate to the application of the device.
- While secure it respects the privacy of the collected data.
- Claimed privacy is verifiable.
- Personal identifiers are removable.
- Encryption keys are secure and managed.

As expected, there are numerous examples of security problems or abuse in the application of IoT devices, with the physical security of the devices being the least. Typical cases are where

- A major auto manufacturer had to recall over a million autos to fix a vulnerability that would allow wireless intrusion into the autos.
- In an Eastern European country, cyber criminals shut down an entire power grid, plunging into darkness and cold millions of residents.
- In another European country cyber spies, off the air, were intercepting TV channel selections to prove their hacking talents.

In conclusion, undoubtedly, the Internet of Things technology holds a high promise for the device manufacturers, for the enterprises that will integrate them and for the consumer who will use them. However, there are challenges ahead, especially in two fronts, namely, in becoming private and secure and in persuading the world that they are private and secure.

Automotive Cybersecurity

Cyberspace is expanding and encompassing totally unaffected domains, such as the automotive industry and the motorist. It is a matter of time when automakers will be offering "Web in the car" as a standard feature. The motorist will simply insert a mobile telephony SIM card and the vehicle will "fill" with Wi-Fi. Wi-Fi will come with Pandora's box* offering unprecedented features†:

- Navigation Support
- Real-time road advisory
- Arrival of selected email
- Emergency Detection and call for help
- Reporting on vehicle's performance
- Reporting on Driver's Performance
- Unlimited entertainment options
- Voice recognition for identity and control
- Remote access and sensing

Basically, the comfort of the living room and the efficiency of the office will be combined in the driver's seat, that is, in the driver's command and control center. Along with this abundance of features—increased safety, efficiency and entertainment—comes a "wide cyber attack surface," to the joy of Web hackers and cyber criminals.

By definition, everything networked, wired or wirelessly, is subject to hacking.‡ Intrusion into a vehicle's local Controlled Area Network (CAN) may inject commands from a remote location able to hijack

---

* https://www.greekmyths-greekmythology.com/pandoras-box-myth/
† http://tf.nist.gov/seminars/WSTS/PDFs/1-0_Cisco_FBonomi_Connected Vehicles.pdf
‡ https://argus-sec.com/car-hacking/

safety and non-safety critical data and functions, possibly affecting the driver's ability to control the vehicle.

Governments foreseeing the upcoming vehicle–Internet integration have prepared extensive studies,[*,†] pointing out the risks that tag along with fast adoption of technologies. Fortunately, cybersecurity standards have been developed[‡] for "Cyber-Physical Vehicle Systems." There have been cases where vehicle controls have been remotely accessed that could potentially create a hazardous situation.

To summarize, in all sectors cybersecurity remains a mixed-blessing, requiring thorough vulnerabilities and risk assessment. Such studies require professional familiar with the automotive industry as well as with cybersecurity. Eventually every vehicle has to be viewed as a multifunction IoT "device" that needs to be protected against possible cyber intrusions.

Vulnerability Assessment Tools

Operating in the Web today is like swimming in shark-infested waters. Internet viruses are usually silently performing their own *mission* copying or damaging files or installing code that will do even more damage. Often, active viruses make a computer slow, or act strangely.

Fortunately, there are numerous[§] anti-virus tools available that can minimize such risks, if not eliminate them. It must be emphasized that the continuous infection of the Internet with new and more powerful viruses make it impossible for anyone to absolutely rely on virus tools. Typically, activities performed by such antivirus tools include the following:

- Collection of the IP addresses of incoming and outgoing traffic
- Tracking of user compliance to organizational policy
- Detection of attack patterns

---

* http://www.nhtsa.gov/staticfiles/nvs/pdf/812333_CybersecurityForModern Vehicles.pdf
† https://www.enisa.europa.eu/publications/cyber-security-and-resilience-of-smart-cars/
‡ http://standards.sae.org/wip/j3061/
§ http://www.thetop10antivirus.com/best-antivirus-software

- Detection of unusual user activities
- Assessment of file transfers integrity
- Analyses of the collected data vis-à-vis cybersecurity criteria

However, having installed a current anti-virus tool in your system is wise, and keeping it in the auto mode is a must. Should there be no auto mode, daily scanning is imperative.

Exercises

1. Access and review the National Training Standard for Designated Approving Authority (DAA) document located at http://staff.washington.edu/dittrich/center/docs/nstissi_4012 .pdf. Summarize it in a twelve-slide electronic presentation.
2. Access and review the *Authentication in an Internet Banking Environment* of the Federal Financial Institutions Examination Council located at http://www.ffiec.gov/pdf /authentication_guidance.pdf. Summarize it in a six-slide electronic presentation.
3. Visit the website www.NordicEdge.se, familiarize yourself with the One-Time-Password technology, and experience it though the Download Two Factor Authentication Trial option at http://nordicedge.com/products/one-time password -server/download/.
4. Access and review the Wireless LAN Security Today and Tomorrow document located at http://www.itsec.gov.cn/docs /20090507163620550203.pdf. Summarize it in an eight-slide electronic presentation.
5. Visit the website http://www.outofblue.net. Understand the presented technology, and express your thoughts as to any vulnerabilities on the side of the clients as well as on that of the server.
6. Visit the websites of Wi-Fi hardware vendors. Understand the technology, and design a WLAN service that will provide Internet access to a three-floor square office building of 30 m on each side. Determine the topology of the APs.

7. Visit the websites of WiMAX hardware vendors. Understand the technology, and design a service that will provide Internet access to a 50-km radius rather flat area.

8. Access and review the following two documents on cloud computing, located at
http://www.us-cert.gov/reading_room/USCERT-Cloud Computing Huth Cebula.pdf
http://res.sys-con.com/download/1288112960/Cloud_101 -WhitePaper.pdf

    Prepare a twelve-slide electronic presentation with the same title.

9. Visit the website of a Cloud Computing provider, subscribe in a free trial option, and build a multiserver and multistorage infrastructure. Describe and document your gained knowledge and experience.

10. Access and review the following three documents, and prepare a twelve-slide electronic presentation with the title Cloud Computing Vulnerabilities.

    • Seven Deadly Threats and Vulnerabilities in Cloud Computing, http://www.ijaest.iserp.org/archieves/15-Jul-15 -31-11/Vol-No.9-Issue-No.1/16.IJAEST-Vol-No-9-Issue -No-1-Seven-Deadly-Threats-and-Vulnerabilities-in-Cloud -Computing-087-090.pdf

    • Cross-VM *Vulnerabilities* in *Cloud Computing*, http:// rump2009.cr.yp.to/8d9cebc9ad358331fcde611bf45f735d.pdf

    • Top Threats *Cloud Computing* V1.0, *https://cloudsecurity alliance.org/topthreats/csathreats.v1.0.pdf*

3

RISKS IN INFORMATION SYSTEMS INFRASTRUCTURE

Cybersecurity is the planet's oxygen; its failure will lead to its suffocation.

Introduction

We may not have realized that every aspect of life involves a risk, where risk is the adverse chance that the hoped for objective will not be met. Risk analysis assesses such mishaps in terms of its probability of happening and on the gravity of the consequence should it happen. Figure 3.1 illustrates the needed balance required to exist between the *pre-sale obligations* and the *post-sale expectations*.

It has to be recognized that there can be no complex system that is 100% perfect or secure. Every design is an approximation to the ideal. In the creation of the end product or service, numerous parameters have to be balanced on selected criteria. The most prominent parameters are the monetary pre-sale cost, the time length of the development process or time-to-market, the product's after-sale life, and the security and availability of that product or service during that life.

Development and use of information systems follow this generic path where, in the process of parameter balancing, vulnerabilities are created, leading into risks. There is no activity in life that is absolutely risk free, and where possible, insurance is purchased or measures are taken to minimize the risk. Therefore, the motto is *risk minimization*, rather than *risk elimination*.

Today, each and every organization operates on an information systems infrastructure that is internal as well as external. In both cases there are embedded risks. There are two factors in assessing the operational

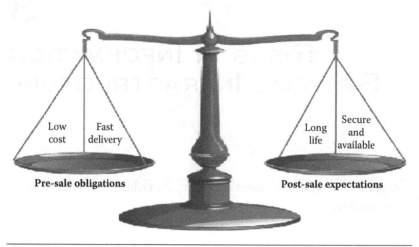

Figure 3.1   Balance in system life cycle.

worth of an information systems infrastructure: the identification of the inherent risks and the availability of appropriate fallback positions.

The external information systems infrastructure is basically the Internet. As for the organizational dependence on the Internet—regrettably—it is almost absolute. As a result, the security of the Internet, the cybersecurity, constitutes a paramount concern for all sectors of society.

The Internet contains vulnerabilities that pose a risk to those who use it, but since there is no choice, the Internet has to be used with its drawbacks. However, users should recognize and assess the risks, making them *affordable* through precautionary measures resulting in systems that are relatively available, reliable, and secure.

Risks in Hardware

In a system, every piece of hardware plays a role in the mission of the organization. Based on the importance of that role, appropriate security measures must be taken. To minimize the security risks, organizations establish official security policies that, as a minimum, must include the following twelve rules.

> **Rule One: Connections Identifications.** Each piece of hardware, considered as a hardware unit, needs to have its connections clearly identified, justified, and protected with specific

security measures, regardless if these connections are physical or wireless. The unit's operational parameters must be explicitly documented. For example, passwords need to have identified their owners as well as their administrators, where the administrators assign the passwords, as well as the renewal policies, which must be known to all cognizant personnel. Unnecessary connections must be removed, and necessary ones must be connected as the need arises. Where applicable, connection logs should be maintained, especially for connections to the Internet, intranet, and to any extranets.

Rule Two: Security Assessment. Security measures must be evaluated on intervals related to developments in technology and in sophistication of attacks. Assessment should include a vulnerability analysis as well as a penetration testing. Security measures must include bidirectional firewalls at all entry–exit points, as well as an intrusion detection and prevention system. Access to the unit must be on a *need-to-access* basis with no *pass-par-tous* passwords. That is, users are granted passwords that access only functions for which they are authorized. At all times, 24/7, each hardware unit has a member of the organization responsible for its security. At no time may a hardware unit be considered as *unattended*.

Rule Three: Vendor Parameters. All operational parameters must be entered by the cognizant personnel, and no hardware may be left with the default parameters, especially user names, passwords, and firewall settings. The existence of any backdoors, trapdoors, or special vendor entry points or interfaces must be known and sealed if possible. Vendors must be continuously accessible for clarifications on vulnerabilities, operational support, maintenance, and repairs.

Rule Four: Security Measures. While most major hardware developers provide their own security measures, most often they are based on proprietary protocols, subscribing to the philosophy that obscurity is build-in security. This is contrary to the fundamental security principle that access must be protected, not hidden, from view. Taking into consideration how mission-critical a unit is, measures must be designed to satisfy the security and privacy policies of the organization.

Where applicable, inbound access should be replaced by a *don't-call-us-we'll-call-you* approach. That is, a caller places a request for data, and the system sends the data to the caller, rather than the caller directly accessing the databases.

Rule Five: Intrusion Detection and Prevention. Embedded should be a 24/7 intrusion detection and prevention system (IDPS), that monitors for external as well as internal intrusions, and reports to the cognizant personnel via multiple modes; such as aural sounds and/or flashing images on monitoring terminal, email, or short message service (SMS). An integral part of the IDPS is a predefined sequence of steps to handle the intrusion. In each and every security-related activity, more than one IT member must be involved. It is very important, and from a variety of viewpoints, that intrusion assessment reports be the result of teamwork, rather than that of a single investigator.

Rule Six: Audits. Frequent technical audits are the backbone of any security policy. Using off-the-shelf security tools, transpired operations can be recorded and reviewed in order to identify trends and possibly recognize aberrations. Audits should include visits to the physical environment of the hardware unit in question in order to possibly discover unauthorized possible tapping points, physical or wireless, and to confirm the enforcement of physical access policy.

Rule Seven: "Blue Team." A *Blue Team* is formed charged with the responsibility of assessing vulnerabilities, threats, and risks. The team is a standing committee of IT and non-IT members that identifies attack scenarios and suggests defense and countermeasures. *Blue Teams* often set up *honey pots* in anticipation of roaming intrusions.

Rule Eight: Job Descriptions. Explicit job descriptions delineate the responsibilities and authorities of each and every member of the organization's cybersecurity structure. A flow diagram illustrating the steps to be taken in case of a cyber emergency is posted. It is most important to recognize that, for the effective fulfillment of responsibilities, sufficient authority must be extended.

Rule Nine: Critical Functions. In any system, while all functions are important, certain functions are more critical or more sensitive than others. For this reason, a hierarchical structure chart must be drawn illustrating the various functions, as they comprise the system's mission. Also shown should be their level of relative importance along with the respective threats and associated countermeasures. Considering that new threats emerge continuously, this chart has to be reassessed on a continuous basis by the organization's cybersecurity committee. This self-assessment process will keep the organization on its toes vis-à-vis the growing threats to cybersecurity.

Rule Ten: Business Continuity. System failure can never be excluded by any mature strategist. Consequently, provisions must be taken, and procedures must be in place to recover from a disabling cyber attack with the losses cut to an absolute minimum. This calls for continuous and multilayered data archiving, for functional redundancy, and for personnel familiarity with the necessary procedures. Such a crisis may not necessarily be caused by a cyber attack. It may be an inside job or an act of nature.

Rule Eleven: Configuration Management. The configuration of any system, and even more of any information system, can never be static. New hardware, new software, new threats, new markets, new technologies, and new ideas demand that IT strategists reconfigure their systems in an evolutionary fashion. However, the fashion may sometimes be revolutionary. As a result, configuration management covers the entire spectrum of a system's elements, including hardware, software, and personnel skills, as well as updates to security policies.

Rule Twelve: Defense-in-Depth.* This is a very old defense concept that has been transplanted into the information systems. Its fundamental principles are two: layered defense and no single point of failure. The successful implementation of this concept calls for appropriate measures to be embedded during

---

* Defense-in-depth is an information assurance (IA) strategy in which multiple layers of defense are placed throughout a system. It addresses security vulnerabilities in personnel, technology, and operations for the duration of the system's life cycle. http://en.wikipedia.org/wiki/Defense_in_depth_(computing).

the entire development process of the system. Such measures would create multiple layers of defense between the entrant and the sought-after resource and would block the entrant's access to unauthorized areas [1].

Risks in Software

Although software and hardware go together, their development, maintenance, and security needs are totally different. The major difference is that software development lacks the finite methodology and metrics that hardware development has generated over the years. Software will never reach the hardware level of metrics because software development is a 100% intellectual process, and as such it is subject to human parameters.

The manufacturing of a hardware product, a personal computer, for example, can be broken down into finite processes with finite steps resulting in a similarly finite skill–man hour requirements. On the other hand, software development strongly depends on the experience, expertise, and available tools of the developers—analysts and programmers—and its cost, especially in time, cannot be determined as easily as with hardware.

"Studies on project failure… suggest that 75% of all US IT projects are considered to be failures" for not meeting the expectations of their sponsors [2]. There are three basic expectations: delivery time, budget, and functional performance. To minimize the failure risks in software development, as a minimum, the following seven rules should be observed.

> **Rule One: Integrated Security.** System development involves several phases, starting with the *concept design* and concluding with the drafting of the *user manual*, with each phase having embedded the necessary security measures. These measures are initially defined in abstract terms, but progressively are mapped from phase to phase during the development process, ending up in concrete steps expected to secure the system.
>
> **Rule Two: Structured Development.** A structured software development must be followed, which calls for a hierarchical organization of software modules where module autonomy is

maximized, rather than code size. This way, a module can be easily described and tested. It may not have the most space-efficient code, but its testing and troubleshooting will be easy and direct.

Rule Three: Project Management. A project must have a skilled professional project manager. There is a misconception that a good analyst or a good programmer can make a good software development project manager. This leads to problems where nonskilled and nonprofessional project leaders fail to follow standard project management rules, managing by intuition.

Rule Four: Project Specifications. Specifications must be explicitly defined, allowing for no more than one interpretation. Most software developments experience problems because of this reason. A very common inherent risk in software is the lack of fault intolerance, which has been accepted in order for the product to reach the market in a prompt and competitive fashion. Also, after a certain point in time, and prior to design initiation, specifications must be frozen. Otherwise, the development becomes a *one thousand and one nights* fairy tale. "System design errors are much more important and costly than coding errors; they are also subtler and more difficult to detect and correct" [3].

Rule Five: Project Planning. A project development timetable must allow for unexpected events—mysterious bugs always appear. Because software metrics cannot be strictly applied, and because software development is a mental process highly dependent on experience, expertise, and available tools, it is impossible to precisely project the time requirements of a software task. Factors like prior experience in the particular field or the particular language, functional complexity, and allotted time-to-market can significantly affect the development outcome. Areas of underestimation in planning include time, manpower, complexity, level of required skills, and capital. Most often, market demand, corporate support, and own level of skills are being overestimated.

Rule Six: Project Testing. A 25% development effort must be allocated to testing the software, relative to the 5% normally allocated to hardware. The testing must optimally follow the

TQM* philosophy, which is test as you go and not test at the end. By testing optimally we mean not too frequent tests nor too few and spaced apart.

Rule Seven: Use of OOL. An object-oriented language (OOL) must be used. This way, software development can benefit from the available modules that have been already developed and thoroughly tested.

Besides the previous risks that affect the functional performance of software, there are security risks that may slide through nominal testing. "All types of software are likely to contain mistakes that have security ramifications" [4]. The following five rules may help in minimizing software security risks, especially cybersecurity risks.

Rule Eight: Patches Currency. To minimize the time-to-market, software developers often release software prematurely and subsequently provide patches that hopefully eliminate already known vulnerabilities. Software users must make sure that they are in the vendor's registered list so that they are notified as soon as a new patch is released. Usually, patches are provided on a regular basis, as the product developers discover vulnerabilities and as malware become increasingly sophisticated.

Rule Nine: Data Validation. Data and their originator must be validated prior to being accepted. Also, data and their recipient must similarly be validated prior to being sent. In addition, data must be validated vis-à-vis acceptance criteria prior to being stored. Furthermore, data must be encrypted while in storage as well as while in transit to bona fide recipients.

Rule Ten: Validation Failure. Data validation failure at any of the above three phases must create an error alert for a subsequent investigation. The alert must be multimodal, including entry into an Errors Log, aural alert, email, and possibly SMS notification to cognizant persons. There must always be more than one person receiving alerts created by possible intrusion attempts.

---

* TQM (Total Quality Management) is a management philosophy that calls for task-by-task testing to discover errors as they are made, rather than conducting a thorough test at the end, often throwing away complete units because a minor part failed at an early stage.

Table 3.1 Rules That Aim at the Minimization of Risks in Information Systems Hardware and Software

HARDWARE	SOFTWARE
1. Connections identifications	1. Integrated security
2. Security assessment	2. Structured development
3. Vendor parameters	3. Project management
4. Security measures	4. Project specifications
5. Intrusion detection	5. Project planning
6. Audits	6. Project testing
7. Blue Team	7. Use of OOL
8. Job descriptions	8. Patches currency
9. Critical functions	9. Data validation
10. Business continuity	10. Validation failure
11. Configuration management	11. Access control
12. Defense-in-depth	12. Antimalware

Rule Eleven: Access Control. Software users must be provided with an access security level that meets—and does not exceed—their authorized needs.

Rule Twelve: Antimalware. The National Vulnerability Database must be frequently consulted for the latest in malware attacks [5]. Antimalware must be installed at the server as well as at the client sides. At the server, there are basically two types of attacks. The first is the Denial-of-Service attack, where the server is flooded with rogue requests aiming at saturating its capacity and preventing it from serving legitimate visits. The second is SQL injection, where access to the server has been compromised and malware is written in the server's database that create illegal activities. "Using this method, a hacker can pass string input to an application with the hope of gaining unauthorized access to a database" [6].

Table 3.1 lists the two sets of rules that aim at minimizing risk in information systems hardware and software.

Risks in People

To effectively increase interdepartmental, interorganizational, or international cooperation, data need to become accessible by a variety of persons from a variety of organizations. However, according to statistics, the number one threat to data security is from someone who is authorized to access the data. People with access to sensitive data or sensitive services, by definition, constitute vulnerabilities. Such insider vulnerabilities can be classified into two types.

The first type is people who, though entrusted with access to sensitive information, behave in a negligent way that exposes such information to unauthorized individuals. This most often takes place in the form of lost mobile phones, lost laptop computers, exposed passwords, unattended terminals, or *loose lips*. Through use of technology and with appropriate training to raise cybersecurity awareness, this type of risk can be minimized.

The second type is people who, though entrusted with access to sensitive information, betray this trust and abuse the authority that has been granted to them. Most such intrusions are highly focused and aim at considerable financial benefits.

Again, there are rules that can be applied that will minimize the people-originated risks. Six such rules can be as follows:

Rule One: Password Granting. Access authorization through passwords or other security mechanisms must be granted only on a need-to-have basis and for a minimal volume of data and time interval. Elevated privileges should have a time-lock, after which they should be reduced to the nominal level.

Rule Two: Password Maintenance. Passwords must be valid for a finite length of time; their renewal must be very dissimilar to the previous ones and must be of a complexity that is proportionate to the importance of the data it protects.

Rule Three: Access Logs. Depending on the level of importance of the protected data, logs must be automatically created listing the access stamp (time, terminal, user, etc.). Real-time alerts need to be generated on unauthorized attempts to capitalize on vulnerabilities, abnormal activities, and out-of-character or suspicious activity.

Rule Four: Technology. Considering that passwords can be lost, creating risks and inconvenience, advanced technologies like the one-time password can be used. In one mode of this technology, upon receipt of the user's name the server sends a password to an authorized mobile phone in the form of an SMS.

The password code is applicable only for the machine that sent the user's name and only for a finite number of seconds.

Rule Five: Tamper-Proof Monitoring. Security safeguards are only as good as the integrity of the monitoring system. Often, intruders neutralize the security monitoring system before proceeding with the hacking attack. Ideally, security supervisory systems need to be automated, producing real-time threat alerts for immediate consideration and action.

Rule Six: Separation. Many incidents of inside damage take place in the time interval between the beginning of rumors about a possible employee termination and the actual date of such termination. There was a time that companies would give a two-week or a month termination notice. However, in the 1970s, the first adverse repercussions appeared. Labor behavior had changed. There were numerous incidents where, when notified of termination, labor would literally smash company property before finally walking out. Terminating an employee for a cause, on a suspicion of cause, or for whatever reason or with whatever excuse needs honesty, confidentiality, indisputable facts, professionalism, decisiveness, and fairness.

Risks in Laptops

Considering that laptop thefts are on the increase, countermeasures should always be used. Laptops and notebooks have become permanent companions, and their exposure or loss can, in most cases, be catastrophic. As a minimum protection, one may install a Full Disk Encryption [8] that normally encrypts everything in the hard disk except the Master Boot Record (MBR).* Total disk encryption can be supported with appropriate external hardware devices.

Full disk encryption cannot protect when a computer is left unattended after boot up. However, proximity technologies can be at your rescue, with a device in your pocket alerting you if you are separated from your protected unit beyond a certain short distance. Table 3.2 presents a nonexclusive list of advice that can minimize laptop-related security breaches. Figure 3.2 illustrates recent laptop crime statistics.

---

* The Master Boot Record (MBR) is a 512-bit sequence located in the first sector of a storage device and contains information about the internal partition of the device.

Table 3.2 Laptop Safety Countermeasures

1. Privacy screen filters [7]	Such filters allow only direct viewing, blocking side viewers.
2. Laptop tracking and recovery [8]	This is a service provided in association with embedded software.
3. Bluetooth proximity lock [9]	This method of laptop data security locks the laptop if an associated Bluetooth device leaves a predefined distance from the laptop.
4. RFID proximity alarm [10]	A pair of RFID devices will sound an alarm if the distance between them exceeds a predefined value.
5. File encryption [11]	Encrypt sensitive files, preferably all files.
6. Password strength testing [12]	Use a strong password to safeguard your laptop. Test its strength using available testing sites.
7. Live backup [13]	Laptop files are being archived on a continuous basis.

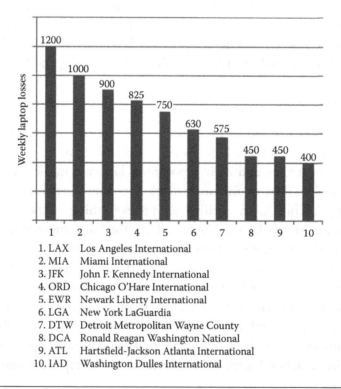

1. LAX   Los Angeles International
2. MIA   Miami International
3. JFK   John F. Kennedy International
4. ORD   Chicago O'Hare International
5. EWR   Newark Liberty International
6. LGA   New York LaGuardia
7. DTW   Detroit Metropolitan Wayne County
8. DCA   Ronald Reagan Washington National
9. ATL   Hartsfield-Jackson Atlanta International
10. IAD   Washington Dulles International

Figure 3.2   Recent laptop crime statistics. (Courtesy of Airport insecurity, http://www.ponemon .org/data-security.)

Risks in Cyberspace

With risks originating in cyberspace, the personal computer is the first line of defense. Therefore, rigorous security measures need to be maintained for effective protection of the digital resources. The following rules could serve as a minimum guard against malware.

> **Rule One: Updated Software.** Software developers provide on a continuous basis updated versions of their software that incorporate stronger defenses against malware. This applies to operating systems as well as applications. It may be an added expense, but keeping the most recent version of the installed software pays in the long run.
>
> **Rule Two: Minimize Content.** Minimize the amount of sensitive content kept in a laptop or notebook, keeping sensitive files in a Web-accessible server and encrypted.
>
> **Rule Three: Admin Account.** Because you are the only user, do not be the administrator at the same time. An unattended computer in the admin mode is totally unprotected. "The privileged administrator account should only be used to install updates or software, and reconfigure the host as needed" [14].
>
> **Rule Four: Compliance.** Following compliance laws or rules, such as the FISMA for federal agencies, is a must and a minimum exercise in data protection [15].

Risks in Legacy Infrastructure

Moving into a new technology can be very costly, especially when the presently used technology has not yet being amortized. So, organizations hang onto old IT infrastructure, hesitating to place hard-earned cash into currently state-of-the-art technology. At this point, one may ask as to what is "old"? Regrettably, in the IT world, typically five years is retirement time.

Keeping and maintaining legacy IT infrastructure can be very costly, as pointed out in a recent report by the U.S. Government Accountability Office (GAO)*. The situation in the private sector is

---

* http://www.gao.gov/assets/680/670745.pdf

not any better as another report* points out, where banking is leading. Typically, legacy IT infrastructure has equipment

- That is impossible to patch
- For which there are no updates
- That are over-customized
- That lack knowledgeable technicians
- That demand higher cyber insurance premiums

In a nut shell, "... *legacy technology is both a security issue and a hindrance to innovation...*" as stated by an FCC official†. Against this backdrop of gloom are the modern IT technologies that provide security, flexibility, automation and intelligence, to mention a few. These technologies are cloud storage and, most important, cloud computing, mobile devices with the power of a desktop PC, and the up- and -coming Internet-of-Things (IoT).

These new technologies with a multitude of embedded features, such as authentication, encryption, compliance to policy mechanisms, and reporting, are by far the most cost effective and with plenty of qualified professionals to look after them.

Risks in Mobile Telephony

In a few short years, the clutter that was on our desk has managed to fit in our palm. We do not, anymore, have an absolute need for a PC with its CPU box, its monitor, and its keyboard and mouse. Neither do we require supporting devices, such as a telephone, an address book, a calendar, or reminders posted all over. Even the photo of our favorite person is not framed anymore.

Today, all of the above features are orderly and conveniently placed in a very ergonomic device referred to as the smartphone, which has become an integral part of our existence. Smartphone features typically include

- GSM Telephony
- Personal Area Network—Bluetooth
- Local Area Network—WiFi

---

* https://www.temenos.com/en/market-insight/retail-insight/banks-are-stuck-in -spaghetti-junction/
† http://www.fiercegovernmentit.com/story/legacy-technology-makes-government -less-secure-less-innovative-say-federal/2015-10-27

- Wide Area Network—Internet
- Additional Wireless Interface—Infrared
- Numerous Physical Interfaces—SD Cards, USB, HDMI, etc.

In addition, these devices are practically free, considering what they offer. The smartphone is the modern-day *treasure box* that needs to be protected against cyber crime that has grown parallel to the Internet's evolution. The pillars of smartphone security can be listed as follows:

- **Availability**—The smartphone must be available 24/7 because effectively it is an integral part of us, like our brain.
- **Integrity**—It must provide correct and accurate information, based on the numerous applications that are continuously being installed.
- **Confidentiality**—The smartphone must protect our privacy through reliable security measures.
- **Authenticity**—When used in our transactions we must be reliably recognized.
- **Non-Repudiation**—And finally, we are committed to a certain action, via smartphone communications, neither side should later deny such commitment.

To safeguard the above five pillars of smartphone security, measures must be in place and must be practiced. Some of these measures are

- Installation of Anti-Malware Software
  Fortunately, there are numerous reliable anti-malware software that can provide protection to a certain extent. However, they must be updated as new versions are made available. The same applies to all installations. Updates offer more features, often including security measures.
- Remote Wipe Option
  This is the ability, via the Internet, to totally or selectively wipe files, or pieces of data residing in the smartphone.
- Use of Secure Passwords
  It is imperative that should the smartphone be lost, its content will be inaccessible.
- Enterprise Mobile Device Management (MDM)

Given that organizations issue members smartphones for business use, a use policy must be in existence, including the monitoring of the applications that are installed in each device.

- Remote Storage

    All of smartphone's content must be duplicated on a regular basis in a non-mobile storage. This way, under no circumstances will one face a catastrophe.

- Use of a Virtual Private Network (VPN)

    VPN is a network technology where the Internet traffic of a device passes through a node that serves as a buffer between the device and the rest of the Internet.

- Use email Encryption

    All email applications include email encryption, so that a mistaken recipient will not be able to read the email contents.

- Report Loss or Theft

    Upon loss or theft of your Internet accessing device, immediately report it to your service provider. Ensure there is a database* of lost or stolen Internet-accessing devices that prevents their subsequent use.

- Minimize Exposure

    Disable application and/or option you do not use, and remove files not needed anymore. Also, when not needed, deactivate wireless features like Bluetooth and Infrared (IR).

- Trust, but Verify

    There are numerous smartphone applications offered in the Web. Some applications are even for free, offering "fantastic" features. Before using them, pass them through a reliable anti-virus software. Some may, indeed, be great for the price, but possibly they are collecting credit card authorizations for later abuse.

- No Jailbreaking

    In the Web lingo, this means, do not tamper with the factory security settings of your mobile device.

- Use the Auto-locking Feature

---

* http://www.telecomabc.com/e/eir.html

When a mobile device is inactive for X minutes, reactivation must require password re-entry. This way, snooping by spyware* is avoided.

- Avoid being spoofed

  While benefiting from an unsecured public Wi-Fi network, it is possible for your data to be copied off the air. Conduct sensitive transactions only in secure Wi-Fi environments.

- Smartphones are Private

  It is true that the purpose of the smartphone is for us to be reachable. However, smartphone telephone numbers must be kept private to avoid being "scanned" and having the phone's contents illegally accessed. So, no public posting of smartphone numbers. If needed, have a non-smart one for public communications.

- Last but not least—Training

  Smartphone users must take every opportunity to educate themselves on the latest cyber defense measures and on the latest cyber-attack types. Over time, smartphones will enter every aspect of our private and of our professional life, requiring life-long cybersecurity learning.

Risk Insurance in Cyberspace

As in risks in the physical world, risks in cyberspace can be similarly passed to insurance companies whose sole line of business is *buying risks*. Since 1995, when the Internet was accepted as an e-market platform, concerns have been raised over hedging potential losses caused by adverse events in cyberspace, such as information theft, vandalism, and denial-of-service.

Enterprises with e-commerce investments are concerned over possible losses should their website become inoperative for whatever reason beyond their control. A website can be down for a large number of reasons, and *involuntary business interruption* has been traditionally an insurable issue. Enterprises often prefer to buy risk insurance rather than implement costly protection countermeasures.

---

* http://www.spyphonedude.com/review/free-cell-phone-spy-software/https:// www.flexispy.com

The ever-increasing possibilities of downtime, due to technical or security problems, have made cyber insurance an option for cyber enterprises to hedge off their risks [16].

It is possible for an organization, through the use of cyber insurance, to minimize losses incurred from adverse cyber incidents. Cyber attacks may cause system down-time, data damage, loss of business, as well as loss in reputation. Cyber insurance premiums are based not so much on the expected compensations, but on the organization's cyber defense posture. That is, cyber insurance premiums are based on the organization's cybersecurity measures and practices. Typically, cybersecurity insurance policies* include

- Loss of Digital Assets
- Business Interruption Costs
- Cyber Extortion Threat
- Security Event Costs
- Network Security and Privacy Liability Coverage
- Employee Privacy Liability Coverage
- Electronic Media Liability Coverage
- Cyber Terrorism Coverage

What is new with cyber risk insurance is that there is no proven methodology on how to quantify the risk in order to subsequently quantify the compensation and, at the end, compute the respective insurance premium. That is, the cyber insurance market has no track record to draw statistics from, and *"Insurance companies are realizing the need to implement greater assessment capabilities... when examining an organization's request for coverage"* [17]. However, numerous insurance companies offer insurance policies in the nine-digit dollar range.

Efforts have been made by insurance companies to identify finite parameters that can be quantified in order to serve as coefficients in cyber risk assessment. Typically, the cyber risk insurance equation includes the following parameters:

- Possibility of *adverse selection*.
- Strong security measures in-place
- Qualifications of data security personnel

---

* https://www.phly.com/Files/Cyber-Liability-Coverage-Synopsis31-5819.pdf

- Monetary worth of protected assets
- Level of *moral hazard*.

Adverse selection is a term in the insurance terminology that describes the existence of hidden adverse preconditions only known to the insured. These are preconditions that are not being disclosed to the insurance company. To counter this risk, insurance companies want the policy to have a certain no-effect initial period and/or a substantial deductible.

Moral hazard is a term also in the insurance terminology that describes the indifference of the insured toward the risk. To counter this risk, insurance companies want a deductible to be included that will motivate the insured to take the necessary precautions toward the risk.

Insurance companies try to assess the risk involved by sketching the profile of the applicant company through the evaluation of various related internal documents. Table 3.3 lists some of the possibly requested documents [18]. Undoubtedly, a review of the above list of documents can paint a very clear picture as to a company's vulnerabilities posture. It also points out the required documents for a corporate security self-evaluation. Cyber-exposed companies can reduce the level of their cyber risk to an acceptable one through their own

Table 3.3 Possible Cyber Insurance Application Attachments

1. Evidence of compliance with ISO 17799 [19]
2. Resume of the chief information security officer
3. Antivirus protection plan
4. Firewall infrastructure configuration
5. Incident detection and response plan
6. Software updating plan
7. Business recovery plan
8. Corporate privacy policy
9. Corporate compliance policy
10. Corporate data security policy
11. Corporate security manual
12. Corporate employee-data access grid
13. Security and privacy certifications
14. Grievances against the company
15. Reports on past security breaches
16. Agreements with partners involving personal data handling

Table 3.4 Comprehensive Corporate
Insurance Policy—Typical Coverage

1. Business interruption
2. Professional liability
3. Employment practices liability
4. Directors and officers liability
5. Key person life insurance
6. Workplace violence
7. Intellectual property

measures together with cyber insurance. The following steps show the relationship of the unprotected raw risk to the protected acceptable risk.

Step One: Assessment of raw risk, **RR**. This is the risk the organization is exposed to when no countermeasures are in place.

Step Two: Assessment of protected risk, $\mathbf{PR} = \mathbf{RR} \times \mathbf{CM}$. This is the new risk that has been reduced by the application of in-house countermeasures, **CM**.

Step Three: Assessment of cyber insurance policies and coverage plans.

Step Four: Selection of suitable cyber insurance, **CI**, policy and plan.

Step Five: Acceptable risk, $\mathbf{AR} = \mathbf{CI} \times \mathbf{PR}$. This is the risk the organization is exposed to after having acquired the selected cyber insurance policy and plan.

Cyber risk insurance is usually a comprehensive corporate policy including a wide spectrum of coverage, including the items listed in Table 3.4.

Exercises

1. Consider an online bookstore, and view it as a system. List six possible vulnerabilities, and describe ways to address the created risk.

2. You have placed an order with an online shoe supplier. List the risks to which you believe you have exposed yourself. Consider the following cases: you have paid via (a) PayPal,

(b) credit card, (c) debit card, or (d) EFT, electronic (bank) fund transfer, often referred to as wire transfer.

3. You are responsible for the supervision of a 100-computer network using all CISCO components. You are about to expand the network and add another 100 computers. For a reduced cost you may use CISCO clone components. Identify any risks that you may be taking and ways to address these risks.

4. Your intranet Wi-Fi network is accessible from outside your company's physical premises. Describe any risks involved and approaches for their elimination, if possible.

5. Visit the National Vulnerability Database, and review the last 50 documented vulnerabilities. Comment on any patterns, trends, or other characteristics you may have observed.

6. You are an IT manager at a bank considering the online account access policy—user names and password. Draft a policy and justify your rules. The basic password parameters are number of characters, life-length, and complexity. Also, specify the measures in the event of wrong entries.

7. Conduct research on software metrics, focusing on their differences from hardware metrics. Summarize your findings in a three-page report.

8. Conduct research on countermeasures against SQL injection attacks. Summarize your findings in a three-page report.

9. Conduct research on full disk encryption. Include hardware supported options. Summarize your findings in a three-page report.

10. Conduct research on the concept of *Defense-in-Depth* as it applies to data security in a corporate environment you are familiar with. Summarize your findings in a three-page report.

11. Conduct research on the concept of *Proximity Alert Using RFID*. Summarize your findings in a three-page report.

12. Conduct research on the state of *Cyber Risk Insurance*. Summarize your findings in a three-page report. Include cases.

13. Visit the website of a publicly held company and try to collect as many as possible of the documents listed in Table 3.3.

4

SECURE INFORMATION
SYSTEMS

Every business is a cyber business.

Introduction

For all practical purposes, every information system is being *hosted* by the Internet, and its security state is, at best, that of the Internet itself. An information system can increase its security by getting out of the Internet, but that may nil its functionality. Therefore, while numerous security measures can be applied onto an individual information system, its overall security is a function of the cybersecurity. The physical aspect of cyberspace, the Internet, is a collection of networks that individually faithfully pass packets to each other, but collectively bear no intelligence that can recognize an individual or a distributed threat. Consequently, "Enterprise to Enterprise security [is] at risk without a global integrated security architecture" [1].

Endless research is taking place to develop effective cyber defense methodologies, but they are mostly addressed to the defense of individual information systems. "Over the past 10 years there has been increased investment by US government agencies... [but] large scale deployment of security technology sufficient to protect the vital infrastructure is [still] lacking" [2]. However, the DETER [3] consortium is creating a cyber physical model where cyber defense technologies can be developed and tested. Eventually, the collective cyber traffic knowledge, now resident in bits and pieces in individual Internet nodes, will be integrated and will create an intelligent system that can recognize and prevent cyber attacks [4].

The security of an information system requires a two-front defense strategy. One front is the borders to the external world, and the other front is the protection of each of the systems resources on an individual basis. The borders are basically the Internet, through which requests come to the information system, which in turn may respond with valuable data to a hacker or may accept a hacker's request as its administrator's command. Here, the ability to discern between bona fide requests and fraudulent ones constitutes successful cybersecurity. The other front is the internal protection of the organization's assets—data and processes. ISO/IEC 17799:2005 "establishes guidelines and general principles for initiating, implementing, maintaining, and improving information security management in an organization" [5]. The fundamental characteristics of a secure information system are its integrity, its availability, and its confidentiality. These characteristics must apply to each and every component of that system. Before developing a strategy for cybersecurity, or for a comprehensive corporate information security plan, it is imperative that first the assets to be protected are identified and inventoried in a secure database.

Assets Identification

Information assets in an organization are identified by name, location, owner, protector, and parameters, and their files must be managed according to a defined corporate policy.

> **Name.** A corporate information asset needs to have an electronic name that defines—directly or through a code—its content and organizational belonging within the enterprise. For example, in the context of an insurance company, the name of a policy file may be *auto/2008/miami/12345/johnson/001 .pdf.* This way, a hierarchical classification of files can be self-explanatory and recognizable by nontechnical personnel. Of course, using non-alphanumeric characters or spaces should be avoided.
>
> **Location.** This is the physical location of the storage medium. Corporate computers need to have all storage areas explicitly identified. All hard drives in the numerous computers of the organization bear identifications based on an assigned pattern. The easiest way would be to simply assign a number to each computer and to internally rename the drives including that number. For example, if a corporate PC is numbered

as 1234, its drives will be renamed as 1234C:, or 1234D:, and so on. This naming requires administrative rights that should be reserved only for IT security personnel. Thus, users will not be able to change the name of the storage devices. Complications are, of course, created when the assets reside in a *cloud*. A *cloud* is an external computing services facility of dynamic addressing and space allocation where the physical location of the data or servers is hard to identify and where stored data and computing resources are being identified only through logical addressing.

Owner. The owner identification may have two parts. One part is the impersonal corporate owner. That is the title of the department or person responsible for the control of the particular asset. For example, the owner may be the *Department of Special Accounts* or the *Associate Director for Special Accounts*. The other part of the asset owner may be the physical person who has create/read/modify/delete rights on that asset.

Protector. The protector identification will similarly have two parts. One part is the impersonal corporate protector, that is, the title of the department or person responsible for the security of the particular asset. For example, the designated protector may be the *Department of IT Security* or the *Special Accounts Security Coordinator*. The other part of the asset protector is the physical person who has the responsibility for the security of that particular asset.

Parameters. The parameters are operational and security related. The operational parameters define the nominal use, while the security parameters define the measures that will secure confidentiality, integrity, and accessibility of the asset. Importantly, the measures must reflect the risk level and harm level should asset security be compromised.

File Management. There are various philosophies on how to best organize files in a given storage space. The following rules may lead to a well-organized database.

- After creating a file, decide whether it should or should not be encrypted. Next, assign level of security. For low level, a general password may suffice. For high security, a unique password may be assigned to each file. Keeping track of the assigned passwords and their location, and possible sharing, may be a problem.

- Create a backup through an automated backing-up mechanism. Be concerned with the security of the backup device and access to it.
- Use a hierarchical directory naming scheme. Depending on the organization-specific activities, the highest naming is usually the years or the projects. So, it becomes multi-project years or multiyear projects.
- Following that may be subprojects or months of the year, depending on the initial selection.
- Then, within the lowest level of directories, individual files can be grouped by type in respective subdirectories.
- All files must have a life cycle—creation date, modification date, and retirement date. At some point in time, the status of their significance may change from *active* to *to-be-deleted* or *to-be-archived*.
- Deleted files should be electronically *shredded*. Electronic *shredding* is a process of repeated overwriting on files, the content of which is to be obliterated beyond recognition. There are various approaches toward this end [6,7]. Table 4.1 lists the most common file shredding algorithms. On certain occasions, electronic shredding will not meet the security policies, and the physical media will have to be destroyed through physical shredding into pieces of 5 × 5 mm or less [8,9].

Assets Communication

The access or transfer of digital information poses a vulnerability, exposing information to risks. However, such risks can be minimized if appropriate precautions are implemented. These precautions include encryption, firewalls, digital certificates, digital signatures, and login controls.

Encryption. "Encryption methods aim at ensuring the confidentiality, integrity and nonrepudiation of information" [10]. Cryptography has been in practice for millennia; however,

Table 4.1   File Shredding Algorithms

ALGORITHM	METHOD
1. One Pass Zeros or One Pass Random	When using One Pass Zeros or One Pass Random, the number of passes is fixed and cannot be changed. When the write head passes through a sector, it writes only zeros or a series of random characters.
2. User defined	You indicate the number of times the write head passes over each sector and pattern to be written.
3. US DoD 5220.22-M	The write head passes over each sector three times. The first time with zeros (0x00), the second time with 0xFF, and the third time with random characters. There is one final pass to verify random characters by reading.
4. US DoD 5220.22-M (ECE)	The write head passes over each sector seven times. The first time with zeros (0x00), the second time with 0xFF, the third time with random characters, the fourth time with 0x96, and then first three passes repeated again. There is one final pass to verify random characters by reading.
5. German VSITR	The write head passes over each sector seven times, each pass writing the following characters: 0x00, 0xFF, 0x00, 0xFF, 0x00, 0xFF, 0xAA.
6. Russian GOST p50739-95	The write head passes over each sector two times. The first pass is zeros (0x00), and the second pass is random characters.
7. Canadian OPS-II	The write head passes over each sector seven times, each pass writing the following characters: 0x00, 0xFF, 0x00, 0xFF, 0x00, 0xFF, random.
8. HMG IS5 Baseline	The write head passes over each sector once, writing zeros (0x00).
9. HMG IS5 Enhanced	The write head passes over each sector three times, writing zeros (0x00), then 0xFF, and finally random characters.
10. US Army AR380-19	The write head passes over each sector three times, first pass writing random characters, then zeros (0x00), and finally 0xFF.
11. US Air Force 5020	The write head passes over each sector three times, first writing 0xFF, then zeros (0x00), and finally random characters.
12. Navso P-5329-26 RL	The write head passes over each sector three times, first writing 0x01, then 0x27FFFFFF, and finally random characters.
13. Navso P-5329-26 MFM	The write head passes over each sector three times, first writing 0x01, then 0x7FFFFFFF, and finally random characters.
14. NCSC-TG-025	The write head passes over each sector three times, first writing zeros 0x00, then 0xFF, and finally random characters.
15. Bruce Schneier	The write head passes over each sector seven times, each pass writing the following characters: 0xFF, zeros (0x00), and then five passes with random characters.
16. Gutmann	The write head passes over each sector 35 times. For details about this, the most secure data clearing standard, you can read the original article at the link.

the use of powerful computers has made decrypting not as difficult as it used to be. There are numerous known encryption algorithms, where their major defense is excessive time to break. Table 4.2 lists the most common file encryption algorithms. Most document processing applications do include easy-to-use and difficult-to-break encryption options, where separate passwords can be applied for read-only and for read-modify protections.

Encryption algorithms are classified into symmetric and asymmetric. The symmetric encryption algorithms use the same key to encrypt and to decrypt a file. Such practice, while protecting files in transit, makes file authentication very difficult because both sides can create an encrypted file. The asymmetric encryption algorithms, on the other hand, have two keys, one for file encryption and a different one for file decryption. In this case, the encrypted file originator uses the so-called *private key*, and the various recipients hold the *public key*. A file that is encrypted with the private key of party X can be decrypted only with the public key of the same party X. This way, authenticity as well as confidentiality are being guaranteed. Figure 4.1 illustrates the principle of file encryption.

Firewalls. Firewalls have been the backbone of data security. Their physical form may be software, or software installed in dedicated hardware. Firewalls serve as gatekeepers attached to the system's communications processor, examining the external traffic vis-à-vis predetermined security criteria. The examined traffic is usually the incoming one, although firewalls may also be used to examine outgoing traffic. In the case of incoming traffic control, firewalls analyze the parameters of the incoming packets, correlating the requested service to the packets' origin. Depending on the protected resources, firewalls allow traffic based on specific *permit-only* or on *permit-all-unless* criteria. Figure 4.2 illustrates firewall options, namely, a network firewall and a private firewall installed in the personal computer.

Digital Certificates. A Digital Certificate, also known as a public key certificate or identity certificate, is to cyberspace what a credit card is to commerce. In the case of the credit card, a third party—that is, the credit card issuing company—vouches on

Table 4.2 File Encryption Algorithms

ALGORITHM	METHOD
RSA	In 1977, shortly after the idea of a public key system was proposed, three mathematicians, Ron Rivest, Adi Shamir, and Len Adleman, gave a concrete example of how such a method could be implemented. To honor them, the method was referred to as the RSA Scheme. The system uses a private and a public key. To start, two large prime numbers are selected and then multiplied together; $n = p \times q$.
DES/3DES	The Data Encryption Standard (DES) was developed and endorsed by the US government in 1977 as an official standard and forms the basis not only for the Automatic Teller Machines (ATM) PIN authentication, but a variant is also utilized in UNIX password encryption. DES is a block cipher with a 64-bit block size that uses 56-bit keys. Due to recent advances in computer technology, some experts no longer consider DES secure against all attacks; since then Triple-DES (3DES) has emerged as a stronger method. Using standard DES encryption, Triple-DES encrypts data three times and uses a different key for at least one of the three passes, giving it a cumulative key size of 112–168 bits.
BLOWFISH	Blowfish is a symmetric block cipher, just like DES or IDEA. It takes a variable-length key, from 32 to 448 bits, making it ideal for both domestic and exportable use. Bruce Schneier designed Blowfish in 1993 as a fast, free alternative to the then existing encryption algorithms. Since then, Blowfish has been analyzed considerably and is gaining acceptance as a strong encryption algorithm.
IDEA	International Data Encryption Algorithm (IDEA) is an algorithm that was developed by Dr. X. Lai and Prof. J. Massey in Switzerland in the early 1990s to replace the DES standard. It uses the same key for encryption and decryption, like DES operating on 8 bytes at a time. Unlike DES, though, it uses a 128-bit key. This key length makes it impossible to break by simply trying every key, and no other means of attack is known. It is a fast algorithm and has also been implemented in hardware chipsets, making it even faster.
SEAL	Rogaway and Coppersmith designed the Software-optimized Encryption Algorithm (SEAL) in 1993. It is a Stream Cipher, i.e., data to be encrypted is continuously encrypted. Stream Ciphers are much faster than block ciphers (Blowfish, IDEA, DES), but have a longer initialization phase, during which a large set of tables is done using the Secure Hash Algorithm. SEAL uses a 160-bit key for encryption and is considered very safe.
RC4	RC4 is a cipher invented by Ron Rivest, coinventor of the RSA Scheme. It is used in a number of commercial systems like Lotus Notes and Netscape. It is a cipher with a key size of up to 2048 bits (256 bytes), which on the brief examination given it over the past year or so seems to be a relatively fast and strong cipher. It creates a stream of random bytes and "XORing" those bytes with the text. It is useful in situations in which a new key can be chosen for each message.

Source: http://www.mycrypto.net/encryption/crypto_algorithms.html

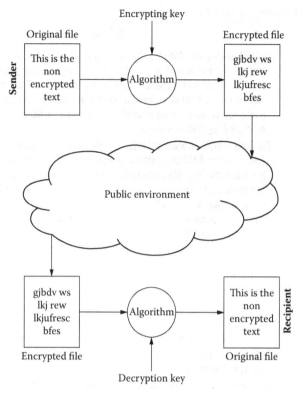

Symmetric encryption method: Encryption key = decryption key
Asymmetric encryption method: Encryption key ≠ decryption key

Figure 4.1   File encryption.

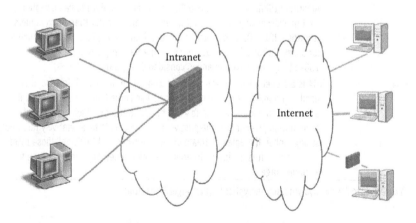

Figure 4.2   Network firewall and private firewall.

the worthiness of the card. Based on that, the merchant offers the buyer the product. Similarly, when our browser retrieves a Web page for us, the digital certificate confirms its validity by communicating with the certificate authority that has granted that website credibility. Browsers with digital certificates can access servers that are programmed to respond to authorized browsers only. Figure 4.3 illustrates the principle of digital certificates.

Digital Signatures. Digital signatures accompany files that are encrypted as well as files that are not encrypted. The digital signature of a file is generated through the convolution of the files over a certain function, creating a unique key. That is, the file is *passed through* a mathematical algorithm, usually a binary one, and at the end, a short numerical sequence—a string—is produced. For all practical purposes, that string is unique to that file in the context of that algorithm. This sequence, which may vary in length from 32 to 512 bits, serves as verifier that the accompanying file is authentic. Figure 4.4 illustrates the principle of digital signature.

Login Controls. Access to resources, in general, and access to information assets, in particular, require tangible controls that are verifiable and auditable. In the latter case, user names and passwords are the most common access control means. There are many viewpoints on the selection of user names and passwords, all aiming to balance between simplicity and effectiveness. Later in this chapter the password parameters are discussed.

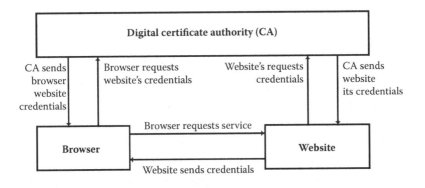

Figure 4.3 Principle of digital certificates.

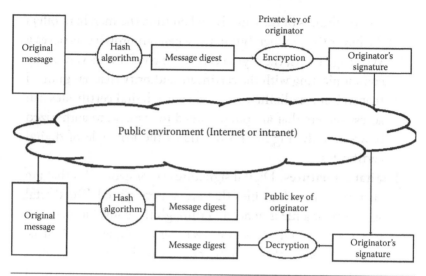

Figure 4.4   Principle of digital signatures.

Assets Storage

Everything in a digital world is files. The files may contain text, spreadsheets, images, videos, music, etc. Continuously, new file types are being established, requiring special applications to *open* them. Their security requirements, however, remain the same. When necessary, the files' content must be inaccessible to the unauthorized user.

For its internal use an organization may develop its own security mechanisms, algorithms, and codes, but to securely communicate with its partners, generally accepted security mechanisms must be employed. The basic principle of securing files against unauthorized access is cryptography, that is, through a certain scheme where files become inaccessible to unauthorized users. Basically, there are two such schemes, steganography and encryption.

In steganography, the files are made secure by being hidden from view. That is, the files are placed in directories that, presumably, no one can think of or the files have names, or extensions, that are misleading. Files can also *hide* inside other files. For example, a text file may *hide* inside a sound file, or an image may *hide* inside another image. Figure 4.5 illustrates the principle of steganography, where a text file is hidden inside a much bigger image file.

There are numerous steganography algorithms. In the case of an image hosting a short text file, the least significant bits of the pixel

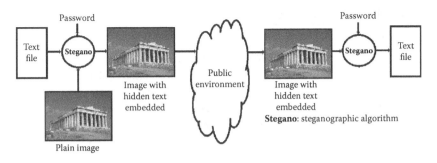

Figure 4.5 Principle of steganography. Text file hidden in an image.

color definition collectively store the short message. Of course, the image color resolution is reduced, but this reduction is invisible. Steganography counts on *security through obscurity,* which is a violation of the fundamental principle of data security which subscribes to security only through encryption—another way of saying it, file security through *reversible obliteration* of the file.

In encryption, a file is secured by being passed through a mathematical algorithm that scrambles the bits and the bytes of the file to a point where only a counterpart algorithm can restore the file to the original version.

Resource Access Control Facility

The Resource Access Control Facility (RACF) is software that grants and administers access control parameters. In the *front office,* the facility issues user names and passwords, while in the *back office,* the facility records and scrutinizes each and every access-related activity.

The facility is under the full control of the designated enterprise information security officer and serves as the issuer of the initial user name and password which will allow the new user to log on to the system for the first time. There is a wide variety of rules and philosophies regarding the selection of a password. Undoubtedly, passwords create inconvenience to users who may lean toward a password that is easy to remember and fast to enter. The complexity of a password must be directly proportionate to the magnitude of the adverse impact a compromise may have.

In the *front office,* which is interacting with the user, the facility enforces the password rules as programmed by the designated

Table 4.3 Typical Password Guidelines

PARAMETER	LIMITS
Length	6–11 Characters. Alpha, numbers, other (symbols/punctuation).
Validity	3–6 Months of validity. Initial passwords single use only.
Reusability	5–10 Password periods must pass before reuse.
Lock-out	2–3 Unsuccessful tries locks out the user name.
Content	No number or dictionary word.

enterprise information security officer. Table 4.3 lists password selection guidelines. Depending on the protected resources, password guidelines may vary.

Special characters and spaces are either encouraged or discouraged, depending on the capabilities of the password analyzer. The process for the selection of a new password may include password strength evaluation, where a certain password strength level must be achieved before the new password is accepted. Password strength meters available online can be used to provide an indication of the strength of a given password [11,12]. For cases where the new password selection is totally up to the user, a random mixture of numbers and letters is recommended. "Organizations should review their password policies periodically, particularly as major technology changes occur (e.g., new operating system) that may affect password management" [13].

In the *back office*, which is transparent to the user, the facility, besides allowing or denying access, keeps track of the behavior of each user name and maintains a log with timestamps and accessed resources. Statistical analyses of the obtained records may reveal compromise attempts. Such real-time monitoring in cooperation with the enterprise intrusion detection system may raise real-time alerts. An enterprise with a large network of extensive external communications and valuable data to guard needs to have a *Security Operation Room* (SOR). In the SOR, all the activities of the corporate information system are monitored and controlled, and this is where intrusion detection reports are directed for assessment.

Securing the Email Communications

One component of a secure enterprise is the email system of the organization, where the security rules may include the following.

Email Server Side

- Keep all administrative controls behind a firewall.
- Install a rigorous administrator authentication mechanism. Preferably, employ a one-time-password (OTP) scheme. "One Time Passwords, generated in advance, called 'prefetch.' They can be printed or sent via email, chat, SMS. Great to have when you have limited access to GSM network, or while out traveling" [14].
- Operate the email server software out of stand-alone hardware that has no unrelated sensitive files.
- Maintain an updated malware detection software, and test all incoming and all outgoing files for malware.
- Maintain an updated list of spam email servers, and flag spam email for the designated recipient.
- Besides attachment, test email content, itself, for active code that may contain malware.
- Maintain a list of words that, if found inside the email text, raise a flag to the recipient or to the administrator.
- Maintain compatibility with all commonly used email clients and webmail browsers.
- Provide support for SSL/TLS encryption [Transport Layer Security (TLS) protocol, Secure Sockets Layer (SSL) protocol]. These are cryptographic protocols that provide security over Internet communications.

Email Client Side

- Email client software should not be installed in hardware— PC or workstations—that are being used as servers or contain confidential information.
- Updated versions of the operating system and of the email clients should be used.
- Hardware used must have updated, self-updating antimalware software that monitors files in real time.
- Email software should run in user mode, contrary to administrator mode, in order to prevent exposure to cyberspace of administrative privileges.

- Email software should be configured to the security features according to organizational policy. Policy must prevent
  - Automatic preview of messages
  - Automatic opening of messages
  - Automatic loading of pictures in messages
  - Automatic downloading of active content
  - Automatic processing of active content
  - Storage of user names and passwords
  - Client from staying active after X minutes of inactivity
- Avoid *read confirmation* and *return receipt*, as they are executable and may connect to malware.
- Email messages from suspicious or unknown sources should be deleted without being opened.
- Spam email may contain active malware in the unsubscribe option.
- Preferably, emails must be viewed as plain text. Advanced formatting, such as HTML and RTF, may allow malware to hide themselves in scripts.
- Confidential communications should be preferably sent encrypted as attached files rather than in the body of the email.

Information Security Management

The three cornerstones of information security are confidentiality, integrity, and availability of data. For these properties to be sustainable, resources are needed, and consequently, upper management support is a prerequisite.

Similarly, the three cornerstones of management are controls, processes, and structures. Table 4.4 lists the basic issues contained within the broad concept of Information Security Management. Figure 4.6 emphasizes the three pillars of management.

Controls. Under controls fall the organizational policies on data security, classification, and accessibility. Security is a costly endeavor; consequently, security levels must be proportionate to the organizational value of the protected data asset. In this context, data classifications take place with security in mind so that

Table 4.4   Information Security Management

CONTROLS	PROCESSES	STRUCTURE
Data Security Policy	Compliance	Security Personnel
Policy document	Legislation	Recruitment criteria
Risks assessment	Copyrights	Ongoing training
Responsibilities	Privacy	Responsibilities
Resources	Audits	Code of conduct
Data Classification	Data Encryption	Physical Networks
Identification	Technologies	Data routing
Classification	Level	VPN
Inventory/storage	Standards	Firewalls
Creation/change	Maintenance	Cloud
Data Accessibility	System Integrity	Incident Management
Authentications	Verification	Policies
Password	Upgrades	Response
Automated audit	Fault	Documentation
Trail	Tolerance	Recovery
Mobile computing	Patches	Data backup

Source: Encryption Methods. Finnish Communications Regulatory Authority, http://www.ficora.fi/en/index/palvelut/palvelutaiheittain/tietoturva/salausmenetelmat.html

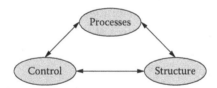

Figure 4.6   Three pillars of information security management: control, processes, and structure.

security resources are allocated in a most appropriate and cost-effective way. User authentications will always be the prime security concern guided by need-to-access and technology efficiency.

Processes. Management, by definition, is the establishment of processes. In this context, the three fundamental processes are compliance, encryption, and integrity of data. There are numerous laws that demand compliance as to data security and data privacy, while others require data archiving for possible future auditing. Data encryption is the infrastructure of data security. However, effectiveness and compatibility determine encryption levels, technologies, and standards. Besides being secure, data must be correct through the use of updated software, verifications, and fault tolerance.

Structures. Regardless of the level of automation, human presence is inevitable. The security structure is headed by the organization's *Chief Information Security Officer*, whose mission is the implementation of the organizational data security policy. This task calls for a team of experts with continuously enhanced skills to defend the organizational data in an efficient and cost-effective manner. The logical structure of the information system also needs to have been designed with security in mind, implemented through firewalls and VPNs. The *cloud computing* concept, described in the previous chapter, poses a new challenge to information systems designers because the dependence on outsourced services becomes absolute.

Over time, increased business opportunities have created a demand for information systems of unprecedented complexity, challenging intersystem interface demands, and stringent interoperability requirements. It has become a perpetual and nonstop race. Technology escalates, and new business possibilities from dreams become reality. However, their implementation is not simple, but it counts on multisystem cooperation, with consequent inter-dependencies that are difficult to fully control.

In this state of flux, from both viewpoints—business and technology—possibilities of failure abound with the main causes being:

- *Technology escalation* with the subsequent lack of critical mass of professionals with experience and expertise.
- *Technology interoperability* with the numerous interface and communications standards.
- *Virtual technologies* with ease in system assembly, hidden complexities, and often unpredictable behavior.
- *New trends* inhibiting the maturity and return on investment of existing successful technologies.
- *Speed of change* is faster than change management can keep track of.
- *Malware* that are always three to six months ahead of the protection software.

With the above challenges, maintaining a secure information system is a difficult but not impossible task requiring a holistic participation of visionaries, developers, and users. "Survivability of the organization depends on the capabilities of the people, actions, and technology that compose the operational process to work together to achieve operational effectiveness" [15].

Encryption Options in Emails

Once an email leaves its origin and before it reaches its destination, there are numerous transmissions and hubs, which are not necessarily secure. An email with no security is like a postcard in the mail. Therefore, an email must be encrypted at the origin and decrypted at the destination.

Typical email applications offer the option of encrypting the email at the origin with a password and will decrypt it at the destination. For enterprises, there are more elaborate email portals that offer advance features, such as

- Secure e-signature, which is digitally signing encrypted files. This is where a code is being created by the sender's private key and is verifiable by anyone with the sender's public key, thus ensuring authenticity.
- Automatic email and attachments encryption, where the sender is using the receiver's public key, thus ensuring confidentiality.
- Mobile device support, allowing full use of the application via smartphones.
- Regulatory compliance with data protection Acts, such as HIPAA, HITECH, CFPB, etc. See Chapter Nine for full descriptions of the Acts.
- Attachment of large files.
- Compatibility with other email applications.
- Centralized management, allowing full auditing.
- Anti-virus and anti-spam protection.
- PGP (Pretty Good Protection)* utilization and removable-media encryption.
- Large storage space.

---

* https://www.symantec.com/products/information-protection/encryption

For increased email security, enterprises may have their own email server, rather than counting on a serviced one in the cloud (physically away from the premises of the enterprise).

Steganography

Besides being encrypted, a file may be concealed inside a much larger file without noticeably affecting the effectiveness of the large file. Typically, such large files are files of images, audio or video. In these files, the asset and its quality are being numerically represented.

In the case of images there are samples of color dots—the pixels—while in the case of audio there are samples of sound. Either way, these samples are being represented by binary numbers corresponding to the quality of the sample.

The simplest way is to dedicate the least significant bit of the binary numbers to enter and conceal the data to be hidden. The impact of this action onto the human perception of the image, audio or video is negligible.

A very common steganography tool is the S-Tools with numerous download mirrors*.

Exercises

1. Research the status and accomplishments of DETER, the Cyber Defense Technology Experimental Research Laboratory Testbed (http://www.isi.edu/deter/), and write a three-page report on its current status.
2. Create a database structure to hold the transcripts of students of a certain college that has six departments with five degree programs each. Select directory, subdirectory, and file names that facilitate file identification.
3. Visit password strength websites, and determine the strength of the following passwords: 123456654321, qwertyuiiuytrewq, MNBVVBNM, ?2wdcgy88ygcsw2

---

† http://www.filewatcher.com/m/s-tools4.zip.278774-0.html

4. It was stated in this chapter to *operate the email server software out of standalone hardware*. Describe what adverse events may happen if this advice is not followed.

5. It is believed that fault tolerance technologies may strengthen data integrity. Explain how, and provide an example.

6. One-time-password (OTP) technologies are being increasingly used in ATM accessing. Identify three other applications, and describe the use and derived benefits.

7. Conduct a two-page research on cloud computing, focusing on the forensics issues.

8. Research the steganography tools, and practice hiding text files in images. Observe possible differences between the original image and the one that is hiding the text file.

9. Develop a text encryption algorithm of your own, and demonstrate its application.

10. Make a comparative study, from the security viewpoint, of five email clients, such as Eudora, Outlook Express, Opera, and Mozilla.

5

CYBERSECURITY AND THE CIO

Cybersecurity is an integral part of any security concept, be it corporate or national.

Introduction

Over time, the position of the most critical person in an enterprise changes. Today, that most critical person is the Chief Information Officer (CIO). At the same level, above or below, or the same person is the Chief Technology Officer (CTO) and the Chief Information Security Officer (CISO) of the enterprise. For all practical purposes, we will consider the CIO as being an all *three-in-one*. Being all three, the CIO is expected to be the organization's visionary, advising on how to leverage technology to achieve the organization's aims. The CIO is responsible for every aspect of information within the enterprise. The CIO's role within the organization can be described as follows [1]:

- Member of the senior administrative/management/planning team
- Manager of the technology and other information resources
- Responsible for IT planning
- Responsible for the development of new systems
- Responsible for policy development and implementation

The position of the CIO demands a certain spectrum in the personality, education, and experience of the person.

Cyberspace is a maze of infinite vulnerabilities, the existence of which is typically discovered by attackers at a cost, at least to the first victim. The role of the CIO is to be aware of all protection mechanisms and have the ability to devise more where needed. This can be hoped for if CIOs enter their tenure with extensive applicable experience and expertise and with the understanding that the position of the CIO is the most life-long learning job.

CIO: Personality

Let us meet the CIO and see what qualifications and career path have brought that person to this position. Figure 5.1 shows the personal and professional qualifications a CIO needs to have to successfully address the demands of the position.

Trust and Ethics

One of the most highly trusted positions in an enterprise today is that of the CIO. The CIO is the bodyguard of the organization's information. The CIO must be self-confident and radiate trust and success. Trust is a personal characteristic, often subconsciously sensed, that makes a person welcome in any environment. Respect for self, others, the organization, and society is a cornerstone to trust. Self-confidence and radiation of success are acquired only through a sequence of prior successes, small and possibly big.

There is absolutely no substitute for consistently ethical behavior. There will be continuous pressures or *rewarding opportunities* to be unethical. Yet the CIO must stand above such temptations, take no risks, and in addition restrain the greed of others who suggest shortcuts to the straight line of ethics.

Figure 5.1 CIO personal and professional qualifications.

Communication and Intelligence

The CIO must be the organization's *great communicator*. This is the person who will have to persuade others for the acquisition of resources, where the word resources leaves nothing outside. The CIO may need capital for a new technology or may need the loyalty and trust of colleagues in all directions of the hierarchy. Persuasion is needed for upward communications, and motivation and inspiration downward communications. In a modern organization, nothing is accomplished through *iron fists*. The CIO has to capture the mind and hearts of all within the enterprise, always remembering that "techie" language can be boring for the nontechies. Outside of the organization, the CIO joins relevant associations, attends fora, participates in conferences, and delivers seminars, thus acquiring visibility and most important polishing skills.

We cannot leave nature out of the CIO picture. Natural intelligence is the algorithm that converts observations to knowledge and knowledge to wisdom. Wisdom coupled with experience usually results in sound judgment. As the saying goes: smart people learn from their own mistakes, while wise people learn from the mistakes of others.

Leadership and Entrepreneurship

Some claim that a leader is born; others believe that a leader can be made. The CIO as a leader must be a level above the followers. This superiority, in the wholesome sense of the word, must be in personal qualities as well as in technical skills. The CIO as a leader, walking through the hallways of the enterprise, as the expression goes, must be viewed as a *guide-by-the-side* and not as a *sage-on-the-stage*.

For the CIO to be received in that manner, that person must be very humble and very knowledgeable and experienced. Everyone in an organization wants to see a friend in the person of the CIO. This is because the CIO is the great gatekeeper, granted with authority that hopefully matches the responsibility that has been placed on that person's shoulders. The CIO and the executives of the enterprise must realize the CIO is a strategic position that provides direction, and the CIO should not become entangled in low-level technical problems. However, the CIO must have the experience to provide direction for the solution of the problems.

The CIO is always looking for opportunities to enhance the organization's business posture, willing to take noncatastrophic risks. The CIO must be a visionary "who can challenge conventional wisdom" [2], with a supervisory style that is well balanced between granting autonomy and applying controls.

Courage and Limitations

CIOs with the above qualifications must be able to foresee the viability of a proposed idea and must have the necessary courage—derived from job security and upper management support—to be able to freely and objectively express their opinions. Equally, the CIO should be able to drop a project that appears to be heading in the wrong direction. With unpredictable technology advances, good ideas may not be as good because new solutions make themselves available continuously. The CIOs, besides recognizing technological limitations, above all should recognize their own limitation, be it human or technical.

Becoming a successful CIO is like going up the stairs, it has to be done one step at a time. Once there, it is not a playground. Being a CIO is a mission and not a pleasant occupation. The CIO is an integral and most critical part of the enterprise. The CIO must have a *love affair* with technology. Millions of engineers, worldwide, are producing new technologies or new malware, and the CIO can never say, "I do not know." The CIO can only say, "At the moment I don't know, but in 48 hours I will have an educated opinion about it."

CIO: Education

University Degrees

The CIO must hold college degrees that indicate an information systems education. The degree(s) must bear the word computer or information, while the respective curriculum must include courses that started with the binary numbers and logic gates and ended with capstone courses that have delved with networks. The CIO is expected to have a technical graduate degree. Many universities now offer MBA degrees in information systems that best prepare CIO position candidates. Table 5.1 lists typical courses that are included in such degree programs [3].

Table 5.1 Typical Courses in MBA in Information Systems

MANAGERIAL AND BUSINESS	TECHNICAL
Information Technology Project Management	Systems Integration
Business Process Innovation	Database Management Systems
Supply Chain Management	Enterprise Architecture
Security and Privacy of Information	Knowledge Management
Management of Information Services	Software Engineering
Information Systems Strategy	Systems Development
Global Systems Sourcing	Mobile Applications Development
International Information Technology Issues	Wireless Networks
Software Requirements Management	Human Computer Interfaces
Software Quality Management	Business Computer Forensics
Business Telecommunications and Networks	Incident Response Systems
Information Systems Legal Framework	Cybersecurity

Source: MBA in Information Systems, Georgia State University, http://www2.cis.gsu.edu /cis/program/mbacis.asp

Certifications

Besides the expected college education, the CIO must have certifications that show technological currency. Depending on the career path the CIO has followed within the information systems profession, current related certifications are expected to be held for such a position.

Table 5.2 presents a partial list of certifications in information systems offered by industry-leading organizations. While university degrees imply broad knowledge on a subject, certification confirms expertise in a particular technology sector.

Continuing Education and Skills Acquisition

The world's benefits from the creation of cyberspace is of unprecedented proportions. Along with that has come a dependence that is dreadful. Internet breakdowns accidental or malicious can cause immeasurable damage.

Consequently, it is imperative for leaders to be aware of this bittersweet situation. Cyberspace has become the infrastructure on which every activity practically stands on. This dependence ranges from smartphones to automated manufacturing, with practically every human activity in-between.

Our absolute reliance on cyberspace demands that leaders be continuously educated in the advances and dangers the Internet is

Table 5.2 Information Systems Certificates

ORGANIZATION	CERTIFICATE
(ISC)²	Information Systems Security Architecture Professional, ISSAP
	Information Systems Security Engineering Professional, ISSEP
	Information Systems Security Management Professional, ISSMP
	Certified Information Systems Security Professional, CISSP
	Certified Secure Software Lifecycle Professional, CSSLP
	Certified Authorization Professional, CAP
	Systems Security Certified Practitioner, SSCP
	International Information Systems Security Certification Consortium
	http://www.isc2.org/default.aspx
CISCO Network Security	Cisco Certified Entry Networking Technician–Security, CCENT
	Cisco Certified Network Associate–Security, CCNA
	Cisco Certified Security Professional, CCSP
	Cisco Certified Network Professional–Security, CCNP
	Cisco Certified Internetwork Expert–Security, CCIE
	CISCO, IT Certification and Career Paths
	http://www.cisco.com/web/learning/le3/learning_career_certifications_and _learning_paths_home.html
ISACA	Certified Information Security, CISM
	Certified in the Governance of Enterprise IT Manager, CGEIT
	Certified in Risk and Information Systems Control, CRISC
	Certified Information Systems Auditor, CISA
	Information Systems Audit and Control Association, ISACA
	http://www.isaca.org
UMUC Certificates	Chief Information Officer
	Homeland Security and Information Assurance
	Homeland Security Management
	Information Assurance
	University of Maryland University College
	http://www.umuc.edu/programs/grad/certificates/
NYU Certificate	Information Systems Security Certificate
	New York University
	http://www.scps.nyu.edu/academics/departments/information-technology.html
GIAC	Certified Incident Handler, GCIH
	Certified Intrusion Analyst, GCIA
	Penetration Tester, GPEN
	Certified Firewall Analyst, GCFW
	Certified Windows Security Administrator, GCWN
	Web Application Penetration Tester, GWAPT
	Assessing and Auditing Wireless, GAWN
	Certified UNIX Security Administrator, GCUX
	Information Security Fundamentals, GISF
	Certified Enterprise Defender, GCED
	Certified Forensic Analyst, GCFA
	Reverse Engineering Malware, GREM

(Continued)

Table 5.2 (Continued)   Information Systems Certificates

ORGANIZATION	CERTIFICATE
	Certified Forensic Examiner, GCFE
	Management Security Leadership, GSLC
	Information Security Professional, GISP
	GIAC, Global Information Assurance Certification
	http://www.giac.org/

bringing to the world. Such education will help leaders identify and minimize cyber risks, while preparing the society for the upcoming benefits and concerns.

The cybersecurity will undoubtedly take the lead, but cybersecurity awareness for all is essential as a driver's license. Many nations have recognized the need for cyberspace education, planning for appropriate educational programs, focusing on three goals*. Namely, to

1. Raise national awareness about the cyberspace risks.
2. Broaden the pool of cybersecurity professionals.
3. Create a globally cooperative cybersecurity force.

CIO: Experience

The CIO must have reached the position *through the ranks*. Education alone will not do it. That is, the person must have served in the IT sector in a meaningful capacity for a number of years. Possibly, the person started as a design engineer or as a programmer, then became an analyst, a few years later a first level supervisor, and so on. Parallel to that, the CIO-to-be was enhancing the background with related courses, seminars, and hopefully acquired a few certificates on the way.

With about ten to fifteen years of experience, and feeling confident about the already acquired qualifications in IT, the CIO-to-be ventures into the market *trying the waters*. The rest of it is a matter of matching the acquired soft and hard skills to the presented opportunities.

On average, about twelve years from college may get one to the CIO position, depending on the size of the organization and if the experience and education cards are played right. While career planning, the

---

* http://csrc.nist.gov/nice/documents/nicestratplan/nice-strategic-plan_sep2012.pdf

CIO-to-be must remember that "recruiters are looking for—proven success stories—not people who have the potential to succeed" [4].

CIO: Responsibilities

With time, IT evolved as an integral and indispensable participant in any organization, and the need for a central figure, the CIO, became apparent. In 1996, it reached the point where, in the United States, a federal law [5] was passed that even included the responsibilities of the CIO within the various departments of the government. The CIO responsibilities are partially listed in Table 5.3 and highlighted in Figure 5.2. It is difficult to prioritize them, so they are listed in alphabetical order.

It is apparent that the CIO's responsibilities cover the entire spectrum of the information systems within the organization. In effect, the CIO is the organization's *Minister of Defense*.

Other responsibilities not explicitly stated in the above act include the following.

Table 5.3   CIO Responsibilities (Clinger–Cohen Act of 1996)

Acquisitions	Performance and results-based management
Architecture	Policy
Business continuity	Process improvement
Capital planning and investment	Program management
Customer relations	Risk management
Innovations	Security
Leadership management	Strategic planning
Operations	Technology assessment

Source: Clinger-Cohen Act of 1996, http://www.cio.gov/Documents/it_management
_reform_act_Feb_1996.html

Figure 5.2   CIO professional responsibilities.

Data Backup and Archiving

The CIO has to design the implementation of plans made by the organization's Data Administrator for the real-time backing-up of the operational data. With the introduction of the *cloud* as a possible backup destination, additional security concerns need to be addressed because of the ambiguity as to the exact physical location of data.

Culture of Security

The CIOs in their capacity as the organization's Chief Information Security Officers bear the responsibility of creating a corporate *culture of security* that will serve as a subconscious guide in everyone's actions. The basic elements of a *culture of security* are, on one hand, the awareness as to the existence of threats and of their potential harm to the organization and, on the other, the adherence to the security rules.

Creating a *culture of security* is not easy, because it creates inconvenience to many. However, through training programs it will be understood that security measures are a very small price to pay for not having security incidents of possibly catastrophic consequences. While the CIO's actual security staff may be small in size, the virtual staff should include each and every member of the organization.

Cyber Training

Considering that technology is endlessly evolving, training of the organization's IT staff will have to be on a continuous basis. The CIO will need to have a career path for each and every member of the IT department, and training will contribute in the realization of a *live* career path. Training may be in-house, external, face-to-face, or online. Certifications must be an integral part of the organization's training philosophy, as well as training by vendors wherever applicable.

Contingency Plans

The CIO, in cooperation with organization's department heads, designs contingency plans for as many adverse eventualities as practically possible.

The CIO has come through the ranks of the organization's operations track and may mistakenly believe that the position is still of the operational level. This is very wrong, and unfortunately many CIOs get lost in technical details. The CIO position is a strategic-level position, and the CIO must be free of the CIO's operations hat. To accomplish that CIOs must "clone" themselves [6]. That is, similar to the ships where the *first officer* is running the ship and not the captain, the CIO needs to have a *first officer* who will handle all the operational IT aspects of the organization. This way, the CIO will be able to concentrate on the strategic role—keeping track of technological advancements, securing resources for the organizational IT needs, and making certain that the morale and trust in the IT cadre are high.

Liability

It is not uncommon for CIOs to carry liability insurance, especially if they are working as independent consultants. There are numerous companies that offer such coverage, often extending to coverages of $5M [7].

CIO: Information Security

There are numerous components to information security. Table 5.4 itemizes the most important ones, classifying them as *internal* and *external*.

Table 5.4   Components in Information Security

INTERNAL	EXTERNAL
Access control—electronic	Access control
Access control—physical	Compliance
Cyber awareness and training	Legal framework
Business continuity	Telecommunications
Operations security	Cryptography
Networks security	Firewalls
Security policy	Malware
Internet use policy	Digital signatures
Intrusion detection systems	Digital certificates

Internal Information Security Components

Access Control—Electronic Here, we have three questions: Who? What? How? Sometimes one more question is added: When? Today's database systems allow access control down to the cell of a spreadsheet. Programming security to that level might be tedious, but these are options technology offers and should be weighed relative to the importance of the protected data. Data access can also be time-locked. Data can be accessible during working hours or after being specifically enabled.

With biometrics still not mainstream access controls, the user name and passwords remain the prevalent access control mechanisms. The password vulnerability can be eliminated with the use of *two-factor authentication.* This is a technology where, once the user name is entered, the server sends the user a one-time password (OTP) via a relatively secure medium, such as an email or an SMS to the user's mobile phone.

The second factor in authentication can be one of several options in addition to the above mentioned. It may be a biometric parameter—fingerprint or voice sample—or may be a device—wireless or USB—that via the login computer sends the server a recognizable and identifiable code [8].

Access Control—Physical In an enterprise, it is often the case where access is granted for specific areas of the facilities. In such cases, combination locks or card swiping devices allow authorized access. In the former case, the drawback is possible loss or compromise of the entry code, while in the latter, the drawback is possible loss of the card itself. A practical solution to physical access can be mobile phone-controlled locks where only authorized phone numbers can unlock and provide access. Such technologies also record a timestamp of the interaction and save all unauthorized entry attempts [9].

Cyber Policies

One of the CIO's major responsibilities is to draft the organization's Information Security Policy. This policy itemizes the rules based on which information travels within the organization and from the organization to other outside ones.

Cyber Awareness and Training   Cyber awareness is "protecting your personal information... and... keeping your computer safe and secure" [10]. The CIO promotes cybersecurity awareness through in-house communications, such as occasional email-newsletters and seminars, emphasizing that cybersecurity is a collective intra-organizational task and mission.

Cyber Awareness can be quantified with the following list of advices:

- Always have a reliable and self-updating antivirus software installed.
- Always use the latest versions of needed software, including the installed operating system.
- Install the patches as soon as they are made available.
- In a Wi-Fi environment, disable the SSID broadcast, and apply the WAP/WEP encryption. Where possible, program the access point to the MAC of the allowed computers (for more see Chapter 4).
- In social networking, understand all the security and privacy measures, and apply them to your maximum protection. Do not post sensitive information and noncomplimentary photos.
- When sending sensitive information, encrypt it and send the recipient the passcode via a mutually agreed medium, such as an SMS, an email, or over the phone.
- Review the cookies options of your browser, and select the one that you feel comfortable based on your surfing needs. Even better, program your browser to prompt you before accepting cookies.
- Program your browser to automatically turn off after X minutes of inactivity and to delete temporary Internet files and possibly the history and the cookies, if appropriate.

Training

Cyber awareness training courses can be found at no cost [11] and may include the following parts [12]:

Intro to Cyber Safety, covering security settings in the personal computer and mobile phone, browser protection settings, document encryption, and password selection.

Malware Attacks, covering viruses and the way they infect computers and mobile devices, and protection through appropriate settings and with the use of antivirus software.

High-End Attacks, covering distributed denial of service attacks and protective countermeasures.

Cybercrime, covering the various schemes of crime in cyberspace and ways to possibly recognize such schemes.

Netiquette, covering the socially and professionally accepted etiquette in interacting over the Internet. This will include chatting, social networking postings, and emails.

Business Continuity

The CIO is responsible for having in place a Business Continuity Plan that has the knowledge and approval of the organization's senior management. The plan is for the "prevention, mitigation, preparation, response, and recovery [of the organization's normal activities] from emergencies" [13]. Detailed information security standards are specified in various published standards [14,15].

To successfully address an emergency that will create discontinuity in the normal operations of the organization, the CIO will need to have performed, as a minimum, the following two tasks:

1. **Business Discontinuity Cause–Impact Analysis.** This is a study that assesses the consequences of a possible adverse situation that will force the organization to interrupt the delivery of expected products or services. In the context of information systems, the adverse situations may be related

to intra-organizational operations or to interorganizational cooperation. Such as,

   a. *Front Office.* Website server shut down, where the causes may be undercapacity to handle legitimate tasks, denial-of-service attack, malware attack, natural disaster, or personnel problem.

   b. *Back Office.* Database storage or computation crash, where, similarly, the causes may be undercapacity, malware, non-malware bug, malware attack, natural disaster, or personnel problem.

   c. **Failure in Dependency.** The organization adds value to a certain product or service, and the supplier has failed. For example, an online education delivery organization is using a leased platform that experiences operational problems.

   d. **Failure in Compliance.** Organization's operations are suspended until compliance is achieved. Losses of certain data may require notification of the government regulators before resumption of operations.

The CIO performs an analysis addressing the above possible business discontinuity causes, and many more, and develops a Business Recovery Plan.

2. **Business Recovery Plan.** This is a plan that has been designed by the office of the CIO, has been adopted by the organization's senior management, and is ready to be implemented should an emergency arise. The plan identifies, by name or by position title, the person who will lead the business recovery process, the responsibilities and the authorities of that person, as well as the line of command to be followed until the organization exits from the state of emergency.

CIO: The Changing Role

As technology becomes more of a critical cornerstone of any organization, the role of the CIO changes "From Technology Steward to Business Leader... In this new world of technology-enabled transformation,... CIOs play an increasingly important role" [16]. The mission of the CIO is no longer to oversee the day-to-day operations of the data processing department, but it is to help the organization's leaders use information and technology to increase the worth of the produced and delivered service to the stakeholders.

The real metric of organizational success is the benefit offered to the stakeholders relative to the available resources. Today, practically every organization leverages on information to maximize that benefit. The aim is to make the offered products or services more productive to the user, more responsive to the market needs, and above all more accessible to the targeted markets.

The CIO is a *revolutionary* with a transformation vision who wants the organization to use technological advances to reach new heights in accomplishments. They may be measurable in efficiency, delivered service, or profits. In this quest, the CIO will find technology as the faithful ally and the organizational culture and bureaucracy as the constant adversary.

To best serve their organizations, CIOs must be granted the necessary resources, visibility, and participation so that they are exposed to organizational problems and concerns in order to provide technology-based recommendations.

Over time, the isolated IT manager was elevated from the *engine room* to became a central figure in the C-Suite bearing the title of CIO. With technology now being at the core of most business activities, the expectations are that the CIO must "... *be a good business consultant to the CEO, the COO and even the CFO.*"*

Adding Business Value through Cybersecurity

The value of most products or services often include certain common components that make them attractive. In cyberspace, these components are privacy, safety and security, collectively spelling *Cybersecurity*.

Therefore, presence of cybersecurity adds value, while lack thereof diminishes value. The more "smart" products and services become, the higher the cybersecurity expectation become.

---

* http://www.ey.com/Publication/vwLUAssets/ey-the-dna-of-the-cio/$FILE/ey -the-dna-of-the-cio.pdf

In the past, education without computer skills was considered deficient. Today, computer skills are being taken for granted, with education without cybersecurity skills as deficient, if not dangerous.

As every aspect of life tries to capitalize on the cyber benefits, cyber crime rides along like parasite living off healthy organisms. As functional value is being embedded in a product or service during the design phase, similarly cybersecurity must be embedded in it.

Exercises

1. Conduct research in CIO job openings and create a list of qualifications for which prospective employers are looking.
2. Conduct research in CIO certificates and create a list of the claimed qualifications to be acquired.
3. Conduct research in CIO liability insurance coverage.
4. Review and research the Clinger–Cohen Act and prepare a six-slide electronic presentation highlighting the objectives of the act.
5. Review and research the Federal Information Security Management Act (FISMA) and prepare a six-slide electronic presentation highlighting the objectives of the act.
6. Develop a Business Disaster Recovery Plan for a video rental store.
7. Conduct research in graduate degree programs, the title of which includes the word *cybersecurity*. In a two-page report, excluding any tables, discuss their respective curricula and express your thoughts as to their adequacy.
8. Consider an online bookstore. Describe the *front office* and the *back office* activities, and highlight possible vulnerabilities.
9. Survey the various CIO job descriptions. Develop a composite of your own with twenty needed qualifications.
10. Review and research the Sarbanes–Oxley Act. Prepare a six-slide electronic presentation highlighting the CIO's compliance obligations.
11. Survey the IT Training opportunities and identify four programs that may benefit an already practicing CIO. Elaborate on the provided competitive advantages.

6

BUILDING A SECURE ORGANIZATION

Though the cyberspace creates new possibilities, respect for personal rights should never be compromised.

Emilienne Sybile Bayiha

Introduction

Today, more than at any other time, two critical facts can be observed with fear. One is that organizations are absolutely based on data; the other is that data are very insecure, regardless if they are in transit or in storage. Considering these two facts, we need to break down the concept of *secure organization* into subcomponents that can collectively provide the necessary infastructure for *confidentiality, integrity,* and *availability*, which is necessary for successful intra- and inter-organizational operations.

A secure organization starts with an information security policy documented in the organization's security manual that each and every member needs to be familiar with. There is no single component that can guarantee information system security in an organization, but a list of components that collectively can provide an acceptable level of security. Such components have been recognized in a wide variety of documents and pieces of literature. International standard ISO17799 explicitly identifies and addresses these components. They are listed in Table 6.1.

Table 6.1   ISO17799 Security-Related Components

1. Business Continuity Planning
2. System Access Control
3. System Development and Maintenance
4. Physical and Environmental Security
5. Compliance
6. Personnel Security
7. Security Organization
8. Computer and Network Management
9. Asset Classification and Control
10. Security Policy

Source: ISO 17799 World, http://17799.macassistant
.com/def.htm

Business Continuity Planning

The prime objective in any enterprise is to provide uninterrupted access to its services or products to all who are authorized to receive them. However, "no organization is immune to business continuity interruptions" [2]. The Business Continuity Planning (BCP) is a printed and otherwise distributed document that describes in an explicit manner the steps to be taken that are necessary to bring the business back in full operation after an interruption or a slowdown. The BCP may be structured into two separate plans, namely, the Business Recovery Plan (BRP) and the Disaster Recovery Plan (DRP), where the former covers minor disruptions and the latter addresses major emergencies. Some of the origins of the events that may have caused the protection plan to fail are shown in Figure 6.1 and may be the following:

- Natural acts—earthquake, flood, and the like—that have directly or indirectly resulted in the disruption of normal operations
- Negligence on the part of a member of the organization
- Failure due to a security process that did not account for a certain event or combination of events
- Civil disturbance, or national emergency
- Indefensible physical or cyber attack onto the information system

A natural act may hit the enterprise directly or may hit another organization that provides the enterprise a critical resource. For example, such an act may result in loss of one or more utilities—power, telephone, water, Internet, gas, transportation, labor, etc. [3–6].

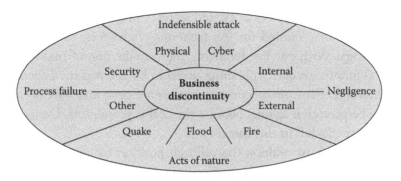

Figure 6.1   Probable causes leading to business discontinuity.

It is very common, due to lack of training or diligence, for persons entrusted with the custody of confidential data to lose or damage data in the process of their duties. This happens repeatedly, but could be mitigated through automated data backing up and through policies where critical data deletion requires the approval of at least two persons. Figure 6.2. illustrates options of automated files backup, namely, USB, intranet, and Internet.

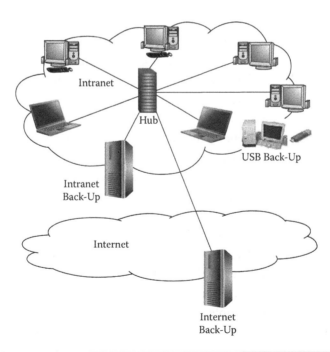

Figure 6.2   Automated files backup: USB, intranet, and Internet.

Information system security, and security in general, always leaves something unaccounted for. As technology advances, so does mal-technology. With patches following the introduction of malware by several months, security planning needs to be updated on a continuous basis [7]. There are certain attacks the enterprise may have decided not to be protected against because the cost is prohibitive. Denial-of-service attacks fall in this category.

The BCP must address the fallback position for each and every known potential cause of possible operations disruption. The development of the BCP is the result of a methodology comprising the following steps:

- Business Impact Analysis
- Business Recovery Strategy
- Drafting of the BCP
- Testing of the BCP
- Training in the BCP Implementation
- BCP Performance Indicators

Business Impact Analysis (BIA)

In this initial phase all the processes of the enterprise are reviewed and classified based on the level of importance in the mission of the enterprise. The analysis reveals existing vulnerabilities identifying cause-and-effect relationships. The potential risks are listed in the BIA report, which serves as a basis for the drafting of the BCP.

The BIA will conclude with a 3D (X,Y,Z) chart illustrating the affected services (X), the vulnerabilities (Y), and the level of the potential losses as the third dimension (Z). Such a chart clearly indicates the priorities an enterprise should have based on the itemized potential losses.

Based on the BIA, and before proceeding with the drafting of steps to be taken after an emergency happens, security improvements must be considered that will reduce the identified vulnerabilities and enhance the security posture of the information system. After this study is completed, the information security team may proceed with the next step of the BCP, which is the Business Recovery Strategy.

Business Recovery Strategy (BRS)

The strategy starts with the identification of the focal point, which is the team that will implement the steps necessary to restore the disrupted operations. Within the organization, all will need to know that this team with an identified team leader will *grab the bull by the horns* when business continuity is challenged. With communications being the most important resource, especially in extraordinary circumstances, the team will have to establish a *communications tree* through which information will be able to travel upward, downward, and to the sides in a reliable and efficient way.

The team, in cooperation with the responsible unit managers, will identify and prioritize the organizational assets that need to be protected and available at all times. For each such asset the required resources will be determined and their availability secured. Availability of a resource, be it data or processes, can be secured through protection or through replication. The team, having established the assets to resources dependency, may now proceed to the actual drafting of the Business Recovery Planning Manual.

Drafting of the Business Continuity Plan

With the critically needed resources known, the plan is being devised to restore them should they, for some reason, become inaccessible. If it is data, replicated databases should be standing by in a different physical or virtual location—server, facility, or in the *cloud*—from where data can be equally accessible.

Of course, replication means that the data will be backed up at *frequent* intervals. The CIO along with the data owner must determine the replication relationship to the nominal storage of the data. The replication may be at predefined intervals or may be on a real-time basis. Also, there might be more than one replication site.

Similarly, the availability of processes will have to be secured through multiple servers which can automatically switch on, replacing the incapacitated ones. This means that, in the case of an extended denial-of-service attack, service will be provided out of different IP addresses with the Domain Name System (DNS) being updated instantly. The DNS converts domain name addresses to IP addresses.

Testing of the Business Continuity Plan

Once the plan is drafted, reviewed, and approved, it has to be tested through a series of emulated emergencies, with the test results feeding back and improving the plan. Before going into sophisticated business continuity failure possibilities, tests for the basic vulnerabilities must be performed, starting with the utilities. What if water service to the operations building is interrupted, or power is lost, or telephone service is lost, or Internet access is not possible, or public transportation stops for whatever reason?

Clients around the world, when going to the Web to access the organization's services, take it for granted that they will be there. Our lives have become so interdependent that, if one service fails, a domino effect of adverse situations will be created. When we drive and see the traffic light to be green, we step on the gas and expect a clear road ahead of us. What if a crossing motorist fails to stop at the red? Certainly, many lives will be disrupted by such a failure.

Therefore, there must be specific step-by-step instructions in that Business Continuity Plan accounting for a long list of possible adverse events that need to be overcome so that business continuity be maintained. Most importantly, each and every recovery solution has to be tested and its validity confirmed. Such testing has to be on a regular basis, where the word *regular* has to be quantified in time units by the Chief Information Security Officer (CISO).

Training in Business Continuity Plan Implementation

It is a fact that learning how to swim cannot be accomplished by reading books alone. Should a swimming book scholar jump into deep waters upon completion of the studies, it will be the first and last jump. Similarly, if there is no training, the recovery will have the success of the swimming scholar. Consequently, proper organizational behavior in an emergency state can be expected only if there is repeated training that continuously takes into account the discovery of new threats and vulnerabilities.

Business Continuity Plan Performance Indicators

The BRP, which covers interruptions as well as disasters, needs to be continuously assessed through selected *indicators* that satisfactorily imply that in case of a real disaster the plan will be effective. The four most representative indicators are

- Indicator one: reporting to management
- Indicator two: involvement of engineering
- Indicator three: testing of the plan
- Indicator four: enhancements to the plan

Through periodic **reporting to management**, the state of preparedness will be emphasized, and appropriate resources will be sought. Senior management needs to be fully aware that risks exist which may result in business interruptions or business disaster. In these reports the BCP committee will be listing the risks as they evolve over time, the potential losses to the organization, the cost to recovery, and the postrecovery impact on the organization.

Because every business is basically a technology-based business, the **involvement of engineering** key technical personnel is imperative in the BCP committee, presenting their continuously adjusted recovery strategies, strategies that are functions of risks and technologies as they both evolve.

Testing of the plan can provide a needed assurance that no business discontinuity will have a catastrophic impact. Through *dry runs* the resiliency of the plan—the ability to recover—will be determined, and the effectiveness of the backup services will be confirmed. Key to any plan is the participation of vendors—with support contracts in place—as well as major customers.

Considering the fast rate of technological evolution, especially in information systems, **enhancements to the plan** are expected, and those responsible need to be in tune with technological advances on one hand and risks on the other hand.

System Access Control

In systems access control, the basic aim is to prevent unauthorized access, making controlled resources available only to authorized users. Additional aims include the detection of attempts by unauthorized users and safeguarding access against mistaken bona fide entries. The system access control process is made of three components: the *credential*, the *reader*, and the *processor*.

Security measures need to be taken in each stage so that a secure system be maintained.

The *credential* is usually a user name and a password, where passwords can be delivered just-in-time and for one use only. The one-time-password (OTP) technology has now become an affordable solution for most applications.

The *reader*, which may be implemented in hardware or in software, must always maintain records of users to be granted or denied access with the timestamps stored in a database. The content of the database is reviewed by appropriate software in search of irregularities. If the *reader* is software, the keystroke biometric features of the user may be recorded and passed to the *processor* as an added authentication parameter.

The *processor* is the most critical component is the access control process. Artificial intelligence may be used to create a user profile in terms of several parameters, such as time of day, entry place, if several, and possibly biometrics [8].

Progressively, the mobile phone is also becoming an integral part of the access control process, as it is becoming relatively inseparable from its user. Physical access technologies extensively use mobile telephony for access requests, where the access control process has a resident processor that is identified by a telephone number and a database of the mobile phone numbers of authorized users to whom access is granted upon calling. The access-granting software records the time/date stamp of the request, thus keeping precise records of the access activity—request, granting, or denial. The use of mobile phones in the access control process goes beyond the impersonal *authorization request* and into *authentication request*, where the request is attached to an actual person. Figure 6.3 illustrates the use of a mobile phone for access control. The medium of communication may be the mobile telephony [9], the Bluetooth technology, or an infrared link.

In access control the *principle of least privilege* should be applied. This means that a user is extended the minimum access rights, just enough to fulfill the assigned responsibilities.

With time, infrastructure security has become reliable to the point of taking second place to application security. Recent statistics indicate that three out of four security breaches are through applications. Application entries are typically safeguarded by user names, passwords,

Figure 6.3 Mobile phone–controlled laptop.

and possibly questions to secret knowledge. Besides the introduction of the OTP mentioned previously, additional parameters can be used to authenticate a user, such as the user's IP address where possible, the PC media access control (MAC) address, or the International Mobile Equipment Identity (IMEI) code in the case of mobile telephony.

System Development and Maintenance

Cybersecurity cannot practically retrofit into an information system. It is not a *security fence* to place around a system, but it is measures that are embedded into an information system during its development process. Development starts with the mapping of the system objectives onto technical specifications, the technical specifications onto technologies, technologies onto designs, designs onto the final product, and the final product onto its maintenance plan. Figure 6.4 illustrates the major stages and issues in system life cycle.

Beyond the system objectives, everything is transformations—there is nothing original, nothing commanding, all implementations.

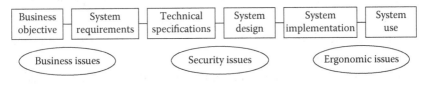

Figure 6.4 Major stages and issues in system life cycle.

So, the system objectives must explicitly include the security features envisioned for this product or service, and the subsequent transformations will simply implement these objectives in the best way possible and as the current technology permits.

In all cases, the envisioned features include security in software and data, protection against loss or unauthorized access, and safeguard of the authenticity, integrity, and confidentiality of the information. In system development, the requirements phase is the stage where the stakeholder individually claims respective ground for the inclusion of features of interest, while collectively stakeholders demand security mechanisms that maximize the confidentiality, integrity, and availability of the system.

In the requirements phase, security measures will be included that will escort data throughout their journey—from data entry, processing, storage, and transmission to their next destination. Later in the analysis and design phases, the defending technologies will be selected; digital signatures, digital certificates, encryption, and the like, where the critical features such as nonrepudiation, authentication, and information integrity will be safeguarded.

At the end of the development, the production—use of the system—will hopefully start along with the required maintenance. Maintenance, in the security context, implies continuous vulnerability study of the system, especially vis-à-vis new threats, and faithful installation of software security patches as soon as they are made available. Last but not least is the training and emergency drills.

Physical and Environmental Security

Physical security mainly pertains to human safety, which must be the number one concern of the Chief Information Security Officer. The CISOs first define the physical perimeter of their territory, then determine the means that need be applied to provide the necessary level of security. It is very important that the level of security be proportionate to the level of the threats and to the worth of the assets that are being protected.

In the physical and environmental sense, threats can be broadly classified into first, unauthorized person attempting to enter restricted areas, and second, unwanted environmental conditions. The first threat is addressed by maintaining an access log where all entry–exit activity is recorded. Visitors should wear an appropriate badge indicating the need or not of an authorized escort and permission or not of carrying an active mobile phone. Video cameras may record activities in critical areas on a 24/7/365 basis. Worth repeating is that the security measures should be compatible with the value of the protected data.

The second threat may include fire, smoke, fumes, chemicals, water, unacceptable ambient temperature or humidity, or loss of utilities. That is, environmental conditions that would adversely affect humans, equipment, or data. Each of these threats may be addressed through appropriate technologies, such as sensors, fire extinction systems, reliable climate control, and voltage regulators with uninterruptible power supplies. If possible, practical, and necessary, have the power company provide two feeds from different power substations.

For each of the above threats, CISOs need to have a plan that has to be reviewed and tested at least once every year. In fact, the organization may have a security week during which all plans are tested, with each and every employee participating to some extent.

Compliance

Compliance is fulfilling a set of standards. New quality control standards are being continuously established in every sector. These standards grant the organization the right to operate or to belong to a special group within its category. The increase in the number of such standards, on one hand, and the organizational dependencies on being considered compliant, on the other, have created a burden over organizations that is being passed on to the *Office of Compliance* headed by a *Compliance Officer*.

The job of the Compliance Officer is to make certain that legal, technical, or even social organizational requirements to which the organization is obliged, or committed to adhere to, are being met. Table 6.2 and Table 6.3 list some of the most commonly required compliance requirements pertaining to information security or protection.

The US Federal Government has the Federal Information Security Management Act (FISMA), which is a law requiring government agencies to produce an annual standardized report showing

Table 6.2   Basic Compliance Regulations in the United States

NAME OF RULE	APPLICABLE TO COMPANIES IN THE UNITED STATES REGULATED BY THE
Sarbanes–Oxley Act (SOX) http://www.soxlaw.com/	Securities and Exchange Commission (SEC)
Federal Financial Institutions Examination Council IT Examination Handbook http://www.ffiec.gov	Federal Deposit Insurance Corporation (FDIC)
Federal Information Security Management Act (FISMA) http://csrc.nist.gov/drivers/documents/FISMA-final.pdf	Applicable to Federal Agencies

Table 6.3   Other Regulations with Data Protection Clauses

REGULATION	ISSUER ORGANIZATION
FEMA 141 Disaster Recovery Planning for Business and Industry http://www.fema.gov/pdf/business/guide/bizindst.pdf	Federal Emergency Management Administration (FEMA)
ISO 15489 Information and Documentation Records Management http://www2.tavanir.org.ir/tech-doc/Mosavab/other/iso_15489-1.pdf	International Standards Organization (ISO)
International Agreements on Intellectual Property Rights http://tcc.export.gov/Trade_Agreements/Intellectual_Property_Rights /index.asp	Bilateral Agreements

compliance to the guidelines of the act. Other guidelines refer to the physical protection and storage of documents. This has been issued by the National Fire Protection Association. Compliance to this standard is a factor in the computation of fire insurance premiums.

In the information security domain the International Standards Organization (ISO) has issued various standards providing important guidelines. A very important one is the ISO27002 on information security management, mainly addressed to CIOs.

The Compliance Officer also oversees organizational compliance to its own policies, especially as they apply to privacy, intellectual rights protection, employee rights, harassment, and human relations at large.

For example, there are standards in various states requiring companies to notify clients should their personal data in their custody be lost. However, in several cases, if the lost data were in encrypted form, no notification is required. Last but not least, Compliance Officers are responsible for reviewing software acquisition records, making sure that all software in the organization are properly licensed.

Personnel Security

A fundamental characteristic of a secure organization is the existence of two types of measures: measures that protect personnel from faulty equipment or abuse and measures that protect the organization against personnel action that may cause harm. While physical safety needs to be everyone's concern, the responsibility for it must be on a particular person—the security and safety officer. This person will be on the lookout for misuse of facilities, fraud, theft, and activities that are contrary to the *Corporate Security Policy Manual*. Table 6.4 provides a partial list of topics that are expected to be included in such a manual.

Security Organization

The organizational structure of the information security personnel should be led by a senior management executive with information security expertise heading a team of experienced and continuously trained professionals. "Roles and responsibilities should be defined for [each of] the information security function[s]" and should be explicitly stated in the organization's Corporate Security Policy Manual [10]. A separate section should be included pertaining to information exchange between external parties—clients, partners, and regulators. Outsourcing has always been a security critical relationship.

Computer and Network Management

Computers, the networked ones in particular, constitute the most fundamental infrastructure of any information system. As such, their

Table 6.4   Corporate Security Policy Manual—Contents

PROTECTING THE ORGANIZATION	PROTECTING THE PERSONNEL
Hiring procedure	Criteria for a healthy, safe, and secure workplace
Security assessment	
Background checks	
Termination procedure	Availability of a first aid facility and medical evacuation procedures
Security issues	
Release of corporate property	
Use of corporate assets	Emergency procedures and training
Property and documents transfer procedures	Procedures for assigning or releasing responsibilities

Table 6.5   Responsibilities of the IT Management Department

1. Ensure the correct and secure operation of information processing facilities.
2. Minimize the risk of systems failures.
3. Protect the integrity of software and information.
4. Maintain the integrity and availability of information processing and communication.
5. Ensure the safeguarding of information in networks and the protection of the supporting infrastructure.
6. Prevent damage to assets and interruptions to business activities.
7. Prevent loss, modification, or misuse of information exchanged between organizations.

flawless performance and interoperability needs to be guaranteed at all times with the availability of properly trained professionals with the responsibilities listed in Table 6.5, as defined in ISO17799 [11].

Asset Classification and Control

In a broad sense everything in an organization is an asset. The assets may be tangible, such as software, hardware, and personnel, or intangible, such as relationships, reputation, and expertise. However, the general perception of assets leans more toward the former. Assets need to be classified into respective categories with their level of significance to the organization clearly identified. Parallel to this level runs the level of security required to protect the asset. By asset control we mean that records must be kept on the life cycle of each asset. The life cycle starts with the decision for their acquisition, followed by their acquisition in accordance with established procedures, their proper use and maintenance, and finally withdrawal or repurposing.

Organizations maintain physical and software asset inventory databases and related policies. However, attention needs to be placed on the intangible assets because these are the ones that effectively guarantee business continuity.

Security Policy

The security policy of an organization is documented into a manual that is made available to all members. Table 6.6 lists major characteristics which may serve as guidelines in the drafting or maintenance of such documents. Table 6.7 lists the most common issues addressed in a security policy.

Table 6.6   Security Policy Characteristics

1. Its objective is to secure the business continuity.
2. It is a live document, as threats and vulnerabilities change.
3. It is imperfect, by definition.
4. It is written in the corporate language, culture, and tone.
5. It seeks to be practical and not theoretical.
6. It is expected to fail and to be subsequently enhanced.
7. It presents the policies in a hierarchical manner.

Table 6.7   Common Security Policy Issues

1. Computer acceptable use
2. Password issuance and renewal
3. Email use, encryption, and attachments
4. Web surfing and social networks
5. Mobile devices computing, communications, storage
6. Remote access authorization and authentication
7. Internet network gateways
8. Wireless BT, Wi-Fi, and WiMAX
9. Servers data and multimedia
10. Incident response plan, the response team

Encryption Key Management

With the decrease in the cost of storage and networking, there has been an explosion in the amount of data that need to be safely stored, and an increase in the communications links that need to be secured. Consequently, the volume of user names and passwords that an organization may have can easily go to hundreds.

Parallel to the large volume of encryption parameters comes the need to meet regulatory requirements and other compliance demands. This need has created an Encryption Key Management (EKM) industry, offering a wide variety of services ranging from encryption keys creation and control to hardware modules for the secure protection of the keys.

EKM Features

EKM services offer an extensive range of features that include

- The creation, distribution and destruction of keys (passwords). For
  - External users (customers, associates, etc.)

- Internal users
- Data handling staff
- Data administrators
- The enforcement of key utilization policies
  - Maintain usage logs
  - Replace keys on expiration
  - Produce and distribute key usage reports
- The support of cryptographic applications
  - Random numbers generation
  - Automated cryptographic operations
- Envelope Encryption
  - Encryption of Encryption Keys
  - Encryption using multiple keys. That is, if the object to be encrypted is large, it can be segmented with each segment having own key.
  - Selection of most suited encryption algorithm, depending on data context.

Key Selection

Selection of the encryption keys takes into account the conditions of the application under which data need to be secure. Such conditions include

- Data security at rest
- Data security in transit
- Data creation at origin
- Data access at destination
- Need for encryption of encryption keys

Under all circumstances, besides data security and confidentiality, concern is also for the integrity of data. A noisy medium, for example, will damage data regardless of the level of confidentiality that has been applied.

Algorithms

There are basically two types of encryption-decryption schemes. One is *Symmetric Encryption*, where the same key is being used for the encryption of data, as well as for decryption of data. The other is *Asymmetric Encryption*, where the data encryption key is different than the data decryption key.

There can be infinite designs of such cryptographic schemes. A very common, and widely accepted, *Asymmetric Encryption* scheme is the RSA Algorithm*. The design of this algorithm uses prime numbers, and it is publicly known. The developer claims that breaking the codes will require very powerful computers calculating for a long time. However, a thorough study[†] prepared by the SANS Institute published the following three conclusions:

> One: "... *there is a backdoor into RSA* (cryptographic system) *and it can be opened by factoring the modulus.*"
>
> Two: "*There is no known method for rapidly and conclusively testing a given number for primality.*"
>
> Three: "... *investigations might one day yield an efficient algorithm for factoring very large numbers into their prime factors, a breakthrough (or not, depending upon how one looks at it) that would render most contemporary public key cryptography systems useless.*"

Exercises

1. Business continuity planning equally applies to the personal level. Develop continuity plans for each of the following four scenarios. Upon arrival at your workplace you noticed that
   a. Your mobile phone was not working.
   b. You left your mobile phone at home.
   c. Your mobile phone has been stolen.
   d. Your mobile phone has been stolen, and a caller is impersonating you.
2. Develop continuity plans for the following scenarios. In your personal computer at home
   a. A virus has corrupted all your files.
   b. Its hard drive was destroyed due to a mechanical failure.
   c. A read-only intruder visited your files.

---

* http://searchsecurity.techtarget.com/definition/RSA

[†] https://www.sans.org/reading-room/whitepapers/vpns/prime-numbers-public-key -cryptography-969

3. Develop an access control plan for your personal computer at home. While physically your computer is safe, virtually it is exposed to the entire cyberspace via the numerous applications that you are using. Elaborate on your password and encryption practice and the handling of emails.

4. Go to your personal computer and classify all your programs into four classifications by level of importance to you. How many of these programs can you reinstall by downloading them online? How many of your programs are backed up in another computer or storage device? What have you learned from this exercise?

5. Go to your personal computer and classify all your files into four classifications by level of importance to you. How many of your files are password protected? How many of your files are backed up in another computer or storage device? What have you learned from this exercise?

6. Research the market and make a comparative study of the available file backup software. Consider all possible file backup technologies, namely, USB, intranet, Internet, and wireless.

7. Develop a BRP for a ten-computer law office network.

8. Develop a Corporate Data Security Policy for a bank. The policy should also cover faxing of documents.

7

CYBERSPACE INTRUSIONS

Cybersecurity is measures that are embedded into an information system during its development process.

Introduction

Intrusion, in the context of information systems, is a violation of established rules as to data access, where the violation may pertain to either reading or modifying protected data. Information systems are defended by dedicated traffic analysis systems designed to detect and hopefully block intrusions. Such systems, made of hardware and/or software, are referred to as Intrusion Detection and Prevention Systems (IDPS, often pronounced "eye-deps"). Depending on the particular application, a system may be an IDS, that is, only Intrusion Detection System with no prevention capabilities, or may be an IDPS, sometimes still referred to as IDS, that has both capabilities, detection as well as prevention. IDPSs implement rules established by the security administrator applicable to protecting access or entry points. Based on these rules, the IDPS passes, blocks, delays, or diverts data traffic. The selected action cannot be at human speed, thus requiring an *expert system*, ideally with *artificial intelligence*, to decide at an electronic speed for the needed action. IDPSs are broadly classified into four types of systems, namely,

- Network-Based
- Host-Based
- Network Behavior Analysis
- Wireless

Table 7.1   Basic Requirements in IDPS

1. SECURITY SERVICES	3. OPERATIONAL CONSIDERATIONS
Monitoring	Scalability
Devices	Reliability
Functions	Interoperability
Capabilities	Reconfiguration
Detection	Documentation
Prevention	Technical support
Reporting	Training
2. CAPACITY	4. COST-EFFECTIVENESS
Computational	Initial cost
Storage	Maintenance cost

Source: Guide to Intrusion Detection and Prevention Systems, NIST, http://csrc.nist.gov/publications/nistpubs/800–94/SP800–94.pdf

The IDPS requirements are a map of the organization's security policy toward intrusions. Table 7.1 lists the basic IDPS requirements.

The implementation of these requirements is based on the available technologies, as applied to the projected needs, with cost-effectiveness as the parameter. There is a wide variety of IDPS tools that can provide events monitoring and information system security, vis-à-vis known threats. The number one target of an intruder is the protection mechanism of the information system. Initially, through a variety of attacks, intruders try to determine the strengths and weaknesses of the IDPS in an effort to recognize the presence of vulnerabilities through which to enter the system and access, or damage, targeted resources. Such resources may be passwords lists, files of sensitive content, or access mechanisms.

IDPS Configuration

Generally speaking, any system is made of three major components: the *sensors*, where data are collected from the environment and are partially processed; the *processor* that makes decisions as a result of data evaluation and correlation; and the *actuators* that, driven by the processor, affect the environment. Similarly, in the case of the IDPS, there are sensors, processing software, and affected units or functions. Figure 7.1 shows an information system monitored by an IDPS. Table 7.2 lists the functions of the major IDPS components.

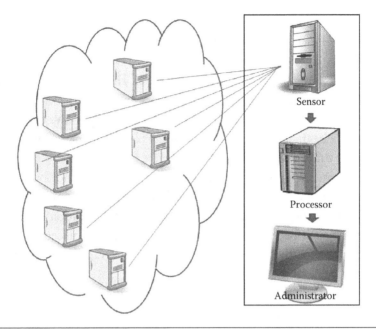

Figure 7.1 Information system monitored by an IDPS.

Table 7.2 Major Components in Intrusion Detection and Prevention Systems

DATA ORIGIN	DATA PROCESSING	CONTROLS DESTINATION
Sensors	Management server	Admin consoles
Agents	Evaluation algorithms	Access authorization
	Parameter database	

Sensors

The sensors are essential components in the intrusion detection process, with their function being to recognize the occurrence of potentially harmful events. The location of the sensors within the information system is critical and of paramount importance. Thus, before identifying sensor locations, the information system topology needs to be carefully decided. Such locations are points of entry into system functions or areas. Typical examples are enterprise interfaces to the outside world, such as connections to the Internet, either via LAN or WLAN, as well as remote access via modems. With organizations divided into departments, sensors may also be placed at interdepartmental points of entry, monitoring access to valuable resources within a department.

Extranet interfaces are also critical. These are entry points where partners will access, and possibly modify if authorized, critical data in corporate databases. There have been cases where an intruder from network A enters corporate network B via the A–B extranet, and while in B, via the B–C extranet, accesses corporate network C, for which the intruder had no authorization. This clearly shows that organization B bears a liability vis-à-vis its extranet partners. Figure 7.2 illustrates this possible intrusion.

The intra-corporate network vulnerabilities should not be underestimated, and sensors must be placed at interdepartmental crossing points. Thus, corporate network topology and the location of critical resources much be clearly known before sensors are placed. Equally important is for the sensors to be properly programmed as to what they will be "looking" for.

Placed in strategic locations, the sensors monitor traffic in accordance to certain criteria. That is, the sensors are looking for the occurrence of certain events, and they report to the agents. The agents are software that receive the observations of the sensors and pass judgment as to the possible threat posed by the event itself or in combination with other events. Agents have *artificial intelligence*, meaning that they make decisions based on criteria that may change based on varying circumstances. Furthermore, through an inter-agents secure communication, agents collectively monitor the entire enterprise network.

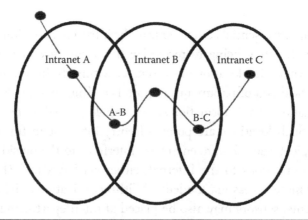

Figure 7.2   Intrusion from network A to network C via network B.

Sensor metrics can be as simple as counting the number of failed user name or password attempts. Based on that number, the agent decides as to the required action. A parameter that can statistically provide a piece of information is the time interval between the submission of the user's name and that of the password. This interval indicates the time it took the user to key in the password.

It is possible for the password webpage to have a short executable code that counts the time intervals between keyed characters. This is applicable to the user name entry or that of the password. The produced *keystroke dynamics* can statistically provide a reasonably reliable semibiometric authentication mechanism, serving as a user's digital identification.

Sensors may be placed *in-line* with the flow of data serving as a firewall. Being in-line, the sensor can block the suspicious traffic, thus preventing the realization of the attempted attack. Sensors may be on the side, *tapping* the flow of traffic and sending the collected data to the IDPS processor. Being on the side, the sensor passively observes the traffic without affecting the speed of the network. Of course, it may not block any suspicious traffic. Either way, the sensors' findings are forwarded to the IDPS processor, from where a blocking action can result. Figures 7.3 and 7.4 illustrate IDPS topology with in-line and passive sensing examples, respectively.

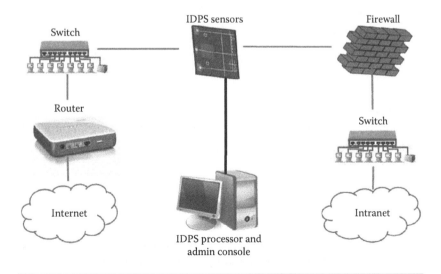

Figure 7.3 IDPS topology with in-line sensing.

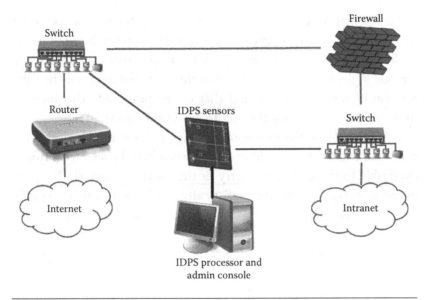

Figure 7.4 IDPS topology with passive sensing.

Processor

The processor collects recorded activities provided by the sensors and agents and correlates them in the search for malware identification or abnormal situations. The performance has to be thoroughly tested—with the IDPS offline and online—with criteria continuously updated to reflect the latest in defense technologies, as well as in the always advancing malware capabilities.

Consoles

The processor delivers all findings to consoles, where administrators oversee the system performance. Sensing and processing parameters may be adjusted by the processor on a real-time basis or by administrators actions.

Network

The IDPS components—sensors, processor, and consoles—communicate with each other using its own network, separate from the production network, which is Web accessible. This way, the IDPS becomes immune to intrusion attacks, because it is physically or logically isolated from the Web.

IDPS Capabilities

The IDPS capabilities vary depending on the sophistication of the system. However, minimally, a Chief Information Officer (CIO) will use the IDPS to independently confirm the firewall's operation, assessing the expected filtering and alerting capability, and also to be notified of nontransactional activities, such as IP or port scanning, which, although not a threat, is the precursor of a possible pending intrusion attack. In the process of overseeing the assigned activity, IDPSs record related information and report to various authorities, as programmed.

Such releases may be *scheduled reports* issued at predetermined points in time, *exception reports* issued automatically because the occurrence of a special event took place, or *on-demand reports* where authorized destinations may receive custom reports. Furthermore, in the event of a recognized intrusion, the IDPS may collect and distribute peripheral information that may later help in the forensics investigation of the intrusion. The basic IDPS capabilities can be classified as

- Information Acquisition
- Information Logging
- Detection Techniques
- Prevention Actions

Information Acquisition

Information acquisition is done by the sensors, which provide the initial processing before forwarding the results to the IDPS processor.

Information Loggings

Events loggings, along with their classification, result in the collection of an extensive amount of data related to detected events. Table 7.3 lists data typically collected by the sensors and sent to the IDPS processor for analysis.

Table 7.3   Sensor Acquired Data

---

1. **Timestamp:** Date and time. Often an IDPS may have its own time clocks to best maintain accurate records.
2. **Addresses:** Source and destination (IP, MAC, IMEI)
3. **Port numbers:** Source and destination
4. **Port types:** TCP, UDP, or ICMP types and codes
5. **Layer protocol:** Network, transport, or application
6. **ID number:** Connection or session
7. **Rating:** Priority or importance for processor to consider
8. **Violation:** Type of violation or alert
9. **Size:** Number of bytes transmitted over the connection
10. **Credentials:** User name, password, any special codes
11. **Payload:** Application-level data exchanged

Detection Techniques

The intrusion detection techniques can be classified into three categories, respectively named

- Signature-based detection
- Anomaly-based detection
- Stateful protocol analysis

In the **signature-based detection**, the IDPS has a database of parameters that indicate a known virus. For example, if a file named love. exe is known to be a virus, its presence will create an alert, and appropriate action will be taken by the IDPS. Also, if a packet's origin or destination has a blacklisted IP, Media Access Control (MAC), or International Mobile Equipment Identity (IMEI) address, again an alert will be created. Possibly, based on the IP address, an entire geographical region can be blacklisted, or a resource can be made unavailable during nonworking hours, for example.

In the case of signature-based detection, blacklists (hot lists) and whitelists are being used. Of course, signature-based detection is not possible on unknown threats. **Blacklists** contain the signatures of *discrete entities* that may be associated with intrusions. Such entities are hosts, port numbers, applications, file names or file extensions, or other quantifiable parameters that can be recognized in network communications. **Whitelists** contain the signatures of *discrete entities* that may raise an intrusion flag, while in reality they are known to be benign.

In the **anomaly-based detection**, the IDPS has a database of profiles that represent the "normal" network behavior. Should something appear to be out of the ordinary, a flag is raised. It is like the passport control at international crossings. If a person is blacklisted, or if something strange is noticed, an alert is raised. These profiles describe the expected behavior of applications, networks, hosts, or even individual users. The parameters of such profiles can be based on statistical information and may dynamically adjust themselves [2]. That is, the use of artificial intelligence may allow these profiles to progressively change without creating an alert. Deviation from these profiles will sound an alarm, and the IDPS will take the appropriate action. In the case of anomaly-based detection, a significant amount of fine-tuning is required. Tight thresholds will result in false alerts, while loose thresholds may fail to recognize malicious activity.

Denial-of-service (DoS) attacks can be recognized using artificial intelligence that monitors the rate of increase in network traffic. "If artificial intelligence is embedded in the Internet routers, the routers can, collectively, create an Internet SCADA able to detect and prevent potential DoS attacks" [3]. However, "anomaly-based IDS are more prone to generating false positives due to the ever-changing nature of networks, applications and exploits [4]." "The major benefit of anomaly-based detection methods is that they can be very effective at detecting previously unknown threats" [5].

In the **stateful protocol analysis**, models of protocol performance are developed and are used, serving as nominal references. In a way, this technique resembles that of the anomaly-based detection, but instead of statistically building up the models of normal operation, here vendor-provided profiles are being used. "When we perform stateful protocol analysis, we monitor and analyze all of the events within a connection or session" [6] and then map the behavior to the available profiles. Though useful, this detection technique cannot detect attacks unless there is a violation of the expected behavior.

Prevention Actions

IDPSs, as their name implies, are expected, after detection, to actually prevent the attempted intrusion. This can be accomplished in a variety of ways, including

- Blocking the access to all services of the targeted resource (database, server, or application).
- Blocking all communications with users bearing a certain identifier, such as IP address, MAC address, user number, or other unique characteristic of a suspected attacker.
- Blocking further activity of the session of the network connection that created the incident.
- Blocking only the infected part of the transaction. This is applicable to an email attachment or to a toxic file that accompanies an HTML file.
- Blocking an attacker's request by altering the network's firewall criteria.

It is very possible that the IDPS may miss an attack, creating a false negative, or may block a bona fide user, creating a false positive. However, through extensive predeployment testing and fine-tuning, the IDPS can asymptotically approach perfection.

IDPS Management

Once an IDPS is acquired, its management is concerned with the implementation, operation, and maintenance of the system. Organizations refrain from in-house IDPS development for two reasons. One is that IDPS, to be powerful, must be very complex. The other is that IDPSs are readily available and are reconfigurable.

Implementation

The implementation of the acquired IDPS product has five steps.

- Step One: Identification of the product's features
- Step Two: Design of the architecture/topology where the product's features are mapped onto the intrusion detection and

prevention requirements of the information system that is to be protected
- Step Three: Installation of the IDPS, which may be application-based or appliance-based software
- Step Four: Progressive testing of the IDPS
- Step Five: Activation of the system, with possible return to any of the steps

Step One: Features
There are numerous IDPSs available. Some are in the form of an application. That is, the IDPS is a software of minimal code making extensive use of routines or modules available in the host's operating system and is, of course, operating-system specific. Others are in appliance form. That is, the software is a self-sustained package with own routines, and it is independent of the operating system of the host. Figure 7.5 shows the control console of an appliance-based IDPS.

Step Two: Architecture
The designed architecture will provide the topology of the applied IDPS, taking into account the monitoring locations and the level of the expected reliability. For increased reliability, sensor redundancy is deployed where multiple sensors monitor the same activity. The IDPS architecture is also concerned with the location of the other IDPS components, like the servers and the administration consoles. The IDPS will interface with the information system it protects in order to collect data and affect necessary actions. Table 7.4 lists the typical IDPS interfaces.

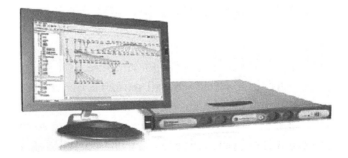

Figure 7.5 Administration control console of an appliance-based IDPS. Enterasys Dragon Network IDS Appliance (Fast Ethernet). (From NIST, Guide to Intrusion Detection and Prevention Systems, http://csrc.nist.gov/publications/nistpubs/800-94/SP800-94.pdf.)

Table 7.4 IDPS Interfaces with Information System

DATA COLLECTED FROM TAPPED SOURCES TO BE ANALYZED	DATA DELIVERED IN RESPONSE TO INCIDENTS
Event management software	Warnings to admin
Login and email servers	Warnings to emails
Paging systems	Automated emails
Network routers and switches	Incident's profile
Firewalls	Firewall reconfiguration
DATA RECEIVED FROM NETWORK MANAGEMENT SOFTWARE	COMMANDS DELIVERED TO PREVENT ATTEMPTED COMPROMISE INCIDENTS
Patch update	Processes terminations
IDPS configuration update	Attachment removal
Admin console commands	Access blocking

Step Three: Installation

Once the IDPS solution has been identified and the topology has been defined, the installation may proceed. Usually, appliance-based IDPSs are simpler to deploy. However, positioning of the sensors remains the most important parameter. Depending on the particular security application, sensors may be placed in front or behind firewalls, at critical subnets, at Web and email servers, and at critical databases.

Step Four: Testing

System testing and operator training should run parallel. Testing is a lengthy process during which detection and prevention criteria are adjusted to minimize false alarms. Operator training will be an ongoing activity, as new threats and software updates are being introduced.

Step Five: Activation

This is the final stage where the system goes into use. Practice has shown that when an IDPS is activated with all sensors active at once, a large number of false alarms overwhelm the operator. It is suggested that the activation of sensors takes place in a progressive manner, so that additional fine-tuning can be implemented. A phased IDPS deployment will best reveal hidden problems and maximize the successful defense of the information system. While in the activation phase, temporary, partial, or total system outages may become necessary for the logical and physical engagement of the IDPS with the production network.

Once in production, a continuous updating of the signatures database will be needed, as well as thresholds adjustments. Considering the importance of IDPS in the secure operation of the information system, it is suggested that administrators' credentials include a two-factor authentication, especially if remote access is used.

Operation

IDPS products are usually operated through a console that employs a graphical user interface, with some offering a command line interface, as well. Using the console, the administrator can perform a wide range of activities including

- Monitoring and analysis of IDPS data
- Configuration and updating of sensor and management server parameters, including the segmentation of the IDPS mission into sectors, thus facilitating operations and troubleshooting
- Setup of user accounts and of the authorization parameters, including specific privileges and sensors to be monitored
- Design and preparation of scheduled, on-demand, and exception reporting

The screen of a typical intelligent IDS console is illustrated in Figure 7.6. Through this console operators can define, edit, store, and retrieve

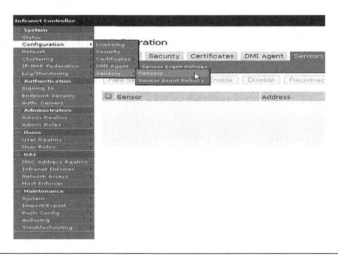

Figure 7.6 Administration console: configuring the connection to the IDPS appliance (partial view). (From IDPS Administrator's Console, Juniper Networks, http://www.juniper.net/techpubs /images/s036695.gif.)

queries. Also, user-defined query filters and alert profiles can be created, and custom reports are prepared.

Maintenance

An IDPS needs to be maintained on a continuous basis. The expected maintenance is basically three parts—confirming proper operation, updating of the software, and training of the responsible personnel. Maintenance is an unavoidable task—performed online and offline— that will affect the expected continuity of service.

Confirming proper operation includes monitoring and testing. Testing can be periodic and may take place in an offline testing environment or while the system is in production—in online use.

Updating of the software includes updating of the threat signatures database; adjusting the threat levels; updating the vendor-provided software through the installation of patches; and reconfiguring the system as new requirements, technologies, and threats call for. After each updating a thorough test is needed. It is advisable that, before applying updates, their authenticity be confirmed through the available mechanisms. Typically, the checksums of the updating files computed by the administrator must match the one provided by the vendor. Also, backing up the old configurations is always a good idea.

Training of the responsible personnel on a continuous basis is an absolutely necessary task in order to develop skills for the best defense of the system. Training is typically in-house, after an initial vendor-provided one, to bring everybody up to speed. The product documentation is always an excellent source of information that operators can rely on, not to mention the expected product vendor support live chat availability.

The successful supervision and operation of an IDPS requires IT professionals with skills in information security and network administration, as well as system administration on which to build their ever-increasing *cybersecurity* expertise with the focus on intrusion, detection, and prevention. Along this objective, joining the *users group* of the particular product is advisable, because this serves as a forum where problems and concerns are brought and, hopefully, solutions are found.

To focus on their core activities, many organizations outsource their information system security to firms dedicated to this field with extensive experience and expertise. Of course, outsourcing has to be evaluated vis-à-vis the organization's mission and constraints.

IDPS Classification

IDPS are classified into the following four general categories.

Host-Based, which analyzes events inside a particular host (a computer) looking for activities that may imply intrusion

Network-Based, which analyzes protocol activity within a particular network (devices or segments) looking for protocol abnormalities

Network Behavior, which analyzes events that may reveal policy violations, presence of malware, or distributed denial of service

Wireless-Based, which examines the wireless network traffic for suspicious activities

Host-Based IDPS

A host-based IDPS is a intrusion detection and prevention system concerned with a single host, that is, with a single computer—workstation or server (Web, email, DNS, or other). This IDPS typically monitors the following six areas and activities:

- External wired interface
- Wireless (Wi-Fi and Bluetooth)
- Modem traffic
- File status (access, modification, and creation)
- System configuration (static or dynamic)
- Running processes (system as well as applications)

Observations in the above areas are compared against templates of expected performance and may cause detection alerts and/or prevention actions. Figure 7.7 illustrates a typical configuration of a host-based IDPS.

The host-based IDPS can be software-based, in which case it is installed inside the monitored host itself, or can be appliance-based, in which case it is a separate physical piece of hardware placed in-line between the monitored host and the path to the Internet or intranet.

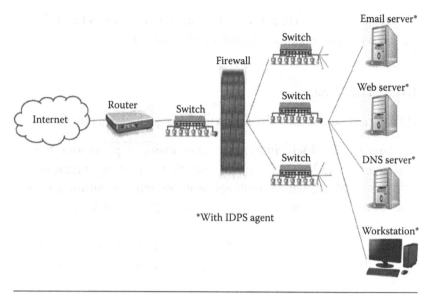

Figure 7.7   Typical configuration of a host-based IDPS. (Courtesy of http://www.enterasys.com.)

In the application-based case, there are two approaches: one, where the agent monitors results of activities, and the other, where pieces of code (referred to as *shims*) are inserted in selected places, such as the OS, operating system code, application code, or protocols, serving as mini-firewalls able to detect and block undesired activity.

In the appliance-based case, the agent is physically outside of the host and does not have the possible microcontrol provided by the *shims*, but it is independent of the OS used. Recorded parameters of detected events include

- Type of event and its level of priority.
- The timestamp, based on assigned source. Most IDPS generate their own timestamp rather than copying one from an external source.
- Associated port and IP (Internet and intranet) addresses.
- File names and their paths (directories, subdirectories, etc.).
- Authorization/authentication credentials (user names).

The host-based IDPS examines codes for malware by executing them in a *sandbox* environment, that is, in an environment where the execution cannot harm other programs, nor can it use forbidden resources. In this supervised execution, the IDPS agent is on the lookout for

- Violations, such as venturing into unauthorized space
- Privilege escalation
- Buffer overflow, stack or heap
- Unauthorized library calls
- Sequences of instructions that may be either copying key-strokes or attempting to install rootkits

The host-based IDPS also checks for the integrity, properties, and access of files. Integrity is checked through checksum testing; if incorrect it indicates that the file content has been altered. Checksum is a residual, a leftover, a binary sequence produced after the passing of a file's content through a predetermined algorithm.

File properties are very important for the security and integrity of the file content. Properties include access privileges—read/write, file authorship, timestamps of access and modification, digital signature, and possibly other parameters depending on the type of file. File access control is the most critical security feature. The placement of a *shim* may detect policy violations and even implement security policies by blocking access.

A host-based IDPS, similarly to other systems, requires *tuning*. This has to take place at the initial activation as well as after the installation or replacement of selected protected files. Also, the whitelists and the blacklists need to be current to prevent false detections. Before deployment, any conflict with other protection systems must be resolved to avoid malfunctioning in both systems.

Because of their continuous vigilance, host-based IDPSs pose a load on the protected host, requiring significant processor time and space in memory and disc. Furthermore, between installation and deployment, extensive testing is required to ensure correct integration of the IDPS into the host. Such testing will have to take place offline, causing the host to be out of service during that period.

Network-Based IDPS

In network-based IDPS sensors can be either application-based or appliance-based and may monitor more than one device or segment in the network. For prevention measures to be applied, sensors must be installed *in-line*. *In-line* sensors must be of very high speed so that they do not create traffic congestion. Should handling of the traffic reach a near-saturation point, traffic has to let pass through unchecked, or low-priority traffic be dropped to reduce the load. When installed as *passive*, observations are only reported, without any ability to block detected events. *Passive* sensors forward the collected data to a *management server*, where they are analyzed and where prevention action may be initiated. Figures 7.3 and 7.4 illustrate network-based IDPS. Network-based IDPSs with *in-line* sensors may intervene and prevent the attempted execution of an event, while network-based IDPSs with *passive* sensors serve as mere observers and reporters of events.

Network-based IDPSs analyze activities in the network, transport, and application layers, and the majority use all three detection techniques discussed earlier in this chapter, namely, *signature-based detection, anomaly-based detection,* and *stateful protocol analysis.*

The detection processes can be distributed to several sensors handled by an IDPS load-balancer. A network-based IDPS is basically an observer looking at the network traffic *passing by*. In that process, the IDPS is on the lookout for violations, as per prescribed criteria. The IDPS reports such violations to the respective IDPS management server, which may apply prevention measures.

The types of collected data include IP and MAC addresses of the communicating hosts, as well as their operating system type and version. Determination of the version leads to information about the existence of possible vulnerabilities that need to be protected. Other collected parameters are numbers of the used ports, applications and their versions, number of hops in the travel between two hosts, and other data that are normally included in communications protocols.

Network Behavior Analysis System

The Network Behavior Analysis (NBA) System, as its name implies, examines the behavior of a finite network, and it is usually appliance-based. The NBA passively observes numerous points and protocol activities in the network and creates a benchmark, which continuously updates itself and constitutes the "normal traffic behavior." NBA uses that model as a benchmark to detect deviations, as well as to recognize trends in the use of the various resources.

NBA is ideal in detecting DoS attacks or persistent attempts to break authorization codes. An NBA sensor can be deployed in either mode, *in-line* or *passive*. In the *in-line* mode, NBA serves as a mini-firewall, blocking requests from suspicious hosts. In the *passive* mode, NBA collects data out of the tapped traffic flow—such as IP addresses of communicating hosts, protocols use, and active applications—and intervenes if necessary, terminating connections that support activities that cannot be trusted. Figure 7.8 illustrates the topology of an NBA intrusion detection system.

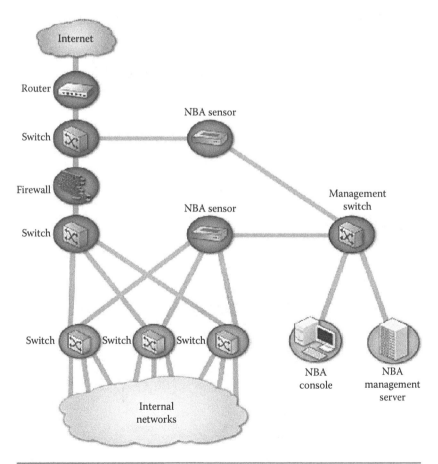

Figure 7.8   Topology of an NBA intrusion detection system. (Courtesy of http://www.juniper.com.)

Wireless IDPS

The wireless IDPS monitors the performance of the wireless local area networks (WLANs). The de facto WLAN technology is the Wi-Fi, officially known as IEEE 802.11. This technology operates in spectra that are subdivided into channels, where communications continuously change channels. Therefore, a wireless IDPS should have one sensor per channel to maximize its performance. If there is only one sensor, that sensor will need to hop from channel to channel, naturally missing traffic activity. Figure 7.9 illustrates the configuration of a WLAN IDPS.

Wireless IDPSs can be stand-alone or embedded in the wireless access point (AP), from where they monitor the network's activities. Although the Wi-Fi technology provides for data security via its Wired Equivalent Privacy (WEP), its encryption strength is considered weak and breakable, and additional measures are needed. Even if an organization has

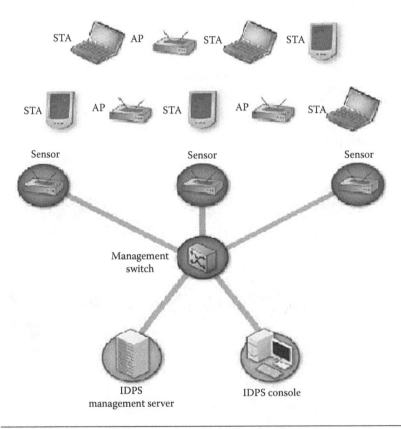

Figure 7.9 Typical configuration of a WLAN IDPS.

no wireless network in operation, a wireless IDPS could be deployed to explore the airwaves and make certain that no unauthorized AP is connected to the organization's network. As a minimum, a Wi-Fi finder should be used to confirm that no unauthorized AP is connected in the organization's LAN. Figure 7.10 displays a typical Wi-Fi finder.

If an organization indeed has operational WLANs, "Solutions are currently available where positioning of RF sensors, can geometrically determine if a client is within the authorized physical area. Such technologies, which need onsite terrain training and fine tuning, have offered 100% security in testing" [9].

The deployment of the sensors needs to take into account various factors, including the following:

- Range of the sensors and the building floor plan
- Topology of the organization's wireless APs
- Topology of the organization's wired network
- Cost of the IDPS versus the worth of the protected data
- The physical security of the devices
- The IDPS technologies to be used

The detected events are assessed relative to criteria similar to those of the other three IDPS types described above. The expected capabilities of the wireless IDPS include the following:

- Recognition of the presence of all wireless device—APs or stations.
- Determination of the physical location of any wireless device— APs or stations. Finding the physical location is through

Figure 7.10 Typical Wi-Fi finder.

triangulation, which will require that several sensors be deployed.

- Recognition of policy violations.
- Ability to execute prevention action while still in detection mode. This is accomplished using two independent RF modules, one listening all the time, while the other transmits information on events.
- Detection of the presence of
  - Man-in-the-middle attacks
  - DoS attacks
- Wireless network scanners used by wardrivers (Wardrivers are persons who drive around streets to locate a wireless network to use or to attack.)

Recorded parameters of detected events include the following:

- Identification of the MAC or IMEI number of the wireless unit suspected in the event.
- Number of channel over which event took place.
- Intranet address assigned to wireless unit by the AP. This address typically is 192.168.1.xx, where xx is the number assigned to the unit.
- Timestamp, based on assigned source. Most IDPSs generate their own timestamp rather than copying one from an external source.
- Type of event and level of priority, as classified by the IDPS.
- Sensor number, should a multisensor IDPS be used.
- Type of applied countermeasure. Typically, termination of connection and prevention of new connection to the suspected unit.

Predeployment of a wireless IDPS requires initialization, where the parameters of legitimate units are entered and fine-tuning is performed to make certain that the protected terrain is properly covered.

IDPS Comparison

Each of the previous IDPS solutions has a unique purpose and, to a certain extent, a unique design. Table 7.5 summarizes their main characteristics.

Table 7.5 Major Types of IDPS—A Comparison

TYPE	PROTECTED DOMAIN	EXAMINED ACTIVITIES	FOCUS
Host-based	A single host workstation or server	Operating system Applications network traffic	Examines all activities, including traffic flow and files properties.
Network-based	Subnets and networked hosts	Layers: network, transport, and application	Focuses on whitelist/ blacklist detections. Analyzes protocols.
Network Behavior Analysis (NBA)	Subnets and networked hosts	Layers: network, transport, and application	Focuses on anomalous behavior recognition. Recognizes DoS attacks.
Wireless	Wireless networks and hosts	Protocol activities and access authorization	Focuses on hosts security and on traffic authorization.

Predicting Cybersecurity Attacks

The acceleration of cybersecurity attacks has made it possible for careful observers to make predictions, most of which have unfortunately come true. Predictors have developed algorithms—methodologies—where the input components include the thorough knowledge of the organization's

- Skills at the C-Suite level
- Skills in the IT *engine room*
- Information system configuration
- Business operations
- Business continuity plan
- Dependency on external entities

In addition, inputted into this prediction algorithm is the current and projected state-of-the-art of the malware technology. The knowledge created out of these exercises helps to better understand the organization's

- Cybersecurity philosophy
- Critical areas vis-à-vis organizational objectives
- Cybersecurity exposure
- Aftermath to a major cyber attack
- Possible cyber defense abilities

Analyses, like the above, should be conducted in an organization on an annual basis, if not on a continuous basis, where besides assessing the front line defensive capabilities, data back up and operational/ functional redundancies should be designed and tested. Typically, such cybersecurity self-assessment consists of four parts, namely,

- The System Security Baseline Configuration, where risk assessment tools bring to the surface vulnerabilities that need to be eliminated or minimized.
- Modeling, Simulation, and Analysis, where attack vectors are simulated, and the cyber exposure is being assessed.
- Vulnerability Demonstration, where actual penetration testing is applied to the system, assessing its performance under *live fire.*
- Allocation of Remediation Actions and Residual Risk, where risk prioritization takes place and remedial resources are allocated, based on how critical the adverse impact may be.

Considering that in the cyber battlefield the offensive weapons are, by far, neither known nor standardized, zero-day vulnerabilities should be expected, and with adequate redundancies and mirrored databases, the cyber damage will be minimized.

Cybersecurity Trends

Cybersecurity confrontation experiences a two-front evolution, namely the cyber attacks that lead the scene, and the cyber defense that trails. In the cyber attacks, traditional attacks like Distributed Denial of Service (DDoS) are on the decrease, with ransomware increasing in number and capability. Regrettably, the availability of cyber currency, such as the BitCoin, facilitates the anonymous payment of the demanded ransom. It is predicted that the use of Internet-of-Things (IoT) devices in critical applications will attract Ransomware-of-Things (RoT) to infect them, holding their unique operation captive until untraceable payment is realized.

In the cyber defense, the eight-character password is being replaced by a multi-factor, usually a two-factor authorization scheme with one being a biometric one. In addition, use of encryption has been increased, as cybersecurity awareness rises. Also, a trend is being observed in the increase of education in the area of cybersecurity, leading to certificates and university degrees. Yet, the demand is not being met, resulting in oversubscribed programs. As cybersecurity awareness increases, we expect to see more compliance regulations that may be welcome by the consumer but not by the affected service providers or product developers. As a defensive measure, to some extent, there will be an increase in *cyber insurance* in an effort to minimize the losses from a cyber attack. As a result of the above, there will be a very high demand for cybersecurity professionals at the enterprises as well as in academia.

Ransomware

Ransomware is the prime concern of cybersecurity professionals because the existence of the so-called cryptocurrencies facilitate the ransom payment, which is presumably untraceable. There are numerous writings on "How cryptocurrencies have aided cyber-criminals using ransomware,"[*] others claiming that "*Ransomware, with the help of crypto currency, is big business, and everyone is susceptible*[†]. Ransomware encrypt a victim's data demanding a ransom to provide the encryption key, "... thereby rendering the data unusable until a ransom payment (usually *cryptocurrency*, such as Bitcoin) is made by the victim."[‡]

One way to make ransomware demands meaningless is by having a 24/7 data back-up software, so that all of a computer's data, files and programs are stored and updated in a Web-inaccessible storage. Another way is to install special hardware that makes the computer's physical storage directly accessible. Either way, all software must be updated as soon as the patches are made available, and all data must be backed-up on real-time basis.

Exercises

1. Research and define *signature-based detection* and explain why it is ineffective to unknown threats. The following source will be helpful: ftp://ftp.tik.ee.ethz.ch/pub/students/2008-FS/MA-2008-06.pdf.

---

[*] https://www.vanillaplus.com/2017/03/23/26146-cryptocurrencies-aided-cyber-criminals-using-ransomware/

[†] http://thirdcertainty.com/videos/ransomware-with-the-help-of-crypto-currency-is-big-business-and-everyone-is-susceptible/

[‡] https://learn-umbrella.cisco.com/ebooks/ransomware-defense-for-dummies

2. Research and define *anomaly-based detection* and explain the necessary steps to initialize a system. The following source will be helpful: http://doc.utwente.nl/61673/1/thesis_D_Bolzoni.pdf.

3. Explain why an organization without any wireless LAN operations in the premises should deploy a Wireless IDPS. Describe such a deployment. The following sources will be helpful:
   - http://www.sans.org/reading_room/whitepapers/detection /inexpensive-wireless-ids-kismet-openwrt_33103
   - http://www.symantec.com/connect/articles/wireless -intrusion-detection-systems

4. Prepare a market research report on Host-Based IDPS products.

5. Prepare a market research report on Wireless IDPS products.

6. Prepare a market research report on Network-Based IDPS products.

7. Prepare a market research report on Network-Behavior Analysis IDPS products.

8. A law office has a single wired LAN of ten desktop PCs and three servers—Web, email, and document. Prepare a configuration report on the necessary IDPS requirements. Include recommended products.

9. A hotel offers free Wi-Fi service in the main lobby area. Prepare a report on the needed protection of clients against war drivers, malware, or other intrusions. The following sources will be helpful:
   - http://www.wardrive.net
   - http://webupon.com/security/securing-business-against -war-driving
   - http://www.sans.org/reading_room/whitepapers/wireless /overview-wireless-intrusion-detection-system_1599

10. Describe the difference between software-based and appliance-based intrusion detection and prevention systems, and state the relative advantages. Consult the following source. http://www .loglogic.com/sites/default/files/appliance-vs-software.pdf.

8

CYBERSPACE DEFENSE

Cybersecurity is an integral part of any security concept, be it corporate or national.

Introduction

Threats against data originate from all azimuths. Data are threatened while in storage as well as while in transit, and data security professionals need to deploy sensors and barriers so that no malware will be able to affect the organization's data. There is a plethora of techniques and tools that protect data, and when properly deployed they maximize information system security.

Data security tools can be generally grouped into PC defense oriented and network defense oriented, with the former concerned with data created or stored at the PC and the latter concerned with data in transit traveling through networks.

File Protection Applications

There are numerous single function, as well as comprehensive, file protection software that, once installed, protect the computer against a wide range of adverse events. Such applications include features listed in Table 8.1 that aim at providing data confidentiality, integrity, and availability.

File Backup

File backup is a fundamental function that every workstation or information system needs to have. File backup may take place offline in an attached removable device or an intranet-accessible storage system or online via FTP in a Web-accessible location [1]. Backup

Table 8.1 File Protection Applications

File backup	File undelete
Disaster recovery	File encryption
History deletion	Loggers
Shredding and wiping	Anti-loggers

storage may take place on a real-time basis, on a scheduled basis, or on demand. Storage may have encryption and compression options. Furthermore, backup storage options often offer "automatic archival of old versions" [2].

Although not advisable, most backup applications offer partitioning of the main disk drive, creating a file backup area. Although this is better than no backup at all, ideally the backing-up space must be in a physically different medium. Figure 8.1 illustrates the various file backup options.

While file backup is undoubtedly a necessary measure, the recovery can be a very time-consuming process to reinstall hundreds of

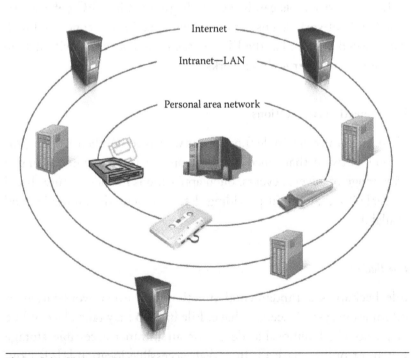

Figure 8.1 File backup options.

applications and files. This can be avoided if, rather than backing up files, an occasional backup is performed of the full image of the drives of concern. This binary image, archived at a frequency to be decided by the data administrator, will be much faster to map back into the drives for a fast and more faithful recovery [3].

The image of a storage medium is a single binary file that contains each and every bit of that medium, including all the sector partitioning bits. Such a medium may be a tape, a USB, or any kind of a disk (hard, floppy, CD, DVD, etc.), where the image is a perfect logical replica of the archived medium.

Disaster Recovery

Disaster recovery pertains to emergency situations where an organization's operational files are damaged beyond acceptable use. Disaster recovery requires that all software of the organization be stored in at least two locations, one on the premises and another out of the premises, and be accessible online.

Disaster recovery systems are made of servers and large storage devices providing a wide variety of features including the following [4]:

- Disk image backup
- Operational and archival files backup
- Application backup (with license numbers storage)
- Bare-metal restore (binary mapping)
- Backup to disk/network share
- Backup to tape and tape libraries
- Backup to online storage
- Remote and centralized management
- Backup catalog and search
- Restore to dissimilar hardware or virtual machine (VM)
- De-duplication

The term de-duplication means the removal of all duplicates, so that whatever is being stored or transmitted is as unique as possible. This way, required storage capacity and disaster transmission time are minimized.

Disaster recovery, which is a very fundamental capability in an organization, requires that a dedicated team be assigned to this task who through training and practice can provide business continuity in a minimum amount of time. Figure 8.2 displays a typical disaster recovery configuration [5]. Figure 8.3 illustrates an advanced disaster recovery configuration, including a secondary data center as well as a fully mirrored data center [6].

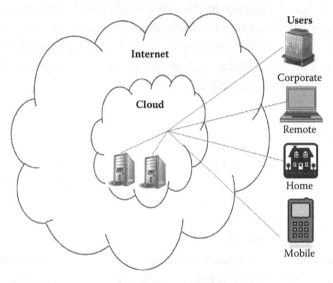

Figure 8.2 Typical disaster recovery configuration. (From Intrapower, Typical Disaster Recovery Configuration, http://www.intrapower.com.au/uploads/images/DisasterRecoveryv2.0.720.jpg.)

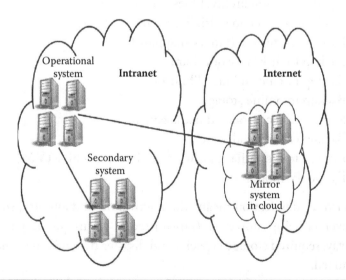

Figure 8.3 Advanced disaster recovery configuration. (Courtesy of EXFO, Inc. HDS, Disaster Recovery Issues and Solutions, http://www.hds.com/assets/pdf/wp_117_02_disaster_recovery.pdf.)

History Deletion

History deletion can be a very important issue in many organizations. In the old paper world, a paper shredder or a fire bin would have permanently eliminated the existence of selected documents. Although there are numerous electronic ways to destroy an electronic document, intelligence agencies often require that the physical medium where the sensitive electronic document resides or resided be physically destroyed into tiny pieces that are less 4 × 4 mm. The message, derived from this option, is that no electronic file erasure is strong enough to be absolutely trusted.

Many Web browsers offer private surfing modes, called *incognito*, *inPrivate*, or other names, where it is claimed that no trace of surfing in this mode is retained in the computer once exited from this mode. According to forensics experts, tools are available that enable the recovery of such files and other data.

Shredding and Wiping

File shredding is the electronic process where a file is written over several times with several patterns so that, according to the e-shredder developer, the file is absolutely destroyed. Many antivirus products do include an e-shredder. In Table 8.6 the most common shredding algorithms [7] are listed and described.

Disk wiping is the concept of totally cleaning a disk and reformatting it. This is needed for portable storage devices, either hard disks or solid state USB devices. Such products "completely and easily erase all live data so as it cannot be recovered with any existing technology" [8].

File Undelete

File undelete can recover a particular file that has been deleted. When a file is deleted, its content is not erased, only its space is added in the list of available sectors. Because of that, a deleted file may be restored, unless it has been actually written over. Several successful tools are available with a sufficient number of search parameters making file discovery and undeleting process shorter than otherwise, though sometimes measured in hours [9].

File Encryption

File encryption is an essential practice in maintaining file security, but having a password for each document may be counterproductive. However, confidential documents do need protection, and an encryption option has to be identified. Office automation suites provide an encryption option where, if necessary, two passwords can be assigned, one read-only, and the other read-modify. One may use external-to-the-suite encryption applications that provide equally strong encryption. Figure 8.4 illustrates the interaction window of a stand-alone file encryption application [10].

Other encryption software enable the creation of "a virtual encrypted disk within a file... [that can be mounted]... as a virtual drive, that can be accessed via a drive letter" [11]. This can be in the main drive or in portable ones. As the files are being stored in this virtual drive, they are encrypted, and they carry the password key of the drive. This is a very interesting technology where there is no need for individual passwords for each particular file.

Loggers

Loggers are software or hardware that copy information as it is being generated and store it in a predefined place. That place can be in the computer where the information was generated, or it can be in a remote place that is network accessible, wired or wireless. A logger may be installed by an administrator to collect statistics for analysis or to clandestinely monitor an unsuspecting user. It is also possible that a

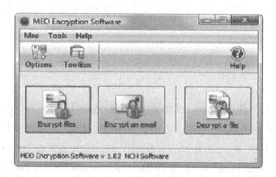

Figure 8.4   Files encryption interactions window. (From MEO Encryption Application, http://www.nch.software.com/encrypt/index.html.)

Table 8.2   Possible Logger Collected Information

Keystrokes	Clipboard entries
Typed passwords	Opened documents
Ran applications	Time activities
Voice chat conversations	
Internet activities—visited websites, emails, FTP	
Captured screenshots at predefined time intervals	

logger is installed in an unprotected computer by a network hacker. Table 8.2 lists some of the possibly logged information [12,13].

The logged information may be stored locally or remotely. In the latter case, communications may take place via

- FTP, sent to a server or database
- Email at periodic intervals
- Wireless means—Wi-Fi or Bluetooth
- Remote login—PC-to-PC communications

The keyboard is the main human-to-machine interface, and it is a very vulnerable entry point. Keystroke loggers operate in a variety of modes, with the easiest being through a software installed for that purpose. Other modes are via acoustic or electromagnetic waves. The depression of each key generates a unique sound based on the mechanical design of the keyboard, and it is possible for these sounds to be recorded and analyzed, leading to the sequence of the keystrokes. In the case of wireless keyboards, the communications can be captured off the air and similarly reveal the keystrokes. In wired keyboards, the connecting cords radiate electromagnetic waves, representing standard sequences of ones and zeros corresponding to the keystrokes.

Anti-Loggers

Anti-loggers are software specifically designed to detect the presence of logging code. Although typical antivirus software do detect many logging modes, dedicated anti-logging software can better serve this very important security need.

Table 8.3 illustrates an actual keystrokes logger report. The word *Kostopoulos* was typed twice. During the first time, the keystrokes encryption was activated, resulting in the writing appearing in bold

Table 8.3 Example of a Keyboard Logger Report

DRPU [14] PC MANAGEMENT—BASIC REPORT	
DATE RANGE: 9/29/2011 TO 9/29/2011	
KEYSTROKES REPORT	
Date:	9/29/2011 1:22:30 PM
Window caption:	Anti-keylogger report—mozilla firefox
Application path:	C:\Program Files (x86)\Mozilla Firefox\firefox.exe
Computer\user:	USER-HP\user
Input keystrokes:	-[Shift]?]yd9u7cfq[Space][Shift][Shift] + Kostopoulos

for emphasis [15]. During the second time, the word was typed after the keystrokes encryption was deactivated. While the keylogger was activated, the installed antivirus software [16] was alerted that this keylogger program may be dangerous [12].

PC Performance Applications

For a PC to work at its best, the files and their interrelations must be error free. Applications are available that scan a PC, identify the errors, and restore the files to their proper status. Such applications include the following features that aim at providing stable PC operation and maximum availability of resources.

- Registry repair
- Anti-rootkits
- Antivirus
- Junk files
- Fragmentation

Registry Repair

In an operating system the files registry—the system's central database—facilitates the inter-file communications and files access. However, over time there is an accumulation of old and loose files that are often corrupted. When registry errors occur, a PC slows down, applications freeze, and the computer itself often crashes. "By repairing these obsolete information in Windows registry, your

Table 8.4 Errors Addressed by Registry Repair Tools

ERRORS IN FILES	ERRORS IN WINDOWS
Applications	Explorer
DLL files	Installer
EXE files	System 32
Blue screen	Browser
Invalid parameters	Run time
Access permission	Utilities

Blue screen: This is the stop error in Windows operating systems when the entire screen becomes blue and certain messages are being displayed.

system will run faster and error free" [14]. Table 8.4 lists the typical errors that are found and repaired by the registry repair tools.

Anti-Rootkits

Rootkit is a spyware-malware that hackers insert in an application or in the operating system to create a trapdoor. A trapdoor is access that bypasses all security controls. Through this trapdoor hackers bypass all security measures and access a resource as an authorized user. "Rootkits can lie hidden on computers and remain undetected by anti-virus software" [17]. Anti-rootkits examine each new program installation for spyware. Removing the spyware from an application is like a surgical operation and has to be done without affecting the nominal performance of the application. Rootkits in programs installed prior to the installation of the anti-rootkit may not be discovered. So, it is recommended that programs be reinstalled after the installation of an anti-rootkit.

Antivirus

A virus is malware that corrupts files, creating operational problems and crashing applications and often the operating system. A most common virus activity is writing over spaces dedicated for the operating system and drivers or over applications code. Typical expectations out of antivirus applications are listed in Table 8.5 [18].

Table 8.5 Antivirus Software Features

• Installation simplicity	• Data backup:
• Malware protection	• Scheduled
• Spyware protection	• On demand
• Anti-keylogging	• Data disaster recovery
• Spam protection	• Controlled Internet access:
• File encryption	• Corporate
• File shredding	• Parental
• Form auto-completing	• Social networks
• Sandbox technologies	• Password management:
• Centralized management:	• Creation
• Report	• Protection
• Updates	• Encryption
• Alerts	• Storage
	• USB password storage

Junk Files

Junk files are files that uninstalled processes have left behind or are no longer associated with any valid application. Resulting in the faster execution of applications, junk file cleaners would remove [19]

- Windows temporary files
- Invalid start menu
- Obsolete files in program files
- Invalid shortcuts
- Invalid msi files
- User defined junk files and folders
- Empty files and folders
- Invalid files and folders

Fragmentation

The term *fragmentation* pertains to the way the hard disk is populated. As the hard disk space is utilized with continuous write and remove operations, empty spaces are created—called fragments. Fragments prevent large applications from being loaded in contiguous sectors. Applications that are stored spread in various noncontiguous sectors in the hard disk require the use on memory management that slows down the execution of the particular application. Defragmentation tries to consolidate all available space together so that large applications can be installed without partitions. Problems caused by file fragmentation include [18]

- Crashes and system hangs/freezes
- Slow boot up and computers that will not boot
- Slow backup times and aborted backup
- File corruption and data loss
- Errors in programs
- RAM use and cache problems
- Hard drive failures
- Overall sluggish domino server performance
- Long-held locks in the console log
- Semaphore timeouts

Protection Tools

As a consequence of being part of cyberspace, an information system is exposed to a multitude of dangers. Fortunately, there is also a multitude of cyber defense applications that minimize this risk. Some applications that are readily available are described below.

Security Analyzer

There is a very useful tool offered gratis that provides an in-depth analysis as to the cybersecurity of a host that is connected to the Web. It is the Microsoft Baseline Security Analyzer (MBSA) [20]. This tool scans your computer and for each detected issue produces a security analysis report stating

- What was scanned
- Result details
- How to correct this

The MBSA may scan a single computer or multiple computers or may retrieve scan reports from prior analyses. Figure 8.5 illustrates the starting page of an MBSA report. The MBSA is a Windows tool, checking and reporting on the following:

- Windows administrative vulnerabilities
- IIS (Internet Information Services) administrative vulnerabilities

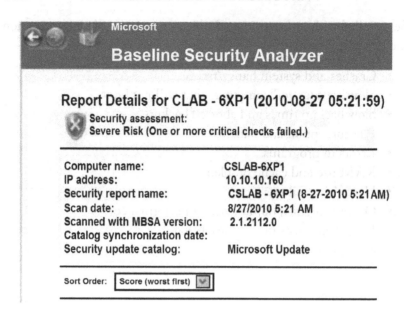

Figure 8.5 MBSA report starting page.

- SQL administrative vulnerabilities
- Security updates

A typical report appears in Table 8.6. Issues checked by the MBSA include

- Local access passwords
  - Presence
  - Expiration
  - Strength
- File system configuration
- Administrative privileges
- Guest accounts
- Incomplete updates
- Windows Firewall
- Events auditing—logon/logoff
- Installed services
- Shared resources—drives

The report presents the identified problems and provides steps for the solution of each problem. It is a very straightforward tool that must be installed in each computer and be ran frequently.

Table 8.6 Most Common Shredding Algorithms

Fast (1 pass)—The fastest shredding algorithm. Your data is overwritten with zeros.

British HMG IS5 (Baseline) (1 pass)—Your data is overwritten with zeros (with verification).

Russian GOST P50739-95 (2 passes)—GOST P50739-95 shredding algorithm calls for a single pass of zeros followed by a single pass of a random byte.

British HMG IS5 (Enhanced) (3 passes)—British HMG IS5 (Enhanced) is a three-pass overwriting algorithm: first pass with zeros, second pass with ones, and the last pass with random bytes (the last pass is verified).

US Army AR380-19 (3 passes)—AR380-19 is a file shredding algorithm specified and published by the US Army. AR380-19 is a three-pass overwriting algorithm: first pass with random bytes, second and third passes with certain bytes and with their compliments (with the last pass verification).

US Department of Defense DoD 5220.22-M (3 passes)—DoD 5220.22-M is a three-pass shredding algorithm: first pass with zeros, second pass with ones, and the last pass with random bytes. With all passes verification.

US Department of Defense DoD 5220.22-M (E) (3 passes)—DoD 5220.22-M (E) is a three-pass shredding algorithm: first pass with certain bytes, second pass with a complement, and the last pass with random bytes.

NAVSO P-5239-26 (RLL)—NAVSO P-5239-26 (RLL) is a three-pass overwriting algorithm with the last pass verification.

NAVSO P-5239-26 (MFM)—NAVSO P-5239-26 (MFM) is a three-pass overwriting algorithm with the last pass verification.

US Department of Defense DoD 5220.22-M(ECE) (7 passes)—DoD 5220.22-M(ECE) is a seven-pass overwriting algorithm: first and second passes with certain bytes and with their complement, then two passes with a random character, then two passes with a character and its complement, and the last pass with a random character.

Canadian RCMP TSSIT OPS-II (7 passes)—RCMP TSSIT OPS-II is a seven-pass overwriting algorithm with three alternating patterns of zeros and ones, and the last pass with a random character (with the last pass verification).

German VSITR (7 passes)—The German standard calls for each sector to be overwritten with three alternating patterns of zeros and ones and in the last pass with a character.

The Bruce Schneier shredding algorithm has seven passes: first pass with ones, the second pass with zeros, and then five passes with random characters.

Peter Gutmann shredding algorithm has 35 passes.

Password Analyzer

There are numerous password cracking methods and software, and knowing the "strength" of the passwords we use can be very important. Many information systems automatically reject the assignment of "weak" passwords. There are various theories as to what constitutes a strong or a weak password, and there are many password meters on the Web to use. Passwords like *password* get a score of 8%, while a password like *Uo5$Pw9#3* gets a 100% score [21].

The passwords in the Windows operating systems are stored in known locations, but in hashed form [22]. That is, the password is rolled through a hashing algorithm, and a code is produced. However, many hashing algorithms are known. Therefore, if the password hashcode matches the hashcode of a known password, it can be concluded that the unknown password has been found.

Among the password discovery applications is the *Cain&Abel Password Protection (C&A)* software. Figure 8.6 illustrates the opening window of the *C&A* application, which has been designed for Microsoft Operating Systems and claims to perform the following [23]:

- It allows easy recovery of several kind of passwords by sniffing the network
- Cracking encrypted passwords using
  - Dictionary Attack
  - Brute-Force Attack
  - Cryptanalysis Attack
- Recording VoIP conversations
- Decoding scrambled passwords
- Recovering wireless network keys
- Revealing password boxes
- Uncovering cached passwords
- Analyzing routing protocols

In the **Dictionary Attack** technique, hashcodes corresponding to actual words are calculated. Each hashcode is compared to the hashcode of the password. Should there be a match, it is presumed that the word corresponding to the matching hashcode is the sought-after

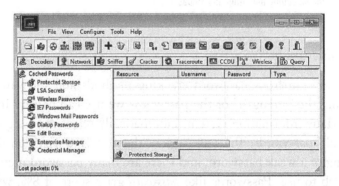

Figure 8.6 Opening window of the *C&A* application. (Courtesy of Cain and Abel, http://www.oxid.it.)

password. The advantage of this method is that it is rather fast and straightforward. However, if the password is not a proper word but contains special characters or numbers, then this technique fails.

In the **Brute Force Attack** technique, the hashcodes of all possible combinations of characters are generated, and eventually the password is found. The process may take long, depending on the available processing power, but theoretically at the end the password is found.

In the **Cryptanalysis Attack** technique, precalculated hashcodes corresponding to actual alphanumeric passwords, called *Rainbow Tables*, are available in databases. The password hashcode retrieved from the PC list is compared to the hashcodes in the database where a match may be found, depending of the size of the database.

Additional services provided by the *C&A* include

Sniffer that analyzes encrypted protocols and examines network traffic

Password Viewer that may reveal the passwords of Microsoft applications

Dumper that dumps the Local Security Authority Secrets (LSA)

Password Decoder that may reveal the passwords of dial-up networking stored in Windows

Wireless Scanner that collects identification and performance parameters on accessible Wi-Fi units and can also capture and decode encrypted 802.11 files

SID Scanner that accesses remote system and extracts security identifiers

VoIP filter that captures VoIP conversations in wav format

LAN Scanner that recognizes the presence of network sniffers and intrusion detection systems

Firewalls

A firewall is a traffic controller for inbound, outbound, or bidirectional traffic. The expected benefits [24] out of a firewall should include

• Controlled access to corporate resources
• Prevention of unauthorized access to applications or information
• Integration with user authentication mechanisms
• Secure deployment of new applications

- Protection of corporate network addresses from the Internet
- Secure remote access to corporate network
- Enterprise-wide intrusion detection and prevention
- Content filtering mechanism

It may be software-only or software installed in dedicated hardware, as shown in Figure 8.7.

In the hierarchical stack, the firewall is usually located in the network layer, but can be found in the transport layer as well. Figure 8.8 illustrates the stack hierarchy.

Firewalls are classified in the following three typical categories.

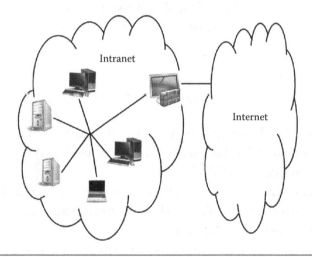

Figure 8.7 Firewall serving as a gatekeeper at the LAN's entry point.

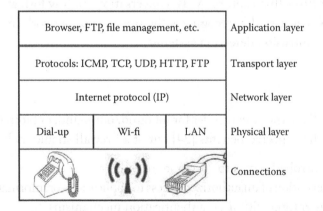

Figure 8.8 Layers hierarchy with typical content.

Packet-Level Filtering

Since everything in a modern network moves in data packets, filtering takes place at the packet level. Packets contain binary numbers or codes that carry the following information:

- Origin of the packet—IP address and port number
- Destination of the packet—IP address and port number
- Protocol information
- Timestamp
- Payload—data, command, or acknowledgment
- Error detection information
- Other—serialization of data, priority, etc.

In Packet-Level Filtering, which is installed in the network layer, firewalls receive packets and assess their potential danger. The assessment, based on the above first three parameters (origin, destination, and protocol), usually concludes in one of the following two options:

- Packets are forwarded to their destination.
- Packets are delayed if suspected of a DoS attack.
- Packets are rejected.

It is a very simple approach to protection, but can be fooled by packets with *spoofed* addresses. The term spoofed refers to the falsification of a packet's parameters, mainly the IP address.

Circuit-Level Filtering

This category of firewalls is usually installed in the transport layer, where it validates a session prior to passing judgment on the credibility of the packets. The criteria are the above first four parameters (origin, destination, protocol, and timestamp), as well as the user's credentials—user name and password. With such criteria, IP spoofing is not the only deciding factor in the assessment of the packet.

Application-Level Gateway

Here, the firewall is an intelligent proxy server shielding the host from the network. The firewall performs data exchanges in a manner that is transparent to the remote system and may control the packets flow based on sophisticated criteria established by the network administrator. This type of firewall often has the ability to encrypt and decrypt data, thus adding increased security. The application-level gateway is by far the most secure firewall, but at the same time the most complex, requiring its own hardware.

Email Protection

Email can be protected in three ways. One is with a powerful email client that provides extensive protection as emails arrive to be viewed. Another is through software installed in the same host with the email client and working with the email client. The third approach is outsourcing, where an organization's email system is resident and is managed in the *cloud*. *Cloud* is a term describing the use of online services that are outsourced and are external to the physical network of the organization. In the cloud, it "is hosted outside... [of an organization's]... network, requiring no additional hardware, software or personnel resources to manage daily security operations" [25].

Advances in malware technologies demand secure email systems where the expected features and benefits include the following:

- Inbound email filtering
- Outbound email filtering
- Antispam filtering in many languages
- Antimalware blocking
- Spam quarantine
- Attachments antimalware inspection
- Removal of regulated content
- Encryption and decryption for storage or transport
- Enforcement of corporate policies
- Disaster recovery
- Email archiving

Advanced filtering systems provide image recognition alerting should the email content or the attachments include images with digital signatures that meet certain characteristics [26].

Additional benefits provided by a cloud-based email system include [27]

- No hardware or software to install or manage
- No up-front capital outlay, setup, or upgrade fees
- 24×7 customer support

- Automatic engagement and synchronization for seamless continuity
- Integrated Web-based administrative console for all solutions
- Notifications on policy violations, blocked content, and quarantined messages
- Protection against attacks

Typical attacks against email systems include DoS and directory copying attempts.

Exercises

1. Download this free disk imaging tool, and practice using it on a USB. Describe your experience. Free Hard Disk and Partition Imaging and Backup Software, http://www.thefreecountry.com/utilities/backupandimage.shtml.
2. Make a comparative study of ten currently available backup software.
3. Make a comparative study of five commercially available disaster recovery plans.
4. Download and install on your personal computer the latest version of the File Shredder offered as a GNU by http://www.fileshredder.org, and practice shredding unwanted files. Warning: the file shredding action is irreversible.
5. Download and install on your personal computer the latest version of the Disk Wipe offered as a GNU by http://www.diskwipe.org, and practice by wiping the contents of a USB storage device. Warning: the disk wiping action is irreversible.
6. Download and install on a USB storage device connected to your personal computer a File Undelete application, and test it by deleting a file currently in the Recycle Bin. Note the file's data (name, extension, size, date deletion).
7. Download and install on your personal computer, preferably in a USB, the latest version of the TrueCrypt offered as a GNU by snapfiles.com, and practice creating files. Warning: record elsewhere the passwords so that you will not get locked out.
8. Download a keystroke logger, possibly from http://www.drpupcdatamanager.com, and observe the produced report.

Download a keystroke scrambler, possibly from http://www
.qfxsoftware.com, and observe the report with the scrambler
on as well as off.

9. Make a comparative study of five commercially available file
encryption applications.

10. Download and use the *File Encryption* application from http://
www.nchsoft?ware.com/encrypt/index.html for a variety of
five different types of files.

11. Download the *Ultra Defragmenter* from http://www.ultradefrag
.sourceforge.net and use it to inspect the fragmentation of your
drives. If needed, defragment your hard disk.

12. Download the Microsoft Baseline Security Analyzer 2.2 (for
IT Professionals), and analyze your personal computer. Write a
report describing your experience as well as the findings (http://
www.microsoft.com/download/en/details.aspx?id=7558).

13. Download the Cain and Abel Password Analyzer, and identify the passwords in your personal computer. Write a report
describing your experience as well as the findings (http://
www.oxid.it).

14. Conduct a comparative study on the email systems in the *cloud*.
Identify advantages and disadvantages to an organization.

9

CYBERSPACE AND THE LAW

Cyberspace is today one of the great legal frontiers.

Stein Schjolber

Introduction

As soon as cyberspace and e-commerce were created in the mid-1990s, cybercrime flourished on a parallel track. Today, in 2012, cybercrime has been doubling every single year in the number of incidents, as well as monetary losses. It is impossible to truly quantify cybercrime because most victims only see further losses in publicizing their inability to defend themselves from this modern day menace. The interesting note is that, of the cybercriminals who have been caught, the vast majority have pleaded guilty. This is because the collected facts—network traffic records—result in airtight cases.

Regarding the promulgation of cybercrime-fighting laws, "the text will need to retain a certain amount of flexibility allowing for the relatively changeable nature of the different forms of cybercrime and the speed with which the new technologies are developing" [1]. Any international treaties to be enforced at the national level need to be adapted in "appropriate and proportionate domestic legislation" [1]. However, it is not easy for international treaties to establish "common definitions of criminal offenses, (and)… security procedures" [1].

While no one will disagree on the need for the establishment of effective anti-cybercrime measures, it is imperative that any such measures in no way should step on the citizens' rights to privacy and individual freedom.

International Laws

Lawmakers and law enforcement agencies, around the world, advocate the need for cyber laws that are written in the cyber language. That is, laws that explicitly define cyber offenses and fully support the acceptance of cyber evidence. International bodies, responding to this call, have convened and produced treaties and conventions that, unfortunately, have fallen short of receiving total acceptance by the member countries.

A country's participation in a particular international agreement becomes effective only if domestic laws are drafted and approved that legislate the intent of the signed international agreement. Table 9.1 illustrates the extent that cyber laws have been incorporated into national legislatures. Of course, over time, more and more countries promulgate cyber laws, and Table 9.1 reflects the current assessment.

Europe

In Europe, in 2004 the Council of Europe accepted a draft of a Treaty on Cybercrime [2], which was offered to countries worldwide. While many countries became signatories [3] to the treaty, only a few have actually promulgated national laws compatible to the treaty. It is of interest that the treaty in Article 47 states: "Denunciation: Any Party may, at any time, denounce this Convention by means of a notification addressed to the Secretary General of the Council of Europe."

Table 9.1   Cyber Legislation Worldwide

EXTENSIVE	SIGNIFICANT	MINIMAL
Australia	Brazil	Belgium
Canada	Chile	Iceland
Estonia	China	Ireland
India	Czech Republic	Italy
Japan	Denmark	Malta
Mauritius	Greece	New Zealand
Peru	Malaysia	Norway
Sweden	Netherlands	Philippines
United Kingdom	Poland	South Africa
United States	Spain	Turkey

And Article 27 states: "Mutual assistance requests under this article shall be executed in accordance with the procedures specified by the requesting Party, except where incompatible with the law of the requested Party. The requested Party may... refuse assistance" [2].

Later in 2006, a controversial addendum [4] was appended to the treaty that attracted a reduced number of signatory countries. The addendum was referring to fear of xenophobic concern surfacing on the Internet. All in all, the initiative of the Council of Europe opened the way for national legislation on cybercrime in many countries and was used as a motivation for a similar treaty at the United Nations.

United Nations

The United Nations (UN) in 2010 received a proposal recommending a Cyberspace Treaty for the UN members. After extensive debate, the proposal was rejected because it contained unacceptable articles. Most of the controversy was created by the following articles:

- **Article 2** of the proposal indicated supremacy of such treaty over national laws, stating that "Serious crimes against peace and security in cyberspace should be established as crimes under international law through a Cyberspace Treaty on the United Nations level, whether or not they were punishable under national law" [5]. This passage was considered ambiguous and offensive to national sovereignty.
- **Article 3.8.3**, referring to the European Union treaty counterpart, stated that "Data... of Internet traffic and transaction data, usually of telecommunications, emails, and websites visited [be retained] The purpose for data retention is traffic data analysis and mass surveillance of data...." The proposal implied that data be retained "for a period of between six months and two years." This article found the opposition of many local and international civil liberties organizations that found the wording offensive, especially the "mass surveillance of data," and clear violation of the fundamental civil rights, the cornerstone of which is *privacy in personal communications* [5].
- **Article 4** was the most controversial. In effect, the article is asking member-nations to accept the International Criminal

> Court [6] as a super-adjudicator in cybercrimes, stating:
> "Anyone, who commits any of the crimes… will be liable for
> prosecution by the Court… The maximum term of imprison-
> ment is 30 years, and also a life sentence may be imposed" [5].

Thus, the UN remains the ideal international forum for discussions
and exchanges of ideas, but is less than ideal for concluding international consensus. However, bilateral or regional agreements very often
suffice until global treaties are signed. The Europol is an example [7].

North Atlantic Treaty Organization

The North Atlantic Treaty Organization (NATO) [8], with defense
and security at heart, is also eyeing a global role in the cybersecurity
arena. A paper appearing on the website of NATO's Cybersecurity
Center suggests that "Global Cyber Security [can be] The Niche for
NATO" [8]. NATO's interest is cyber terrorism and cyberwarfare,
but the cybercrime door was left open as stated in the organization's
Cyber Security Policy.

Although in many state-members of NATO the Internet is extensively used, it plays no role in their national security, nor does it constitute an absolute social or economic pillar. Therefore, the attitude of the
membership will not be uniform toward investing against cyber terrorism or cyberwarfare, considering "the prevailing reluctance of [mem-
ber-] nations to engage in [costly] international binding initiatives" [9].

In the 2011 articulation of the alliance's *Strategic Concept for
the Defense and Security of the Members of the North Atlantic Treaty
Organization* adopted by Heads of State and Government in Lisbon,
the cybersecurity issue was addressed as follows [10]:

> Article 12. Cyber attacks are becoming more frequent, more organized
> and more costly in the damage that they inflict on government admin-
> istrations, businesses, economies and potentially also transportation and
> supply networks and other critical infrastructure; they can reach a thresh-
> old that threatens national and Euro-Atlantic prosperity, security, and
> stability. Foreign militaries and intelligence services, organized criminals,
> terrorist and/or extremist groups can each be the source of such attacks.

The alliance maintains a Cyber Security Defense Center of Excellence in Tallinn, Estonia, with a mission "to enhance the capability, cooperation and information sharing among NATO, NATO nations and partners in *cyber defense...* [and] be the main source of expertise in the field of cooperative cyber defense... within NATO, NATO nations and partners" [11].

In a recent Cybersecurity Conference at the Center, the following ten rules were presented as the cornerstone to effective cyber defense at the sovereign state level [12]. The second rule, however, is totally unacceptable, because it places blame on the public sector of a state for an action that could have been originated by a rogue or clandestine organization operating in that state.

1. **The Territoriality Rule:** Information infrastructure located within a state's territory is subject to that state's territorial sovereignty.
2. **The Responsibility Rule:** The fact that a cyber attack has been launched from an information system located in a state's territory is evidence that the act is attributable to that state.
3. **The Cooperation Rule:** The fact that a cyber attack has been conducted via information systems located in a state's territory creates a duty to cooperate with the victim state.
4. **The Self-Defense Rule:** Everyone has the right to self-defense.
5. **The Data Protection Rule:** Information infrastructure monitoring data are perceived as personal unless provided for otherwise (the prevalent interpretation in the EU).
6. **The Duty of Care Rule:** Everyone has the responsibility to implement a reasonable level of security in their information infrastructure.
7. **The Early Warning Rule:** There is an obligation to notify potential victims about known, upcoming cybersecurity.
8. **The Access to Information Rule:** The public has a right to be informed about threats to their life, security, and well-being.
9. **The Criminality Rule:** Every nation has the responsibility to include the most common cyber offenses in its criminal law.
10. **The Mandate Rule:** An organization's capacity to act (and regulate) derives from its mandate.

INTERPOL

The International Criminal Police Organization (INTERPOL) "is the world's largest international police organization, with 190 member countries... [with an outstanding] high-tech infrastructure of technical and operational support" [13]. INTERPOL plays a leading role in training law enforcement agencies around the globe on the best ways to defend against cyber attacks and malware, focusing on [14]

- Trend analysis of cyber attacks
- Practical use of digital forensic tools in cybersecurity incidents
- Evidence analysis and recovery techniques
- Technical analysis of malware and botnets

INTERPOL maintains a cybersecurity international alliance at the front line of defense—the law enforcement agencies—aiming at

- Promoting the exchange of information among member countries through regional working parties and conferences
- Delivering training courses to build and maintain professional standards
- Coordinating and assisting international operations
- Establishing a global list of contact officers available around the clock for cybercrime investigations
- Assisting member countries in the event of cyber attacks or cybercrime investigations through investigative and database services
- Developing strategic partnerships with other international organizations and private sector bodies
- Identifying emerging threats and sharing this intelligence with member countries
- Providing a secure Web portal for accessing operational information and documents

Impediments to Cyber Law Enforcement

International treaties can be drafted and signed and hopefully followed by the promulgation of national laws that effectively address cybercrime. This is only part one in the endless fight against cybercrime. Part two is the actual removal of the cybercriminals from society. Presently, in this there are several areas that need definition or improvement, with some listed below.

- **National bureaucracy.** In most countries the court systems are overloaded, and cases are scheduled to be heard one or two years after the accusation has been formalized and deposited. Until then the accused, if guilty, may be free to commit more cybercrime.
- **Cyber-skilled judges.** Most often, crimes committed in cyberspace involve network intrusions and security violations that are part of highly sophisticated fraud schemes. Judges without special and continuous training may not understand why the accused is guilty or innocent of the charges.
- **Authentication of evidence.** If the header of an email has the email address of the accused, that in itself is not necessarily proof of guilt or innocence.
- **Loss of evidence.** With a long gap between the commitment of the alleged crime and the court hearing of the case, electronic evidence may be lost or altered.
- **Access to evidence.** Evidence may be in servers in a foreign country, and special data extradition procedures may be required.
- **Comprehensive legislation.** With cybercrime schemes ahead of law enforcement by several months, added delays are introduced into the process.
- **Cybercrime investigators.** With the Internet explosion and the parallel explosion in cybercrime, there is no country in the world that has sufficient cyber police personnel to pursue each and every case of alleged cybercrime.

By all standards, the cyber legal system is in its embryonic state. However, it is improving throughout the world, and there is a justified hope that cybercrime will be contained in the near future.

Cyber-Related Laws in the United States

Before the creation of cyberspace as it is known today, there was another *space*—though not identified as such—the *Dataspace*. With the advances in semiconductor physics and chemistry, analog computers evolved into digital ones, and hardware size started reducing, progressively reaching today's size and computing power.

The *Dataspace*—the era of digital storage of information—started in the 1960s and in the mid-1970s was in full bloom. Many companies started having minicomputers for their operational and accounting needs, and at the same time concerns started being raised on the privacy of data and on computer security, resulting in the promulgation of laws for the protection of data, privacy, and national security. Table 9.2 displays a partial list of federal laws, related to data, that were promulgated in the United States. The laws printed in bold are elaborated below.

Table 9.2   Data-Related Federal Laws Promulgated in the United States

TITLE	YEAR
The Fair Credit Reporting Act	1970
The Privacy Act	**1974**
The Family Educational Rights and Privacy Act	1974
The Foreign Intelligence Surveillance Act	1978
The Right to Financial Privacy Act	1978
The Cable Communications Policy Act	1984
The Electronic Communications Privacy Act	1986
The Computer Security Act	**1987**
The Video Privacy Protection Act	1988
The Driver's Privacy Protection Act	1994
The Communications Assistance for Law Enforcement Act	**1994**
The Freedom of Information Act	1996
The Telecommunications Act	1996
The Clinger–Cohen Act	1996
The Health Insurance Portability and Accountability Act	1996
The Children's Online Privacy Protection Act	1998
The Gramm–Leach–Bliley Act	1999
The USA PATRIOT Act	**2001**
The No FEAR Act	2002
The Sarbanes–Oxley Act	2002
The Homeland Security Act	2002
Confidential Info Protection and Statistical Efficiency Act	2002
The Federal Information Security Management Act	**2002**
The Protect America Act	2007
The Health Information Privacy and Security Act	2008
The Cybersecurity Act	**2010**
The Commercial Privacy Bill of Rights Act	**2011**

National Cybersecurity Protection Act of 2014

The National Cybersecurity and Critical Infrastructure Protection Act of 2014 is the cornerstone US law that fully addresses the Internet and the possible dangers that it comes with, aiming at "Securing the Nation Against Cyber Attack."

Most important is that the law provides a legal definition as to what a "cyber incident" is. Namely,

> A "cyber incident" as an incident, or an attempt to cause an incident, that if successful, would: (1) jeopardize the security, integrity, confidentiality, or availability of an information system or network or any information stored on, processed on, or transiting such a system; (2) violate laws or procedures relating to system security, acceptable use policies, or acts of terrorism against such a system or network; or (3) deny access to or degrade, disrupt, or destruct such a system or network or defeat an operations or technical control of such a system or network.

The law brings in the National Institute of Standards and Technology (NIST) to facilitate public-private collaboration on cybersecurity for the development of a voluntary, industry-led set of standards and processes to reduce cyber risks to critical infrastructure.

The law also amends the Homeland Security Act to add provisions entitled the **Homeland Security Cybersecurity Boots-on-the-Ground Act,** which develop cybersecurity occupational categories—a very first in the Federal Government. In brief, the law recognizes the need for the creation of a cybersecurity army.

Cybersecurity Workforce Assessment Act of 2014

The Cybersecurity Workforce Assessment Act—Directs the Secretary of Homeland Security, to conduct an assessment of the cybersecurity workforce of the Department of Homeland Security (DHS), which shall include information on

- The readiness and capacity of such workforce to meet its cybersecurity mission;
- Where cybersecurity workforce positions are located within DHS;

- Which such positions are performed by permanent full-time equivalent DHS employees, by independent contractors, and by individuals employed by other federal agencies;
- Which such positions are vacant;
- The percentage of individuals within each Cybersecurity Category and Specialty Area who received essential training to perform their jobs; and
- In cases in which such training was not received, what challenges were encountered regarding the provision of such training.

Cybersecurity Workforce Recruitment and Retention Act of 2014

This is a very important law because it authorizes the Secretary of Homeland Security to establish positions in the Department of Homeland Security (DHS) as necessary to carry out the responsibilities relating to cybersecurity. Furthermore, it requires the DHS to provide the Government with guidance identifying acute and emerging skill shortages in cybersecurity.

Commercial Privacy Bill of Rights Act of 2011 [15]

The objective of this act is "To establish a regulatory framework for the comprehensive protection of personal data for individuals under the aegis of the Federal Trade Commission, and for other purposes." It has been recognized that

- The proliferation of personally identifiable information (PII) has created concerns that this may lead to compromises in data privacy, data security, and equally important data integrity.
- Abuse in the collection, storage, distribution, and use of PII has already resulted in a wide variety of crimes, mostly cyber-crimes, adversely affecting the growth of a trustworthy electronic commerce.
- There is lack of, and at the same time a need for, a legal framework that will provide a uniform and comprehensive government position as to the handling of PII.

Having taken into account the above, US lawmakers drafted and enacted this law, which directs the attorneys general of the fifty states along with the Federal Trade Commission (FTC) to establish detailed rules for a uniform states-wide legal regime that will protect PII in a comprehensive manner. The highlights of this law are as follows:

- **Accountability.** All entities covered by this act—holders of PII in the process of their business—must "have managerial accountability [over data in their custody]." In the present context, *managerial accountability over data* means the existence of policies regarding the collection, processing, storage, physical and virtual security, distribution to third parties, and use of data classified as PII.
- **Privacy by design.** In all aspects of data handling the privacy of the data must be of prime concern. This can be accomplished using "appropriate management processes and practices throughout the data life cycle."
- **Transparency.** Data collectors, in cyberspace and elsewhere, must "provide clear, concise, and timely notice to individuals" regarding the management of the collected PII.
- **Individual participation.** Holders of PII must "offer individuals a robust, clear, and conspicuous mechanism" to allow or to forbid the use of their PII and to be able to change this status at any time.
- **Data minimization.** Data related to an individual, collected in the process of a service, must be minimized and be "as [it] is reasonably necessary."
- **Constraints on distribution of information.** Collectors of PII passing such data to third parties must "require by contract that such third party" fully comply with this law as to the management of the data. Furthermore, transfer of PII data to "unreliable third parties [is] prohibited."
- **Data integrity.** Collectors of PII must make every effort, through appropriate policies, practices, and mechanisms, to ensure that utilized "personally identifiable information... is accurate [especially when such information]... could be used to deny consumers benefits or cause significant harm."

- **Enforcement and penalties.** This law directs the FTC to promulgate cognizant regulations and pursue their enforcement. Penalties shall be based on the extent of the violations and on the length of time these violations were committed.
- **Safe Harbor provisions.** The law grants the FTC the authority to enact *safe harbor* programs. *Safe harbor* is a legal term referring to the modification, reduction, or elimination of a party's liabilities vis-à-vis the provisions of a certain law. Such waivers of legal obligations are extended on the name of the greater good. Such programs would apply to data collectors, under the jurisdiction of this law, as long as the intent of this law remains in effect, which is the protection for the privacy of the individual.

The Commercial Privacy Bill of Rights Act of 2011 does not provide specific rules on the issue of PII management, but it empowers the FTC, which oversees trade and is best suited for such a task, to draft rules and measures that will eventually protect PII and minimize abuse and cybercrime.

Cybersecurity Act of 2010 [16]

The objective of this act is

> To ensure the continued free flow of commerce within the United States and with its global trading partners through secure cyber communications, to provide for the continued development and exploitation of the Internet and intranet communications for such purposes, to provide for the development of a cadre of information technology specialists, to improve and maintain effective cyber security defenses against disruption, and for other purposes.

It has been recognized that

- Cyberspace is an integral part of the American society and a very important infrastructure for all aspects of life, with the White House identifying it as a strategic national asset.
- The Internet is not as secure as it should be, considering on one hand its importance and value to the United States and on the other the increasing threats in the form of cybercrime and terrorist attacks.

- There is a need for a comprehensive national security strategy, as well as for an increase in the quality and quantity of cybersecurity professionals.

Driven by the above concerns, the US lawmakers drafted and enacted this law, directing the implementation of the law to the US president, rather than to a government agency, as in most cases. Following are the law's main points:

- **Certifications.** The law addresses the need for qualified cybersecurity professionals, prerequisite to which is "cybersecurity accreditation, training, and certification programs."
- **Cybersecurity Scholarships.** The law directs the National Science Foundation to "establish a Federal Cyber Scholarship-for-Service program to recruit and train the next generation of information technology professionals." The program is to provide 1,000 graduate and undergraduate full scholarships per year for programs leading to cybersecurity. Furthermore, talent is to be sought even among high school students, "to promote computer security awareness in secondary and high school classrooms."
- **Cybersecurity Competitions.** The law directs the National Institute of Standards and Technology to establish cybersecurity-focused competitions and other challenges with prizes, in order to "attract, identify, evaluate, and recruit talented individuals for the Federal information technology workforce... [and in order to]... stimulate innovation in basic and applied cybersecurity research."
- **Cybersecurity Workforce Plan.** Recognizing that cybersecurity requires cyber warriors, the law addresses the need for a plan, for each and every government agency, that will provide quality and quantity in its cyber defense. The plan shall include "cybersecurity hiring projections... long-term and short-term strategic planning to address critical skills deficiencies... recruitment strategies... cybersecurity-related training" so that cyberspace will be secure.
- **NIST Cybersecurity Guidance.** The law recognizes the National Institute of Standards and Technology (NIST) as the technological authority in the area of cyberspace and

cybersecurity and directs it to "promote auditable, private sector developed cybersecurity risk measurement techniques, risk management measures and best practices" that can later serve as standards in assessing cybersecurity preparedness.

- **Cybersecurity Knowledge Development.** The law emphasizes the need for the continuous development of knowledge, skills, and professionals with expertise in the design of "complex software-intensive systems that are secure and reliable... [that] guarantee the privacy of an individual's identity, information or lawful transactions."

- **Cybersecurity Advisory Panel.** Having placed the president as the focal point for its implementation, the law calls for the creation of a panel made of qualified "representatives of industry, academic, non-profit organizations, interest groups and advocacy organizations" that will advise the president on "matters relating to the national cybersecurity program and strategy."

The Cybersecurity Act of 2010 serves as a starting point for the creation of a cybersecurity awareness plan that, through policies, guidelines, and extensive appropriations, will result in qualified cybersecurity professionals who will defend the public as well as the private sector against cybercrimes and cyberwarfare.

Federal Information Security Management Act of 2002 [17]

In 1987, US lawmakers, having seen the growth of data processing and the increasing use of computers, passed a law—the Computer Security Act of 1987—which provided some rudimentary, by today's standards, guidelines regarding the security and general treatment of data. In 2002, it was realized that the threats had been multiplied by several orders of magnitude and that managing the security of systems and data required an organized approach.

The Federal Information Security Management Act (FISMA) establishes benchmarks that federal agencies, and federal contractors, need to meet that are quantifiable and measurable. FISMA directs the agency heads to establish and implement policies and procedures to minimize the risks and the threats to government information systems. The responsibility for the creation of the necessary standards was placed on the NIST, with the objective to have uniform information security standards throughout the government that will ensure data integrity, availability, and security.

FISMA constitutes a milestone in the articulation of compliance rules for information security, and its purpose includes the following objectives [18]:

- To provide a comprehensive framework for ensuring the effectiveness of information security controls over information resources that support federal operations and assets
- To provide for development and maintenance of minimum controls required to protect federal information and information systems
- To provide a mechanism for improved oversight of federal agency information security programs
- To recognize that the selection of specific technical hardware and software information security solutions should be left to individual agencies from among commercially developed products

The highlights of FISMA are as follows:

- **Responsibilities.** The law places all responsibilities on the agency head to provide security to all information in the custody of the agency, where the level of security should be "commensurate with the risk and magnitude of the harm resulting from unauthorized access, use, disclosure, disruption, modification, or destruction of" the information in custody.
- **Planning.** Agencies are free to develop their own security program for the protection of their information, even if their information is not on their own premises—this applies to contractors and satellite sites.
- **Reporting.** Compliance with the spirit and letter of FISMA will be demonstrated in an annual report that the head of each agency will prepare with a distribution that will include the following:
  - Director of FISMA in the Department of Commerce
  - House Committees on Government Reform and Science

- Senate Committees on Government Affairs, Commerce, Science and Transportation
- Appropriations Committees
- Office of the Comptroller General (OCG). The OCG will attest "on the adequacy and effectiveness of information security policies, procedures, and practices, and compliance with the requirements of... [FISMA]."
- **Independent evaluations.** Annually, each agency will have an independent evaluation conducted by the agency's Inspector General "appointed under the Inspector General Act of 1978... or by an independent external auditor, as determined by the Inspector General of the agency."

The 2010 FISMA report of the Securities and Exchange Commission (SEC), an agency of the federal government, can be viewed online [19]. The report, prepared by an independent contractor, contains the findings of the Inspector General with specific recommendations for the enhancement of the SEC information system vis-à-vis data security.

USA PATRIOT Act of 2001 [20]

The objective of the USA PATRIOT (Uniting and Strengthening America by Providing Appropriate Tools Required to Intercept and Obstruct Terrorism) Act, also known as the Patriot Act, is "To deter and punish terrorist acts in the United States and around the world, to enhance law enforcement investigatory tools, and for other purposes." This law was proposed and enacted in an aftermath of the 9/11 attacks on public and private property in the United States. It is a very controversial law which restricts previously enjoyed civil liberties in the name of national security. Below are issues this law addresses that pertain to information collection and processing [20].

- **National Electronic Crime Task Force.** Recognizing the need for information in combating crime, in general, and terrorism, in particular, the law directs for the creation of "a national network of electronic crime task forces,... for the purpose of preventing, detecting, and investigating various forms of electronic crimes, including potential terrorist attacks against critical infrastructure and financial payment systems" [20].

- **Information interception.** The law grants authority to cognizant US government agencies "to intercept wire, oral, and electronic communications relating to terrorism, computer fraud and abuse offenses." There can be "Seizure of voice-mail messages pursuant to warrants" [20].

- **Disclosure of records.** An Internet Service Provider "*may divulge a record or other information pertaining to a subscriber or a customer… if the provider reasonably believes that an emergency involving immediate danger of death or serious physical injury to any person requires disclosure of the information without delay*" [20].

- **Telemarketing fraud.** The law is concerned with charitable telemarketing fraud and requires that such activities fully disclose "*the name and mailing address of the charitable organization on behalf of which the solicitation is made*" [20].

The Patriot Act mainly focuses on measures to assist federal law enforcement agencies in their fight against terrorism and financial crime. Although civil liberties groups claimed that many provisions of the Act are unconstitutional, and that the Act "*expanded the government's authority to pry into people's private lives with little or no evidence of wrongdoing*" [21], the Act was extended to June 1, 2015.

Communications Assistance for Law Enforcement Act of 1994 [22]

The Communications Assistance for Law Enforcement Act of 1994 (abbreviated as CALEA) requires that companies in the telecommunications sector provide law enforcement agencies with access to private communications and to records of such communications. The act falls in the domain of the Federal Communications Commission (FCC). "*In response to concerns that emerging technologies such as digital and wireless communications were making it increasingly difficult for law enforcement agencies to execute authorized surveillance, Congress enacted CALEA on October 25, 1994.*" However, the telecommunications industry has not designed nor built its facilities and services to necessarily accommodate this objective, and additional infrastructure is needed to "comply with the CALEA obligations set forth" in the law. Below are the main points of the act [22].

- **Requirements.** Telecommunications companies providing services to the public must be able to intercept "*all wire and electronic communications carried by the carrier... of a subscriber...*" It is stated that this service to a law enforcement agency must be "*... pursuant to a court order or other lawful authorization...*"
- **Compliance cost.** Apparently, installing equipment that will facilitate the implementation of CALEA has a high cost that telecommunication companies are not willing to carry.
- **Encryption.** Should a subscriber employ their own encryption technology, "*A telecommunications carrier shall not be responsible for decrypting,... unless the encryption was provided by the carrier and the carrier possesses the information necessary to decrypt the communication.*"
- **Capacity.** Another issue is the capacity to intercept that a telecommunications company should maintain, which will "*be based upon the type of equipment, type of service, number of subscribers, type or size or carrier, nature of service area, or any other measure; and shall identify, to the maximum extent practicable, the capacity required at specific geographic locations.*"
- **Rogue eavesdropping.** To protect government secure radio communications, the act makes it illegal for hackers to listen to communications that are "*... encrypted, or transmitted using modulation techniques the essential parameters of which have been withheld from the public with the intention of preserving the privacy of such communication...*"
- **Safe harbor.** Compliance with the directives of CALEA can be waived under special circumstances, under the authority of the US Attorney General and the FCC. Usually, such waivers only extend the date of compliance to allow the telecommunications company to properly equip itself.
- **Costs.** In telecommunications, technologies are always advancing, and, consequently, CALEA compliance will add costs onto the respective companies that are not supported by revenues. "The Attorney General may, subject to the availability of appropriations, agree to pay telecommunications carriers

for all reasonable costs directly associated with the modifications performed by carriers... (in order) to comply with [CALEA]. The authorized appropriations for the 1995–1998 fiscal years were $0.5 billion.

- **Penalties.** Supporting the law enforcement agencies in their mission is not a voluntary task, but a legal obligation. The act states that "a telecommunications carrier, a manufacturer of telecommunications transmission or switching equipment, or a provider of telecommunications support services [found not to be in compliance with CALEA may be fined]... up to $10,000 per day for each day in violation."

Civil liberties groups watching over CALEA are very concerned of CALEA's possible expansion to include Internet telephony. *"This expansion is of significant civil liberties concern because it would require VoIP providers to build all their products with surveillance backdoors that can be accessed by law enforcement and will likely be misused by hackers and criminals"* [23].

Computer Security Act of 1987 [24]

This law was the precursor of FISMA [25], and its purpose was to improve *"the security and privacy of sensitive information in Federal computer systems... [and to create] a means for establishing minimum acceptable security practices for such systems..."* Some of the law's highlights were as follows.

- **The Authority.** The law points to the need for the development of computer security *"standards and minimum acceptable practices"* and assigns the NIST to the task with the help of the National Security Agency.
- **The Program.** The program would establish policies, *"standards, guidelines, and associated methods and techniques for computer systems... [as well as] technical, management, physical, and administrative standards and guidelines for the cost-effective security and privacy of sensitive information in Federal computer systems."*
- **Prior Related Law.** This law also amended the Federal Property and Administrative Services Act of 1949, streamlining it with the technology and management practices of 1987.

- **Training.** The law placed significant emphasis on training, stating that each Federal agency shall provide for the mandatory periodic training in computer security awareness and accepted computer security practice[s] of all employees who are involved with the management, use, or operation of each Federal computer system... Such training shall be designed

  1. To enhance employees' awareness of the threats to and vulnerability of computer systems
  2. To encourage the use of improved computer security practices

Privacy Act of 1974 [26]

By the early 1970s, it was realized that cross-referenced and cross-searched databases could very quickly result in a wide variety of records about an individual and that such power should be prevented from being abused. This was a victory for civil liberties groups who were very concerned that technology was working more for records retrieval and less for records protection. Some of the act's highlights follow.

- **Conditions of disclosure.** The key issue is personal information disclosure, and the law stated that *"No agency shall disclose any record which is contained in a system of records by any means of communication to any person, or to another agency, except pursuant to a written request by, or with the prior written consent of, the individual to whom the record pertains...."* However, disclosure of records would be allowed for official use. This clause was aimed at blocking unofficial disclosure of personal records.
- **Freedom of Speech Amendment.** There is a very strange clause in the law, (under Agency requirements 7), stating that *"Each agency that maintains a system of records shall... maintain no record describing how any individual exercises rights guaranteed by the First Amendment unless expressly authorized by statute or by the individual about whom the record is maintained or unless pertinent to and within the scope of an authorized law enforcement activity."* Loosely expressed that means that the US government should not tag citizens based on how outspoken they are.

- **Accuracy of records.** Considering that accuracy is the most important attribute of records, the law explicitly directs that agencies must *"maintain all records... with such accuracy, relevance, timeliness, and completeness as is reasonably necessary to assure fairness to the individual in the determination."*
- **Mailing lists.** In the early 1970s, data automation facilitated the creation of categorized mailing lists for commercial purposes, and the law wanted to make certain that there was no abuse of personal data in the custody of the government. The law stated: *"An individual's name and address may not be sold or rented by an agency unless such action is specifically authorized by law. This provision shall not be construed to require the withholding of names and addresses otherwise permitted to be made public."*
- **Minimum of records.** The law concerned with the compilation of private unrelated data on individuals explicitly states: *"Each agency that maintains a system of records shall... maintain in its records only such information about an individual as is relevant and necessary to accomplish a purpose of the agency."*

Cybercrime

Cybercrime has been a byproduct of cyberspace, serving as a black stigma in the optimism the Internet had given the world. Cybercrime has been growing over the past two decades, having reached the annual level of over half a billion dollars in 2009 [27]. "Indeed, driven by the prospect of significant profits, cyber crime innovation and techniques have outpaced traditional security models and many current signature-based detection technologies" [28].

A new underground industry has developed, that of *cybercrime hubs.* These are legitimate companies with as many as fifty employees that offer Internet services, ranging from website design and website advertising to Web hosting and domain name registrations. Progressively, these cybercrime companies turn hundreds of thousands of Internet hosts—computers connected to the Internet—into their zombies by installing malware [29].

The installation of malware is made under false pretenses. For example, they have an array of websites where visitors are offered presumably needed software for free. In effect, this software is malware that redirects the DNS pointer located inside the host to a rogue one that misdirects the user's Web interactions, resulting in the compromise of user sensitive data.

What is surprising is that a significant amount of cybercrime is still not for financial gain but only to do harm. Equally surprising is that many organizations apply more resources into employee Internet abuse than into cyber protection. Relative to the required resources, cybercrime is the most cost-effective and physically safe of all crimes, with new threats being continuously recognized. It is not possible to make an all-inclusive list of crimes that can be committed over the Internet.

One fact is evident, that hackers are being replaced by organized crime, and that increased cyber defense spending does not necessarily result in increased cybersecurity, but risk prioritization does. Appendix 9.A at the end of this chapter lists most of the commonly occurring crimes over the Web.

Trends in Cyber Abuse

Trends indicate that cybercrime is not the only cyber abuse, and new very innovative illegal schemes make their appearance on the Internet daily. There is an abundance of mobile phone applications that have been designed without a security consideration in mind and numerous applications with cybercrime in mind [30–32].

The general public in good faith downloads and installs applications without having any way of knowing if they are safe or not. The result is that malware applications infect the initial phone as well as those they communicate with, plus they make the content on the phone illegally accessible. Table 9.3 lists cyber abuses that have been on the rise [28,33].

Combating Cybercrime

Being connected to the Web is a vulnerability in itself. Therefore, it is a good practice to connect to and disconnect from the Web on a need-basis. The ease in the commitment of cybercrime has turned the Internet, this wonderful human creation, into a minefield. However, an

Table 9.3 Types of Cyber Abuses on the Rise

Cybercrime hubs (organized crime)
    Rogue DNS servers
    Fake ISP services
    Ads replacement
    Zombie development
Underestimation
    Potential damage
    Defense cost
Terrorism
    Communications
    Recruiting
    Libeling
Unreported events
    Records losses
    Records exposures
Espionage
    International
    Industrial
    Political
Online banking
    Illegal transactions
    Malware installation
    Wire mules
Illegal intelligence gathering
    Foreign
    Domestic
    Business
    Personal
Underground economy
    Information
    Records
    Malware
    Keyloggers
Money laundering through
    Online gambling
    Online banking
    Online investment
Need for increased corporate awareness
    Preparedness
    Training
    Crime detection

(*Continued*)

Table 9.3 (Continued)   Types of Cyber Abuses on the Rise

Authentication spoofing
Identity theft
URL misdirection
Cybercrime in social media
Phony friends
Phishing
Malware installation
Misleading offers

awareness and the use of protection software like the ones mentioned in the chapter on intrusions can minimize the risk. The philosophy in combating cybercrime should be not so much maximizing security as minimizing risk. There is a subtle but important difference in these two concepts, where the former is only the means, while the latter is the true objective.

At the corporate level, cybersecurity should not be viewed as a technical exercise, but as a top management responsibility that is delegated to the chief security officer of the organization. As such, cybersecurity should be the top management's most important project.

There are many cybercrime protection software that filter-out questionable websites and filter-in only selected websites and email correspondents. Such software provide "inbound and outbound messaging security, (highly) effective antispam and antivirus protection, advanced content filtering, data loss prevention and encryption for email" [34]. No corporate cyber activity can be considered insignificant from the security viewpoint. However, certain areas require special attention due to increased cybercrime. One such area is password management. A considerable amount takes place with compromised passwords. At least this type of cybercrime can be combated with the deployment of one-time passwords (OTPs) [35]. Table 9.4 lists four areas—weak links—that are in the forefront of cybercrime.

In our defense measures against cybercrime, there are two fronts. The first is our technical fortification. That is, the installation in our computers of the best possible antivirus suites. There are numerous such highly reputable software even for the smartphone [36], mobile phones that have Web access. Unfortunately, cybercrime malware is

Table 9.4 Weak Links in Cyberspace Interactions

AREA	CONCERNS
Access management	Management of access credential and access mechanisms, such as issuance of passwords, codes, user names, and deployment of OTPs
Web applications	Online transactions, website navigation, intranet portals
	Log-on systems, cross-Internet communication and cooperation tools, security settings
Unattended entry equipment and devices	ATM, cards with RFID communication links, Wi-Fi access, USB devices
Telephony mobile and landlines	Smartphones, mobile telephony services, automated interactions— voice or keyed, automated voice response

leading in the technology, with the malware security industry lagging by three to six months. The second defensive front is our awareness of the existence of Web-based fraudulent offers and refraining from falling into cybercrime traps.

For example, there are websites that that have fantastic offers for products or services. Some will charge your credit card, and they will never deliver. In this case, you may alert your credit card company and try to get refunded. However, there are other fraudulent e-commerce websites that, after you place an order, will reply that such product is out of stock and that your credit card will not be charged. Indeed, your credit card is not being charged, but the cards credentials are sold to cybercriminals. "Technology can only take us so far, and the rest is education and vigilance on the part of computer users" [37]. There are numerous organizations dedicated to fighting cybercrime, and our awareness of their existence is important in our own fight. Appendix 9.B lists a number of prominent organizations concerned with the fight against cybercrime.

The liability in the commitment of a crime, be it in the physical world or in cyberspace, falls on the shoulder of the victim. For example, if someone with a fake card deceives an ATM and steals money out of your account, the liability would be with the bank. However, if someone using a keystroke collection scheme hacks your bank codes and attacks your account, the bank may deny "liability for the loss because the log-on was authentic. The bank is not responsible for the integrity of the customer's computer" [38].

Cybercrime in Banking

According to a variety of news releases, hundreds of banks are being cyber attacked every day with total losses close to one billion dollars. One Asian bank alone had $101M stolen with only $20M recovered.[*]

Apparently, these activities required extensive skills in electronic funds transferring, as well as Internet protocols. Even certain US banks have been *dysfunctional* due to cyber attacks.[†,‡]

Because it is impractical to run physical wires, or dedicated wireless links, from a bank's central IT center to each and every ATM machine, banks are using the Web as a communication link with the ATM machines falling in the category of Internet-of-Things (IoT), with its pluses and minuses.

Many enterprises, including the banks, believe that cybersecurity can be enhanced through the purchase of more equipment. However, according to an FBI official *"It's not enough to build up walls and harden the systems, you need human capital to understand the threat."*[§] Where that *human capital*, cybersecurity professionals, have experience and expertise and have been keeping up to date on a daily basis.

For all enterprises, including the banking sector, allocating millions for cybersecurity, is *unjustifiable*, but the Royal Bank of Scotland did not hesitate to double it's cybersecurity budget to half a billion dollars. The cybersecurity need is dual, with experienced strategists in the C-Suite and techies in the IT *engine room*.

Cybercrime in e-Commerce

Practically every commercial activity tries to take advantage of the benefits of the Internet, at the same time exposing itself to cybercrime. Laws around the world have itemized cybercrime into over one hundred types, and with stiff penalties, but that has not discouraged

---

[*] https://www.ft.com/content/39ec1e84-ec45-11e5-bb79-2303682345c8

[†] http://www.telegraph.co.uk/finance/newsbysector/banksandfinance/12082198/hsbc-online-bank-platform-payments-are-down-glitch.html

[‡] https://www.theregister.co.uk/2016/09/28/natwest_online_payments/

[§] https://www.finextra.com/blogposting/12685/the-threat-is-real-battling-cybercrime-in-banking

criminals from seeking illegal gains. So, according to global statistics, the volume of e-commerce doubles annually.

The fight against cybercrime has become a cooperative fight with merchants, government and consumer, together to at least minimize that plague. There has been a consensus as to the preventive measures consumers must follow, which include the following*:

- Keep the computer's operating system and the installed applications all up to date.
- Use the best possible antivirus application. Never rely on the free versions.
- Use secure networks. Avoid public Wi-Fi spots, where in the same physical area there might be servers operated by cyber criminals.
- Shop through trusted websites. Cyber criminals set up websites with "outstanding deals," just to get the credit card parameters of the buyers.
- Avoid having the same password for many critical uses. Thus, if compromised, it will not work in other websites.
- Avoid the convenience of the auto-fill—especially with financial data.
- Avoid being entrapped in Internet games, awards, lotteries and the like. Many such public websites are virus infected.
- Do not let anyone know your passwords.
- Change your passwords frequently, depending on how critical the access is.
- When available, attend cybersecurity awareness classes.

Cybersecurity in Maritime

In today's maritime, Internet access is as available as it is in a major city. Thus, there can be online and real-time communications 24/7. With appropriate Internet-of-Things (IoT), devices the central office may monitor each and every activity on the ship, such as

- GPS location
- Speed

---

* https://www.researchgate.net/publication/306401151_Cyber_Crimes_-_Threat_for _the_e-commerce

- Pitch and yaw
- Level of fuel
- Status of the hauls
- View fixed and mobile cameras on board

Similar to other cyber supported activities, the operation of a ship in the middle of the ocean requires marine cybernetics* services that include:

- Stress and robustness testing
- Penetration and network segregation testing
- Antivirus scanning and software patches and updates
- Authentication auditing
- Portable and IoT devices security
- Vulnerabilities assessment
- Traffic anomalies
- Network equipment monitoring

On the maritime cybersecurity issue, the European Network Information Security Agency (ENISA) recommends cybersecurity awareness training that includes all members in the maritime domain, from stevedores, terminal operators, and sailors, to chief engineers and captains.[†]

Appendix 9.A: Cybercrime Activities

ACTIVITY	DESCRIPTION
1. Cyber defamation	Posting of false information of chats, blogs, and websites.
2. Cyber stalking	Tracking of a person's activities through unwelcome visits to websites that have relevant information.
3. Cyber bullying	Making anonymous threats via Web postings.
4. Virus spreading	Installation of malware through emails or websites.
5. Impersonation	Pretending, using email or chat, to be someone else.
6. Identity theft	Collection of sufficient personal information of other persons to the point of claiming their identity.

(Continued)

---

[*] https://www.dnvgl.com/services/cybersecurity-and-network-resilience-82950?gclid=COui6Zzl99ICFQKBswod5HYF-w

[†] https://www.enisa.europa.eu/publications/cyber-security-aspects-in-the-maritime-sector-1/at_download/fullReport

ACTIVITY	DESCRIPTION
7. Fake auctions	Websites that display valuable products, administer auctions, collect fees, but never deliver.
8. Ponzi/pyramid	This is an investment scheme where there are high promises that are never realized.
9. Fake lotteries	Lotteries that collect charges for possible winnings that are never realized.
10. Fake storefronts	E-commerce websites that collect but never deliver.
11. Credit card abuse	Use of valid credit or debit card information to make unauthorized purchases over the Web.
12. Fake services	Typical are astrology, technical advice, private investigations, genealogy, and antivirus software.

Appendix 9.B: Cyber Resources: Organizations Concerned with the Fight against Cybercrime, a Partial List

ORGANIZATION AND URL	ACTIVITIES
The Carnegie Mellon Computer Emergency Response Team (CERT) http://www.cert.orgoordination	Coordination Center • Receives reports on Internet security problems • Analyzes product vulnerabilities • Publishes technical documents • Presents training courses
The Federal Computer Incident Response Center (FedCIRC) http://itlaw.wikia.com/wiki/Federal _Computer_Incident_Response _Center	Part of the Department of Homeland Security Information Analysis and Infrastructure Protection Directorate. Among other activities: • Provides federal civilian agencies with technical assistance • Provides coordination and analytical support and encourages development of quality security products and services • Fosters cooperation among federal agencies for computer security and communicates alerts and advisory information
Internet Storm Center (ISC) http://www.incidents.org http://isc.sans.edu/index.html	ISC provides a free analysis and warning service to thousands of Internet users and organizations, and is actively working with Internet Service Providers to fight back against the most malicious attackers.
The Institute for Security Technology Studies at Dartmouth College http://ists.dartmouth.edu	Serves as a principal national center for counterterrorism technology research, development, and assessment with a significant focus on cyber attacks.

(Continued)

ORGANIZATION AND URL	ACTIVITIES
The National Infrastructure Protection Center (NIPC) http://www.nipc.gov	Serves as the national focal point for threat assessment, warning, investigation, and response to cyber attacks. A significant part of its mission involves establishing mechanisms to increase the sharing of vulnerability and threat information between the government and private industry.
The System Administration, Networking and Security (SANS) Institute http://www.sans.org	The institute is a cooperative research and education organization through which system administrators, security professionals, and network administrators share lessons learned. SANS provides system and security alerts, news updates, and an education center for counterterrorism technology research, development, and assessment with a significant focus on cyber attacks.

Exercises

1. In a three-page report summarize "Directive 2002/58/EC of the European Parliament and of the Council" located at http://eur-lex.europa.eu/LexUriServ/LexUriServ.do?uri=OJ:L:2002:201: 0037:0037:EN:PDF.

2. In a two-page report summarize the "Cybersecurity Challenge" speech located at http://www.nato.int/nato_static/assets/audio/audio_2010_02/20100202_?100202-jamie-lecture6.mp3.

3. In a two-page report summarize the paper "Global Cyber Deterrence" located at http://www.ewi.info/system/files/Cyber DeterrenceWeb.pdf.

4. In a two-page report summarize the paper "Terrorism in Cyberspace—Myth or Reality?" located at http://www.cyber crimelaw.net/documents/Terrorism_in_cyberspace.pdf.

5. Research the issue of JPEG files, where executable code can be hidden in the file header. Summarize your findings in a two-page report. The following link may give you a head start: http://www.sophos.com/en-us/press-office/press-releases/2002/06/va_perrun.aspx.

6. Prepare a ten-slide presentation highlighting The Fair Credit Reporting Act of 1970 (http://www.ftc.gov/os/statutes/031224 fcra.pdf).

7. Prepare a ten slide presentation highlighting The Federal Information Security Management Act (FISMA) of 2002. The document can be found at http://csrc.nist.gov/drivers/documents /FISMA-final.pdf.

8. Prepare a ten slide presentation highlighting The Homeland Security Act of 2002. The document can be found at http://www.dhs.gov/xlibrary/assets/hr_5005_enr.pdf.

9. Prepare a ten-slide presentation highlighting the two Internet-related proposed legislations: The Stop Online Piracy Act (SOPA), located at http://judiciary.house.gov/hearings/pdf /HR%203261%20Managers%20Amendment.pdf; and its Senate companion, the Protect IP Act (PIPA) located at http://www.leahy.senate.gov/imo/media/doc/BillText-PROTECTIP Act.pdf.

10

CYBER WARFARE AND HOMELAND SECURITY

Victory and defeat are far from being recognizable in cyberspace.

Paul Cornish
Chatham House

Introduction

Cyberspace is a unique institution that supports all aspects and sectors of a society, and consequently, the security of that space is of absolute importance to all governments for their respective societies. Countries, one after another, are forming government agencies concerned with the security of that space. Similarly, in the United States the Department of Homeland Security (DHS), among numerous other responsibilities and in cooperation with other government agencies, has been assigned the task of cybersecurity.

DHS has recognized that there is a need to create a "resilient cyber ecosystem" [1], meaning that cyberspace is not an isolated support system but a multidimensional ecosystem that has to operate perpetually and in a resilient manner, free of threats or possibilities of breaking down. Furthermore, the defense of that ecosystem has to be thorough and of "automated collective action[s]" [1]. That is, the security of cyberspace has to be automated, because there can be no stop-examine-decide process with human intervention—it is just too slow. The cyberspace defense system must implement its decision to act at electronic speeds, where these actions are collective, meaning they are implemented at distributed locations of information centers. In this case, "artificial intelligence at the network node level will recognize and avert threats on a real time basis" [2].

Cyberspace day-by-day is becoming more and more important in every aspect of life. It is offering unprecedented and irreplaceable convenience that is making society its hostage. We have two choices. We either refuse to use cyberspace and pay the consequences, which are isolation and inefficiency, or we fully enjoy its unlimited benefits, knowing well that its failure can be catastrophic unless we take all the necessary precautions. DHS has come into the picture with full recognition of the dilemma, and it is steadily increasing its experience and expertise trying to reach the asymptote—a secure cyberspace.

Cyber Warfare

Cyber warfare is an expected hostile activity that adversaries will attempt to capitalize on if an advantage is perceived to be gained. "Simply put, cyber warfare is a new but not entirely separate component of a multifaceted conflict environment" [3]. "Today in cyberspace, intelligent adversaries exploit vulnerabilities and create incidents that propagate at [electronic]... speeds to steal identities, resources, and [to create] advantage" [1]. In cyber warfare it is difficult to say who has the upper hand, because no one knows exactly how many "holes" are in cyberspace. In the warfare context, cyberspace is the electronic space including the Internet, as well as the airwaves regardless of frequency. Numerous cyber attacks have taken place, but none has been explicitly attributed to an apparent political or military adversary [4].

All major powers—United Kingdom, France, Germany, Russia, and China—in a variety of ways have acknowledged having incorporated "cyberwarfare as a new part of their military doctrine.... the French may see a legitimate role for economic cyberwarfare in the pursuit of national objectives." The Russians look at "cyberwarfare as an act of war for which any response... is deemed justified" [5]. Furthermore, it is believed that "Russia retains the right to use nuclear weapons first against the means and forces of information warfare, and then against the aggressor state itself" [6]. The Chinese view it as another warfare and have created the Blue Army [7].

An event that took place in Siberia, the explosion of a gas pipeline in 1982 [8], is claimed to have been the first known act of cyber warfare. According to Western publications, the event was the result of sabotage where the Supervisory Control And Data Acquisition (SCADA) of the pipeline system was mal-programmed to cause the explosion. This is a computerized system that supervises and controls an industrial process. Figure 10.1 illustrates a typical pipeline control SCADA where the main control room has two-way communication with remote sites.

One side says that "It was a Trojan program inserted [by the CIA] into the SCADA system software that caused a massive natural gas explosion along the Trans-Siberian pipeline in 1982" [9]. The program "reset pump speeds and valve settings to produce pressures far beyond those acceptable to pipeline joints and welds" [10]. The other side claims that "it was caused by poor construction rather than sabotage" [11].

If indeed it were a hostile act of attributed origin, like a bombardment for example, then the United States would have been guilty of an *act of war*, with all the legal and moral consequences the Soviet Union could raise. Because a cyber warfare victim has a difficult case, if not impossible, to prove the cyber attacker's identity, the future will be full of cyber attacks. If in the above case of the Siberian pipeline, the officials, former or past, of the attacker claim responsibility, the cyber victim country has every right to reparations. Therefore, if at the moment of the cyber warfare solid evidence does not point to a guilty party, nothing prevents right to reparations once the guilty party confesses or the origin of the act is proven in an international court.

That is, once the perpetrator of a deliberate damaging cyber act is identified, the cyber victim, be it an individual or an entire state, has rights to reparations. Recognizing the important role cyberspace will play in the future, all major powers have developed cyberspace commands wanting to create cyber warriors ready to attack or defend when the moment comes.

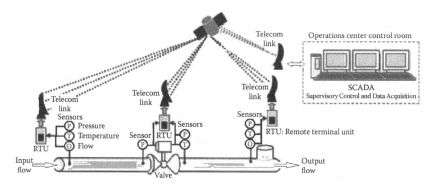

Figure 10.1 Remote Supervisory Control and Data Acquisition (SCADA) system. (Courtesy of Ookaboo, Pipeline SCADA, http://images.ookaboo.com/photo/m/Pipeline_Scada_m.jpg.)

It has been said that cyberspace is an *equalizer*, in the sense that anyone can put up a powerful website without the visitor knowing the full organization behind the website facade. Similarly, warfare in cyberspace is an *equalizer*, in the sense that military or economic or political strength play no role, with malware skills being the only arsenal. It is quite possible that through cyber warfare minor geopolitical goals may be achieved without a military confrontation.

Table 10.1 lists some of the most publicized cyber attacks that could be considered as cyber warfare. In all cases, there has been no indisputable evidence that particular sovereign states were behind the attacks. It has to be recognized that neither the IP origin of the attacks nor the accomplished goal, if any, can absolutely link the attacks to governments. Most accusations are justified speculations.

A weak link in the cyber warfare scenario is the trapdoors telecommunication manufacturers create for the law enforcement agencies to facilitate their mission in fighting crime. Trapdoor is a term in the security context referring to a mechanism that bypasses the security authentication and/or authorization procedures in order to obtain unrestricted resource access. This is the equivalent of a master key in physical locks. Considering that no information of value can be kept secret, the trapdoor codes or other information can leak to enemy hands.

Cyber Weapons Convention

About a century ago, the world powers realized that atomic power could be used for destructive use as well. Thirty years later the explosion of two atomic warheads proved to the world the possible level of destruction. Similarly today, the world powers—visible and invisible—are developing defensive and offensive cyber arsenals of Cyber Weapons (CW), continuously testing them for all eventualities. Again, similarly with the atomic weapons, some "cool heads" are pointing out the need for a *Cyber Weapons Convention* (CWC) [13]; a convention—*an international arms control treaty for cyberspace*—to which signatories will agree not to use their CW in prohibited scenarios [13].

It is said that in open hostilities the first victim is the truth. Undoubtedly, the second victim will be cyberspace. However, unlike all other weapons, where the launching origin cannot be hidden or

Table 10.1   Cyber Warfare Attacks—A Timetable

1999. Russia–USA

"In the US, the Navy's Web site was hacked, reportedly by Russians who support the Serbs.
 Erasing the Navy's information, they left blisteringly obscene insults against the US."
http://business.highbeam.com/409220/article-1G1-54299338/serb-supporters-sock-nato-and-us
 -computers

1999. Serbia–NATO

"The war in Yugoslavia has spread to the Net with NATO suffering attacks on its computer
 systems from Serbia."
http://news.bbc.co.uk/2/hi/science/nature/308788.stm

2001. China–USA

"Chinese hacker groups... organized a massive and sustained week-long campaign of cyber
 attacks against American targets...."
http://www.dtic.mil/cgi-bin/GetTRDoc?AD=ADA395300

1999–2001. India–Pakistan

"Sympathizers on both sides of the Kashmir conflict have used cyber tactics to disrupt each
 other's information systems and disseminate propaganda."
http://www.dtic.mil/cgi-bin/GetTRDoc?AD=ADA395300

1999–2001. Israel–Palestine

"By the end of January 2001, the conflict had struck more than 160 Israeli and 35 Palestinian
 sites...."
http://usacac.leavenworth.army.mil/CAC/milreview/download/English/MarApr03/allen.pdf

2007. Estonia

"A three-week wave of massive cyber-attacks on... Estonia, the first known incidence of such an
 assault on a state...."
http://www.guardian.co.uk/world/2007/may/17/topstories3.russia

2007. Israel–Syria

"Syrian air defense was reportedly disabled by a cyber attack...."
http://www.ccdcoe.org/articles/2010/Geers_Cyber%20Attack%20Deterrence.pdf

2008. Georgia

"The methods of cyber attacks against Georgia primarily included defacement of public websites
 and launch of Distributed Denial of Service (DDoS) attacks against numerous targets...."
http://www.carlisle.army.mil/DIME/documents/Georgia%201%200.pdf

2009. Kyrgyzstan–Russia

"Kyrgyzstan became the latest country to come under cyber attack from computers based in
 Russia, security researchers said this week. The denial-of-service attacks, which began on
 January 18, disrupted the networks...."
http://www.securityfocus.com/brief/896

2010. China–Germany

"Germany experienced a significance increase in cyber attacks in 2010, many originating in
 China, and plans to set up a special center next year to counter the problem...."
http://www.thenewnewinternet.com/2010/12/28/germany-blasted-with-cyber-attacks-in-2010-plans
 -cyber-defense-center/

(Continued)

Table 10.1 (Continued)   Cyber Warfare Attacks—A Timetable

2011. China–USA

"US Secretary of Defense Robert Gates answered the question nobody dared to ask—Would the US launch military attacks on China in response to Chinese cyber attacks? His answer—yes, if the cyber attacks were perceived as acts of war."
http://www.whiteoutpress.com/articles/wach/us-and-china-threaten-war-over-cyber-attacks578/

2011. China–USA

"The Chinese military has accused the US of waging a global Internet war against multiple nations in an effort to bring down governments...."
http://rt.com/usa/news/china-usa-internet-war/

2011. France

"The French finance ministry has confirmed it came under a cyber attack in December that targeted files on the G20 summit held in Paris in February."
http://www.bbc.co.uk/news/business-12662596

2011. Kosovo–Serbia

"Kosovo hackers... (attacked) websites belonging to the Serbian Orthodox Church."
http://www.balkaninsight.com/en/article/kosovo-hackers-kosovo-broke-into-serbian-web-sites

2011. International Monetary Fund

"Officials at the International Monetary Fund report . . . "a very major breach" of its computer systems."
https://www.infoplease.com/world/cyberwar-timeline

2011. Asia

"Malware, named Mahdi after the Messiah in Islam, infiltrates . . . computers of government officials, embassy employees, and other businesspeople in Iran, Israel, Afghanistan, the United Arab Emirates, and South Africa."
https://www.infoplease.com/world/cyberwar-timeline

2012. Flame

A malware named flame ". . . attacks computers using Microsoft Windows, . . . "Its development is believed to have been state-sponsored. Flame also has a kill command, wiping out all traces of it from the computer."
https://www.infoplease.com/world/cyberwar-timeline

2012. Saudi Arabia

"Hackers, . . . infiltrate the computer networks of Saudi Aramaco, a Saudi Arabian oil company, and wipe out the hard drives of about 30,000 computers.
https://www.infoplease.com/world/cyberwar-timeline

2012. Banking

Major U.S. Banks ". . . were hit by a distributed-denial-of-service attack that denied customers access to the banks' websites for several days."
https://www.infoplease.com/world/cyberwar-timeline

2013. Press

"The New York Times website is shut down for about 20 hours after being hacked, . . . The attackers accessed the site through Melbourne IT, the vendor that registers domain names."
https://www.infoplease.com/world/cyberwar-timeline

(Continued)

Table 10.1 (Continued)   Cyber Warfare Attacks—A Timetable

2014. US–China

"American officials announced that Chinese hackers had breached the computer network of the Office of Personnel Management in March.
https://www.infoplease.com/world/cyberwar-timeline

2015. US–China

The "White House said that the Social Security numbers and other personal identifying information of some 4 million current and former government employees had been breached. . . . The government said it believes that the hack originated in China.
https://www.infoplease.com/world/cyberwar-timeline

2016. US Elections

"Hackers have breached databases for election systems in Illinois and Arizona, according to state election and law enforcement officials."
http://edition.cnn.com/2016/08/29/politics/hackers-breach-illinois-arizona-election-systems/index.html

2017. Wannacry

A ransomware malware named Wannacry ". . . spread around the world, . . . temporarily crippled National Health Service hospitals and facilities in the United Kingdom, hobbling emergency rooms, delaying vital medical procedures, and creating chaos for many British patients." The ransomware demanded payment in the BitCoin, a presumably secret and anonymous cryptocurrency.
https://www.wired.com/story/2017-biggest-hacks-so-far/

---

disputed, the launching origin of the CWs can remain unknown forever. Eventually, a CWC will be drafted and signed, but it will be difficult to enforce while many questions remain unanswered, such as,

- How can one inspect the presence of CWs?
- Should there be a minimum number of CWs?
- What facilities should be excluded from such attacks?
- Can the true origin of an attack be located without the slightest doubt?

Cyber warfare is only a decade old, versus all other types of warfare, and no formal or informal "ethics, norms and values can apply" [3].

Cyber Terrorism

Terrorism is another type of hostile confrontation, often between sovereign powers which anonymously attack each other's interests. Typically, terrorism involves direct or indirect acts of violence against specific targets or against a certain innocent population by groups that have no formal link to any sovereign power, that is, to any country. Terrorists have utilized a wide variety of weapons as a means to accomplish their aims, and cyberspace has not been left out. As for a definition, one may safely say that cyber terrorism is the use of cyberspace to commit, or threaten to commit, violence. Use of cyberspace may be accessory to a crime. For example, a terrorist organization maintains a website in order "to solicit money for their various causes or disseminate coded messages, either explicitly or steganographically" [14]. Stenography is the practice of concealing messages inside unrelated files. For example, text messages can be concealed inside image files without visibly affecting the displayed image.

For terrorism, cyberspace is the most cost-effective weapon, as well as the safest from the terrorists' viewpoint. Cyber terrorism may be identified as

- **State-sponsored.** As of now, no country has accepted having conducted cyber hostile activities against anyone. Such *actors* are usually highly skilled with a focus on particular enemy targets.
- **Extremist groups.** Such groups use cyberspace for publicity, recruitment, and fund-raising, as well as for cyber attacks on targets they consider hostile. Such groups fall in the following general categories:
  - Political
  - Religious
  - Ethnic
  - Ideological
- **Organized crime.** These are groups that have a certain expertise in a particular sector and commit extortion based on threats of harm—economic or physical. Their motives are always financial gains.
- **Individual crime.** These are isolated individuals who commit, or threaten to commit, cyber crimes. In this case, the motives may or may not be financial gains.

As for tools, a minimal research on the Web can produce effective hacking tools. The counter cyber terrorism professionals document terrorist incidents through the identification of six main parameters that collectively define the incident. These are

- **Perpetrator.** The person or group that has committed the act of cyber terrorism.
- **Action.** The terrorist cyber activity that has been committed or threatened to be committed.
- **Cyber resource.** Usually, this has three parts.

  - The virtual cyber location, defined by the URL.
  - The logical location, defined by the identity of the server or database.
  - The physical location where the data are residing. With cloud computing this location may be difficult to pinpoint.
- **Means.** The malware or intrusion technique used in the attack.
- **Cyber vulnerability.** The weak point in the cybersecurity of the attacked resource.
- **Motivation.** Usually, this has two views.
  - The publicized "noble" motivation
  - The ulterior hidden motive
- **Affiliation.** Usually, this has two identities.
  - The entity claiming responsibility for the action
  - The entity suspected to be the beneficiary of the action

The above constitute the starting point in the classification of the incident. Such incidents range from the defacement or temporary distributed denial-of-service (DDoS) attack of an official website to the destruction of accessible public records or interference in the controls of a power grid. Against the warning of cybersecurity professionals, many critical infrastructures utilize the Internet as an operational intranet because of the derived cost benefit, rather than building and maintaining their own network that is physically and logically isolated from the Internet.

Currently, several power generation sectors are exposed to the Internet, and "With the recent advancements in smart grid systems and the increasing use of information technology in power infrastructures, such attacks are likely to take place, specially in large scales using sophisticated intrusion techniques" [15]. Figure 10.2 illustrates the four major sectors within a power utility organization. An attack

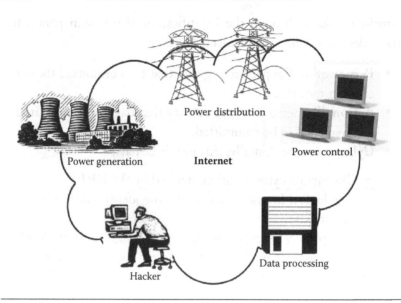

Figure 10.2   Hacker-threatened power generation system.

at the *generation* may result in the destruction of large turbines, shutting down power and causing human casualties [16]. An attack at the *distribution* and *power control* may leave large areas with no power service; while an attack at the *data processing* may destroy important possibly irreplaceable records.

Experts say that a "Mouse click could plunge city into darkness" [17] and have urged power utilities to "Disconnect electrical grid from Internet" [18] stating that "Any nation's critical infrastructures—communications, power grids, water supplies, gas lines, military, and the like—and their networks must have nothing to do with the Internet. Such infrastructures must have their own intranets, accessible only from selected locations and physically and virtually secure" [19].

Furthermore, the Commander of the US Cyber Command, referring to the cyber vulnerabilities in the electrical power grids, has stated that "cyber-attacks over the Internet are shifting from data theft to physical assaults" [20]. The possibility of a destructive cyber terrorist attack is within the realm of reality, and every measure needs to be taken to prevent it.

Considering that terrorism usually is the "left hand" of sovereign powers, cyber terrorists are virtual civil servants who are as trained and as well skilled, if not more, than the legitimate law enforcement agents who are after them. Terrorism in cyberspace is at its infancy, and its actions will eventually overshadow the physical ones.

Cyber Espionage

Cyberspace has made espionage less dangerous and more rewarding in many cases, and it is "one of the most prevalent of cyber activities" [3]. Organizations for the convenience of access and for the apparent cost-effectiveness very often use the Internet as their intranet. Consequently, data are exposed to illegal access and are frequently compromised. Organizations sometimes set up *honey pots* to lure cyber spies into them and reveal their cyber origin. *Honey pot* is a term in network security used to refer to files with false information placed in a website to misinform spies and reveal their IP address.

Such espionage may be political, military, industrial, commercial, or personal, in an effort to obtain information in an illegal or unauthorized manner. It was made public that cyber espionage silently snooped on the official records of dozens of countries and organizations, with intrusions having taken place during 2006–2011 [21]. The countries ranged from the United States to Vietnam, while the organizations included Olympic Games Committees. It was surprising that this cyber espionage was the work of a single computer. This was confirmed when all the cyber victims' IPs were counter spied out of it. Figure 10.3 illustrates the coverage of the cyber espionage.

Economic espionage is on the rise because use of such information may result in large legal profits [22]. Typically, cyber espionage uses no passwords because such information is difficult get, if at all. Cyber espionage starts with an email to a custodian of sensitive information, like a company's CEO, from a sender who is impersonating a highly reputable and trusted organization. The email comes with an attachment. The recipient, not suspecting the fraud, executes the attachment that displays a rather useful or interesting piece of information. During the execution of the attachment, a malware is installed in the recipient's computer that grants the sender full access to the recipient's computer. With such privilege, the sender not only searches the computer, but also accesses websites that require user names and passwords that usually cyber users leave inside for their convenience,

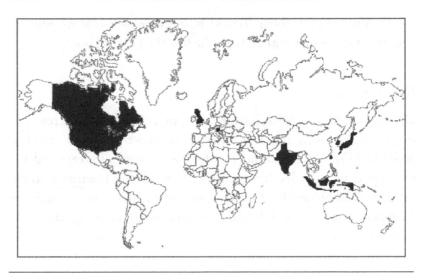

Figure 10.3 Countries affected by one spy's cyber espionage: United States, Canada, South Korea, Taiwan, Japan, Switzerland, United Kingdom, Indonesia, Vietnam, Denmark, Singapore, Hong Kong, Germany, and India.

rather than entering them each time they need to access their email or other services.

Espionage has been recognized as a unfriendly act, but not as an act of war, and similarly, cyber espionage is expected to be "tolerated," with diplomatic repercussions rather than war-like actions. However, once open hostilities commence between two adversaries, cyber warfare and cyber espionage will definitely follow, if not already in place.

Homeland Security

In the United States to address security issues, other than military defense, a cabinet-level government department was established on November 25, 2002, by the Homeland Security Act of 2002 [23]. "The Department of Homeland Security [DHS] has a vital mission: to secure the nation from the many threats… [including] cybersecurity…. [The] duties are wide-ranging, but our goal is clear—keeping America safe" [23]. The DHS was initially created by the transfer, from other government departments, of various agencies that were directly or indirectly responsible with the country's domestic security [24]. Table 10.2 lists the agencies that comprised the

Table 10.2 Initial Agencies That Were Incorporated into the New DHS Department

AGENCY	ORIGINAL DEPARTMENT	CURRENT AGENCY OR OFFICE
US Customs Service	Treasury	US Customs and Border Protection US Immigration and Customs Enforcement
Immigration and Naturalization Service	Justice	US Customs and Border Protection US Immigration and Customs Enforcement US Citizenship and Immigration Services
Federal Protective Service	General Services Administration	Infrastructure Protection and Security Directorate
Transportation Security Administration	Transportation	Transportation Security Administration
Federal Law Enforcement Training Center	Treasury	Federal Law Enforcement Training Center
Animal and Plant Health Inspection Service (part)	Agriculture	US Customs and Border Protection
Office for Domestic Preparedness	Justice	Responsibilities distributed within FEMA
Federal Emergency Management Agency	None	Federal Emergency Management Agency
Strategic National Stockpile National Disaster Medical System	Health and Human Services	Returned to HHS, July 2004
Nuclear Incident Response Team	Energy	Responsibilities distributed within FEMA
Domestic Emergency Support Teams	Justice	Responsibilities distributed within FEMA
National Domestic Preparedness Office	FBI	Responsibilities distributed within FEMA
CBRN Countermeasures Programs	Energy	Science & Technology Directorate
Environmental Measurements Laboratory	Energy	Science & Technology Directorate
National Biological Warfare Defense Analysis Center	Defense	Science & Technology Directorate
Plum Island Animal Disease Center	Agriculture	Science & Technology Directorate
Federal Computer Incident Response Center	General Services Administration	US-CERT, Office of Cybersecurity and Communications—National Programs and Preparedness Directorate

(*Continued*)

Table 10.2 (Continued)   Initial Agencies That Were Incorporated into the New DHS Department

AGENCY	ORIGINAL DEPARTMENT	CURRENT AGENCY OR OFFICE
National Communications System	Defense	Office of Cybersecurity and Communications National Programs and Preparedness Directorate
National Infrastructure Protection Center	FBI	Office of Operations Coordination Office of Infrastructure Protection
Energy Security and Assurance Program	Energy	Office of Infrastructure Protection
US Coast Guard	Transportation	US Coast Guard
US Secret Service	Treasury	US Secret Service

Source: http://en.wikipedia.org/wiki/United_States_Department_of_Homeland_Security#cite_note-44

initial DHS structure. The DHS organizational chart appears in Figure 10.4 [25]. (Note: In the United States the top-level governmental entities are called "Departments," while in most parts of the world they are called "Ministries." Therefore, the DHS should not be confused with a private organization calling itself the *Ministry of Homeland Security* [26].)

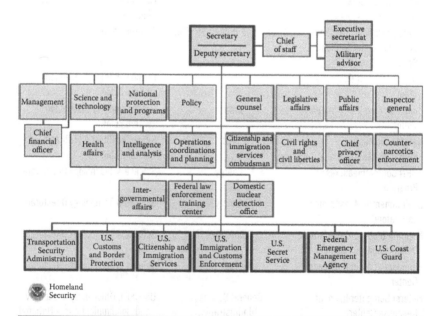

Figure 10.4   Organizational chart of the US Department of Homeland Security. (Courtesy of DHS, DHS Organizational Chart, http://www.dhs.gov/xabout/structure/editorial_0644.shtm.)

National Cyber Security Division

Within the DHS is the National Cyber Security Division (NCSD), the mission of which is to work "collaboratively with public, private, and international entities to secure cyberspace and America's cyber assets" [27]. The division's strategy is

- To build and maintain an effective national cyberspace response system
- To implement a cyber risk management program for protection of critical infrastructure [27]

The DHS-NCSD is hosting the United States Computer Emergency Readiness Team (US-CERT) that provides cyber-related security bulletins, technical security alerts, and security tips, as well as valuable information on releases on vulnerabilities of major software. US-CERT is also the place to report a cyber-related incident [28]. Recognizing that there is no time to be lost, the NCSD is "moving aggressively to build a world-class cybersecurity team, and we are focusing on key priorities that address people, processes and technology" [29].

One of the DHS directorates is the Science and Technology Directorate, which supports programs that promote cybersecurity awareness and increased capabilities for the public as well as the private sector. Under this directorate is the Cyber Security Research and Development Center that provides direction for future cyber security R&D. Activities of the center also include cybercrime prevention, wireless security, the reliability and integrity of the Domain Name System (DNS), and cooperation with other cyber-concerned government agencies.

The DNS is the array of servers distributed around the world with databases that convert domain names such as *www.xyz.com* to IP addresses such as 34.167.86.94. Should these servers be attacked, then the *www-based* cyberspace will collapse. Maintaining a DNS cache in the PC can be make surfing faster and less reliant on DNS servers. A DNS Cache is a two-field database maintained in a PC that has the domain names and the respective IP addresses of the visited Web pages.

Cybersecurity Preparedness

The NCSD sponsors various activities and initiatives aiming at the enhancement of cyber defense skills and capabilities. The major two are

- **Cyber Storm.** This is a biennial cyber defense exercise that attracts international participation and where new cyber defense skills are tested. The first *Cyber Storm* exercise took place in 2006. Through these exercises the preparedness in responding to cyber incidents is being assessed, along with information sharing and coordination among partners. Participants in the *Cyber Storm* of 2010 were other US government agencies, states within the union, numerous countries, and many private sector organizations. *Cyber Storm IV* is expected to take place in 2012.
- **National Cyber Alert System.** This program improves concerned cyberspace *residents'* awareness of the current threats and vulnerabilities in cyberspace. Concerned individuals may register [30] to receive monthly updates, as well as bulletins, on the state of cybersecurity. The major initiatives follow:
  - Cyber Security Alerts—Technical
  - Cyber Security Alerts—Non-Technical
  - Cyber Security Bulletins
  - Cyber Security Tips
  - Vulnerability Notes
  - Current Activity

Subscription to the alert system is a free public service provided by the DHS, and several thousand subscribers benefit from these monthly alerts.

Cyberspace Security Challenges

Any government agency responsible for the security of cyberspace is facing numerous challenges that can be grouped into social, economic, technological, and political. Society expects the authorities to provide security in a manner that is transparent, efficient, effective, and does not in any way step on grandfathered civil liberties, especially the right to privacy and the right to express one's own opinion.

A very important factor in fighting crime is to be able to look into the past. The ability to data mine records and extract valuable crime-solving information cannot be replaced by post-crime information. However, storage of cyber records across the board, just in case the cyber surfer may commit a crime in the next five years, should not be acceptable in a free society.

Sociologists and law makers will always be challenged in their pursuit of finding the right balance between civil rights and security, a balance that is subject to social norms that evolve along with technology. Consequently, a cybersecurity policy can only be complete if it has a respective "privacy impact assessment" [31].

There is no endeavor that is not economically challenged. Funds going into any sector, be it cybersecurity or street beautification, have to compete with the demands of other sectors. Although more resources will result in better cybersecurity, responsible managers will have to do their own balancing act, spreading the available resources among the various cybersecurity subsectors, hoping to maximize the overall security. Through "quantification of the economic value of security and assurance" [32], a manager can best calculate the cybersecurity return-on-investment.

Considering that cybersecurity requires highly skilled cyber warriors, or cyber defenders, available funding can be instrumental in educational programs and specialized training, with continuing education being the cornerstone of success.

An important challenge within cyber economics is the cybersecurity metrics. Metrics are the result obtained after processing related measurements. The challenge is what the measurements should be and how the results should be processed. Corporate management and government administrations do not hesitate in approving cybersecurity appropriations, but being non-techies themselves, they are looking for a tangible way, though parametric, to measure the return-on-investment. Measuring the efficiency or the effectiveness of a security measure, that stood guard but was never confronted, is a challenge in itself. The acronym of good metrics, that is, "**s**pecific, **m**easurable, **a**ttainable, **r**epeatable, and **t**ime-dependent" [33], forms the word **smart**.

In the cyberspace context, the answer to the question: *Are we secure enough?* is always no. This is because not only is the network exposed to known and unknown cyber risks, but each and every member of the organization through surfing, emailing, and social networking creates additional vulnerabilities that the enterprise cybersecurity measures cannot necessarily protect against. That is, the "degree of understanding of security issues among computer users" [34] in an organization is a major factor in assessing the level of cybersecurity in a system.

Effective use of technology is the number one factor in practically every sector, especially in cybersecurity. The Internet is a very complex system, and the identification of the origin of a cyber attack can have no margin of error. The challenge here is the development of a cybersecurity that is ergonomic; that is, it uses automated processes and procedures that best support the professionals in their mission.

Once the origin of a cyber attack has been absolutely identified, the political challenge is to classify it. Such classification may range from nuisance to cyberwarfare, with all associated consequences. In most cases, retaliation will be in kind rather than responding through another mode.

Distributed Defense

As cyberspace is becoming an integral part of practically every aspect of modern life, the threats against its safe and reliable operation are on the increase. Thanks to cryptography, communications content is relatively secure, while the prompt delivery of communications can be impeded by denial-of-service (DoS) attacks. Cyber antimalware have been successfully protecting against *viruses*.

However, DDoS attacks appear to remain out of control. Such attacks come in large bursts of thousands of requests, overwhelming the computational capacities of Web hosts. Typically, this happens

- Through repeated requests that incapacitate the server's resources, attacking servers, network, or terminal devices
- Through the injection of false messages, such as *connect, disconnect*, or *error messages*, that disorient the server operations.

The Internet was not designed with the cyber criminals in mind, and it is totally vulnerable to sophisticated DDoS attacks, which have become the prime concern of all cyber security officers. Also very concerned are custodians of DNS servers. Saturation, or malfunction

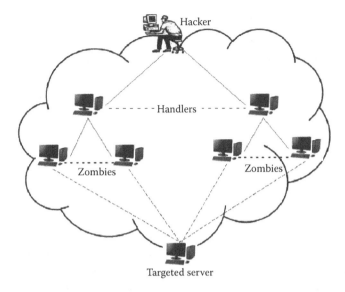

Figure 10.5   Basic topology of a distributed denial of service (DDoS).

of such servers, will result in the inaccessibility of thousands of web-sites. DDoS attacks have been on the increase in frequency and in strength, having reached the level of close to 50 Gbps in a single attack. Figure 10.5 illustrates the basic topology of a DDoS.

Cybersecurity Countermeasures

DDoS countermeasures start with the detection of a potential attack, proceed with an assessment of the attack's potential, and end with the necessary actions that need to be taken. Such actions include delay or rejection of suspected packets and, if possible, forward and backward notifications of the Internet nodes about the suspected DDoS attack. The increased speed of networks, coupled with the equally increased size of computer memory and storage, now allows for the incorpora-tion of advanced algorithms in the network nodes where traffic can be monitored, assessed, and controlled. This way, "security capabilities are built into cyber devices in a way that allows preventive and defen-sive courses of action to be coordinated within and among communi-ties of devices" [35].

The deployment of such algorithms in Internet nodes can collec-tively create a *traffic forecasting* system where destination servers will be informed of the impending traffic, its volume, and, equally important, its origin. Presently, there is no such system in place. However, significant research is in progress that points to the need for an Internet SCADA. Any Internet SCADA system has to be of a well-defined scope, of measurable effectiveness, of controllable complexity, and of practical scalability, focusing on an early-warning type of DoS detection [2].

Cyber Defense Ecosystem

Numerous cyber defense research activities point in one particular direction, that is, the creation of special artificial intelligence software that will be embedded in each Internet node, where it will collect traffic information. Collectively, and in cooperation with each other, such software will serve as an Internet SCADA that will be able to detect and prevent potential DoS attacks. Figure 10.6 illustrates an Internet host protected by security-intelligent nodes providing defense-in-depth.

Presently, the Internet is merely a global grid of interconnected routers that facilitate the end-to-end communication between Internet clients and Internet servers, without any cybersecurity potential. While administering this traffic, the Internet nodes access data that collectively may result in most valuable information. Based on

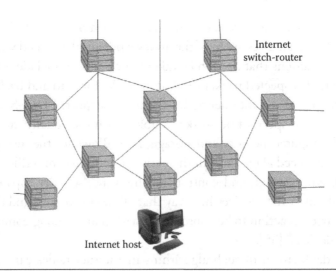

Figure 10.6   Internet host in a cyber defense ecosystem.

statistical assessments and other packet observations, an Internet SCADA—a cyber defense ecosystem—will be able to monitor related traffic and dynamically establish criteria able to possibly recognize suspected DDoS attacks.

All technology-supported services have started minimal in size and functionality and progressively have grown into powerful and useful social resources. Similarly, the Internet started as a text messaging platform and has grown in being an integral part of everyone's life. Today, the functionality level of the Internet nodes can be compared to that of the mobile phones of the 1990s—minimal and nonintelligent. For the Internet nodes, the next step is to go beyond the packet-passing stage and to collectively become an infrastructure that supports server security and load projections, at least as a start. As a system, the Internet nodes are an underutilized resource. Once security-related intelligence is entered into them, a cyber defense ecosystem will be created.

Cybersecurity Training

Cybersecurity training is the responsibility of all persons who expose their computers to cyberspace. The degree of training will vary depending of one's involvement. If we look at the two ends of the spectrum, we see cyberspace users at one end and cybersecurity professionals at the other end.

Cyberspace users have a responsibility to themselves and to the cyberspace community to maintain a healthy PC that is free of malware that may infect others via cyberspace. As a minimum, a PC must have a live antivirus software that examines each and every file before it is opened or installed on the PC. Cybersecurity users need to have a security awareness, especially as it applies to the acceptance of files and applications from unknown sources, because user acceptance may override the capability of a firewall or antivirus to protect a PC. Such awareness needs to be reinforced through frequent seminars—webinars, even better—and knowledge of the risks associated with social networking.

The cybersecurity professionals must have a wide spectrum of skills and expertise focusing in one or more specializations. Table 10.3 identifies the four major specializations within the broad field of

Table 10.3   Specializations within Cybersecurity and Respective Skills

SYSTEM ADMINISTRATIONS	PENETRATION TESTING
Policies and compliance enforcement	Techniques
Federal	Intrusion
Corporate	Hacking
Firewalls and patches	Web applications
Installation	Languages
Currency	Protocols
Server maintenance	Networks
Database	Layers
Networking	Protocols
Web and email	Operating systems
CYBER AUDITING AND FORENSICS	**CYBERSECURITY MANAGEMENT**
Recoveries	Leadership skills
Password	Project administration
Files	Knowledge acquisition
Cryptography	Communication skills
Malware	Policies and compliance awareness
Analysis	Federal
Tools	Corporate
Techniques	Investigations
Devices	Policies
Storage	Procedures
Mobile	Documentations
Formats	Legal aspects
Networks protocols	Intellectual property
Incident response	Privacy
Intrusion detection	

cybersecurity and the required respective skills. Cybersecurity professionals have chosen a career that is characterized by intense life-long learning and technology legislation monitoring.

Cyber Simulation and Exercises

A large amount of resources is being continuously allocated toward cybersecurity, and powerful claims are made as to the level of preparedness. However, there are no reliable metrics to assess and to *calibrate* the cyber defense strength. There has been no real cyber war to test the defensive and the offensive capabilities of potential adversaries. In lieu of that, there is the option of cyber war simulation.

Over the years, simulations have been made using large arrays of cyber hosts—computers—and servers. It is not easy to botnet a large number of hosts to bombard a particular server and create a DoS attack. Fortunately, cyber warfare simulation software have been developed that may emulate attacks in the millions. Figure 10.7 illustrates an advanced system that "simulates blended application traffic and current attacks at 120 Gigabits per second (Gbps) and the load of 90 million concurrent users,… Military units tasked with protecting national cybersecurity can create the world's most advanced and cost-efficient cyber ranges, delivering realistic cyber war simulations to hone cyber defenders' knowledge and instincts for protecting military networks and installations" [36].

Considering the dependence a modern society has on the Internet, and how "cyber warfare is subtle and devastating" [37], governments have been very concerned over Web vulnerabilities. As a result, cyber exercises are important mechanisms being held in order to [38]

- Assess preparedness measures against
  - Cyber threats
  - Natural disasters
  - Technology failures
- Enable authorities to target specific weaknesses
- Increase cooperation among relevant stakeholders
- Identify interdependencies

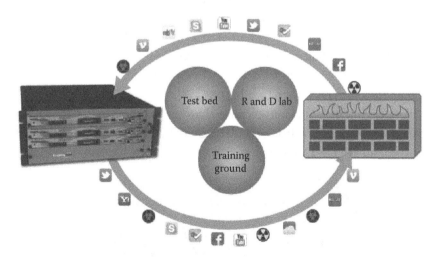

Figure 10.7   Cyber warfare simulation and firewall testing and calibration. (Courtesy of Breaking Point Systems, Inc. Cyber Warfare Simulation and Firewall Testing, BreakingPoint Systems, Inc., http://www.breakingpointsystems.com/cyber-tomography-products/breakingpoint-firestorm-ctm/.)

- Stimulate continuity planning
- Train and educate people
- Create a level of confidence as to cybersecurity

Cyber exercises require extensive [37]

- **Planning**, for attacks and counterattacks, spoofing and intrusions, disruptions and degradation
- **Testing**, [for the evaluation of] different strategies and tactics for limiting damage, identifying vulnerabilities, and creating redundancy
- **Training**, [for] personnel to recognize problems and to adapt and respond effectively

Three such major exercises are shown in Figure 10.8:

- **Cyber Endeavor**, a US government, industry, and academia exercise
- **Cyber Storm**, a United States–organized multinational exercise
- **Cyber Europe**, a European Union–organized regional exercise

Cyber Endeavor is an annual event organized by military entities of the US government that "provides a grass-root, working level and environment for operators, thought-leaders, and practitioners to collectively discuss and identify potential solutions to the most critical, pressing Cyber challenges and problem sets facing..." cybersecurity. The event includes a Cyber Symposium, Cyber Games and Competitions, and Cyber Exhibitions [38].

Cyber Storm is a cyber exercise that has been taking place every two years since 2006. It is organized by the National Cyber Security Division of the US Department of Homeland Security, and it provides

Figure 10.8 Three global cyber warfare simulation exercises.

an assessment for the US readiness in the event of cyber warfare. Participating are public and private sector organizations, as well as international entities [39].

Cyber Europe was the very first European cybersecurity exercise, with the objective to create a cyber defense community among state members. Participating were seventy public sector organizations from twenty-two countries, with some additional ones participating as observers. The exercise was organized by the European Network and Information Security Agency (ENISA), a European Union Agency. One of the recommendations was that such exercises be held at the national level as well to develop experience and expertise [40].

The common aims of the exercises were to

- Create, test, and enhance communications policies and procedures for various cyber attack scenarios
- Identify areas of improvement and assess value of policies and issues
- Assess information-sharing mechanisms
- Identify critical interdependencies between cyber and physical infrastructures
- Raise awareness of the role of cybersecurity in national security and in the economy
- Develop familiarity with available tools and technologies for cybersecurity

Warfare Information in an Information Warfare Terrain

In an information war the most valuable warfare information is the knowledge about the existence of zero-day vulnerabilities. That is, knowing what *holes* exist in the adversary's cyberspace and how to inflict maximum damage through their exploitation.

It is now *old news* that every national ministry of defense has a *cyber combat division*, and every ministry of foreign affairs has a *cyber information department*. It is now in the open that cyber warfare is a reality. On January 20, 2017, the White House's website posted:

> "*Cyberwarfare is an emerging battlefield, and we must take every measure to safeguard our national security secrets and systems. We will make it*

a priority to develop defensive and offensive cyber capabilities at our U.S. Cyber Command, and to recruit the best and the brightest Americans to serve in this crucial area."

This website posting tells the world to *do the same*. The difference between conventional warfare and non-proliferation treaties is that the sizes of armed forces and capabilities are well known or can be reasonably estimated. It is impossible to know the size of a country's cyber force, or *information warfare force*, to be more correct because, cyber warfare is limited to cyberspace, that is the Internet space, while in information warfare, the entire electronic space is included.

The spoofing of GPS signals that can mislead GPS-supported activities, such as navigation, is a powerful defensive measure against enemy drones. A perfect example is when "[t]he government of Iran announced that an American unmanned aircraft, detected in Iranian airspace, was brought down by its cyber warfare unit stationed near Kashmar and brought down with minimum damage."†

At the state level, cybersecurity is not so much threatened by the self-taught cyber-criminals and cyber-terrorists, but by the well-funded, well-educated and well-skilled state-sponsored cyber-actors. As a result, "… *there is a pressing need for all sectors and governments* (to create a state cyber-defense/offense entity) *to prevent, detect, recover from, and defend themselves against cyberattacks.*‡

In the creation of a state cyber-defense/offense entity, there are four main challenges, namely,

- How to distinguish between the *nominal* mission and the *real* mission of the endeavor.
- How to determine its most effective qualitative and quantitative size and structure.
- How to grant it autonomous, but legitimate authority.
- How to select the government agency, under which to be, without disrupting the existing domestic political balance of power.

---

* https://www.whitehouse.gov/making-our-military-strong-again
† https://en.wikipedia.org/wiki/Iran%E2%80%93U.S._RQ-170_incident
‡ http://www.rand.org/randeurope/research/projects/reforming-nato-cyber-acquisition
  -process.html

The main difference between conventional warfare and cyber warfare is that in conventional warfare the attackers and their locations are well identifiable, while in the cyber warfare it is practically impossible to determine the location or the identity of the attacker.

Developing a National Strategy for Cybersecurity

As cyberspace imposed itself on the world, governments recognized its inevitable dominance, and one after another realized the need for a National Cybersecurity Strategy. It has to be a strategy that balances the need for national protection and the need for civil rights protection. Namely, the citizens' rights to speech and the citizens' rights to privacy. Furthermore, it has to be accepted that there will be no absolute protection, and that this strategy will need to be updated as society and technology evolve. In general terms, such strategy should include the following:*

Create a cybersecurity work force with a centralized emergency support team, serving as a trusted point of contact and as a national coordinator on cyber issues.

Establish a cybersecurity awareness educational program, publicize cybersecurity best practices and build a cybersecurity culture.

Build a secure and reliable cyberspace information sharing government agency.

Give citizens and organizations an opportunity to provide their input into a national dialogue.

Articulate the national priorities, principles, policies and programs.

Specify the roles and missions of each government agency and non-government organization involved.

Stipulate goals, milestones, and metrics to measure and communicate the extent of progress in addressing the issues.

Foster international cooperation on cybersecurity.

---

* http://download.microsoft.com/download/b/f/0/bf05da49-7127-4c05-bfe8-0063 dab88f72/developing_a_national_strategy_for_cybersecurity.pdf

Similar to any modern-day strategy, any National Cybersecurity Strategy must recognize the relevant needs and articulate the way those need be addressed. In this case, the Strategy must meet the following principles*:

Risk-based. Cyberspace is full of a wide variety of risks.

Threat Modeling. Address all possible threats, let it be cyber-crime or espionage.

Outcome-focused. Articulate and focus on the desired final result.

Prioritized. Set clear priorities among the objectives of the strategy.

Respectful. Include protections for privacy and civil liberties.

While the establishment of a National Cybersecurity Strategy is adopted in many countries, Austria has adopted "self-regulation" to encourage the private sector to set its own standards on Cybersecurity, with the state creating the necessary regulatory framework.

In conclusion, the purpose of a National Cybersecurity Strategy is to serve as a focal point for the nation's defense against this invisible though real threat to a country's national interests.

Exercises

1. Research Cyber Storm III and prepare a three-page report summarizing your findings. The following sources will give students a head start:
   - http://www.dhs.gov/xlibrary/assets/nppd-cyber-storm-iii-final-report.pdf
   - http://www.pcworld.com/businesscenter/article/206554/cyber_storm_iii_simulates_largescale_attack.html
   - http://www.dhs.gov/files/training/cyberstorm-iii.shtm
   - http://www.nextgov.com/nextgov/ng_20100929_4557.php?oref=rss??zone=NGtoday
2. Research the published cyber warfare incidents and prepare a table similar to Table 10.1. List the reported incidents not included in the table, and elaborate on each incident.

---

* http://download.microsoft.com/download/b/f/0/bf05da49-7127-4c05-bfe8-0063dab88f72/developing_a_national_strategy_for_cybersecurity.pdf

3. Study the document A Guide to Security Metrics located at http://www.sans.org/reading_room/whitepapers/auditing /guide-security-metrics_55. Develop a 12-slide electronic presentation describing the guide.

4. Research the availability of Cybersecurity Training Programs and prepare a three-page report summarizing your findings, focusing on the program contents. In your survey include academic as well as certificate programs.

5. Research the Impact of Social Networking on the Society and develop a 10-slide electronic presentation, or a three-page report. The following three papers may provide students an introduction to the topic:
   - http://www.ec.ubi.pt/ec/06/pdf/neelamalar-new-media .pdf
   - http://myconvergence.com.my/main/images/stories/PDF _Folder/jan2010/MyCon06_50.pdf
   - http://ftp.jrc.es/EURdoc/JRC54327.pdf.

6. Research the Impact of Social Networking on Cybersecurity and develop a ten-slide electronic presentation, or a three-page report. The following three papers may provide students with an introduction into the topic:
   - http://download.pwc.com/ie/pubs/security_for_social _networking.pdf
   - http://www.us-cert.gov/reading_room/safe_social _networking.pdf
   - http://www.cio.gov/documents/guidelines_for_secure_use _social_media_v01-0.pdf

7. Research the *topic of Cyber Warfare Simulation* and prepare a ten-slide electronic presentation. The following three papers may provide students an introduction to the topic:
   - http://www.scs.org/magazines/2010-07/index_file/Files /Article_Stytz.pdf
   - http://scs-europe.net/services/ecms2005/pdf/abs-03.pdf
   - http://iac.dtic.mil/iatac/download/Vol12_No3.pdf

8. Study the document Emerging Cybersecurity Issues Threaten Federal Information System, located at http://www.gao.gov /new.items/d05231.pdf, and summarize it in a 10-slide electronic presentation, or a five-page report.

9. Research the extent of published Cyber Espionage and prepare a ten-slide electronic presentation, or a four-page report,
summarizing your findings. The following three papers may
provide the student with an introduction into the topic:
   - http://pages.uoregon.edu/joe/cyberwar/cyberwar.pdf
   - http://www.nartv.org/mirror/ghostnet.pdf
   - http://commlaw.cua.edu/res/docs/articles/v19/19-1/11-v19
     -1-O-Hara-Final.pdf

10. Study the White House document, the Comprehensive
National Cybersecurity Initiative, and summarize it in an
eight-slide electronic presentation. It is located at http://www
.whitehouse.gov/sites/default/files/cybersecurity.pdf.

Digital Currencies

Introduction

Typically, digital currencies are private monetary values that exist only in ledgers. That is, a digital currency—offered and administered by a private organization—is bypassing the conventional banking system and governmental currencies, allowing monetary worth to change ownership for the purchase of goods and services. Because these currencies have no physical aspect to protect, their protection and integrity is safeguarded by heavy cryptographic means, and for that they are referred to as cryptocurrencies.

Parallel to the *soft* cryptocurrencies, that is currencies that exist only in database-ledgers, also exist *hard* cryptocurrencies, that is, currencies that have a physical representation. Examples of such currencies are the *peercoin*[*].

While the most well-known cryptocurrency is the Bitcoin[†] with its Marketplace[‡], there are numerous other such currencies publicly or privately available[§]. The use of cryptocurrencies allows anonymity in the transaction, thus offering privacy over the performed transaction[¶].

The Blockchain Concept

Physical monetary units, such as paper money, are numbered to indicate their uniqueness and are made relatively difficult to duplicate.

---

[*] https://www.peercoin.net/
[†] https://www.bitcoin.com
[‡] https://coinmall.io/?aff=bitcom
[§] https://en.wikipedia.org/wiki/List_of_cryptocurrencies
[¶] http://www.payoutmag.com/press-releases/802-titcoin-receives-two-web-a-tech-xbiz-nominations/

Similarly, metal monetary units, such as gold and silver coins, have their own intrinsic value, and their duplication is impractical.

On the other hand, the digital currency units are traced through their use, as they are being utilized, changing owners in the process. This tracing is being implemented via a highly secure open ledger—a database—that records all transactions digital currency units go through. Each transaction is referred to as a *block*, and the ledger keeps track of each and every transaction that takes place within a particular cryptocurrency system.

Each transaction, that is each use of the digital money, has a timestamp and a link as to where that digital money came from. Cryptocurrency management organizations claim that *"By design blockchains are inherently resistant to modification of the data"**. Because the *blocks* are linked to each other—they are *chained*—the concept is called *blockchain*.

In a general sense, the concept of creating a *blockchain*, that is the recording of a sequence of events permanently stored in a database, is applicable to many areas, including the medical[†] field and the military[‡].

Cryptocurrencies

There are numerous organizations[§] that issue cryptocurrencies. It is believed that they are over seven hundred digital currency issuing organizations. OneCoin claims that *"Regulatory challenges related to cryptocurrencies are mainly linked to the anonymity of transactions and the decentralization of financial dealings."* Monero claims that it *"... is a secure, private, untraceable currency."* Many such organizations employ external auditing supervision in order to establish reputation on maintaining integrity and above all privacy. Authorities are primarily concerned over two main issues regarding the cryptocurrency industry, if we may call it that way.

The first is that the possibility that criminal/illegal activities are concealed behind the anonymous transactions. It is believed that

---

* https://en.wikipedia.org/wiki/Blockchain_(database)
† https://www.healthit.gov/sites/default/files/5-56-onc_blockchainchallenge_mit whitepaper.pdf
‡ http://dtic.mil/doctrine/education/jpme_papers/barnas_n.pdf
§ https://en.bitcoin.it/wiki/Comparison_of_cryptocurrencies

cryptocurrencies "*... have been quite a debatable vehicle for payments due to the poor regulations and high attractiveness for international criminal activities.*"[*] The US Federal Bureau of Investigation is very concerned over the use of cryptocurrencies for criminal-illegal activities, having made many arrests on such crimes.[†]

The second concerns cryptocurrency integrity, whereby the minting of the respective currency corresponds to the available conventional monetary assets. If unregulated, cryptocurrencies may become insolvent, unable to convert crypto money to conventional money— dollars, euros, etc.[‡] Addressing such possibilities, insurance companies offer coverage over cryptocurrency losses due to cyber crime, such as theft, hacking, or insolvency.[§]

There are numerous cryptocurrencies, and new ones pop up continuously. The most visible to the public are the following:

Bitcoin[¶]	Ethereum[**]	PeerCoin[††]	DASH[‡‡]	Litecoin[§§]
VeriCoin[¶¶]	CLAMCoin[***]	DogeCoin[†††]	Factom[‡‡‡]	Monero[§§§]
OneCoin[¶¶¶]				

Bitcoin

Bitcoin is the most well-known of the cryptocurrencies. According to the Bitcoin organization "... the supply of Bitcoin is mathematically limited to twenty-one million bitcoins and that can never be changed"

---

[*] https://letstalkpayments.com/why-cryptocurrency-is-a-perfect-vehicle-for-crime/

[†] https://www.fbi.gov/@@search?SearchableText=bitcoin&pageSize=20&page=1

[‡] https://www.law360.com/articles/531713/cryptocurrency-exchange-insolvencies -may-force-reg-action

[§] http://insurancethoughtleadership.com/why-insurers-caught-the-blockchain-bug/

[¶] https://www.bitcoin.com/

[**] https://ethereum.org/

[††] https://www.peercoin.net/

[‡‡] https://www.dash.org/

[§§] https://litecoin.org/

[¶] http://vericoin.co/

[***] http://www.clamcoin.org/

[†††] http://dogecoin.com/

[‡‡‡] https://www.factom.com/

[§§§] https://getmonero.org/home

[¶¶¶] https://www.onecoin.eu/en/

and "... the Bitcoin network is unstoppable and uncensorable."* The last statement concerns crime prevention agencies, worldwide, while it is a clear invitation for illegal activities. This statement is not unique to Bitcoin coin, but applies to all digital currencies that maintain uncensorable accounts. A law firm specializing in cyber matters states: "This digital currency (the Bitcoin) that is processed via the Internet is not subject to oversight by a central issuing authority."

Cryptocurrencies might not be *subject to oversight by a central issuing authority*, and also be *uncensorable*, but there is a US law in the books, covered in Chapter Nine, the Communications Assistance for Law Enforcement Act of 1994[†], that obliges telecom companies "... pursuant to a court order or other lawful authorization, to intercept all of the subscriber's wire and electronic communications...." It is hard to believe that cryptocurrencies are above this law.

Cryptocurrency Wallet

In the cryptocurrency context, the *wallet* is an account that is anonymously maintained by the cryptocurrency issuing organization, or by a third party. Such accounts may be uni-currency or multi-currency. Using the *wallet*, one can "Make direct person-to-person transactions, pay invoices, request or send payments by email."[‡]

The crypto currency wallet may also be a hardware device that holds the cryptocurrency account password. Such device interfaces via a USB connection, and it may hold passwords for other accesses as well[§].

Cybercrime in the Cryptocurrencies Domain

Undoubtedly, the use of digital currencies provides privacy and anonymity not offered by the conventional funds transferring institutions. However, this privacy, and especially the offered anonymity, has made cryptocurrencies cryptocriminals' heaven.

---

* https://www.bitcoin.com/getting-started
† https://www.congress.gov/bill/103rd-congress/house-bill/4922
‡ https://www.cryptonator.com/
§ https://cryptojunction.com/wallet/keepkey/

One type of cybercrimes that is being harbored by the anonymity of cryptocurrencies is the cyber extortion—the demand for ransom—for the prevention of future attacks, or for the restoration of already-locked data. Ransomware, as it is named in cyberspace, is illegal software self-installing in Web-connected computers with the ability to encrypt, or to delete, directories or files that can be decrypted only through a password, or through a remote deactivation by the cyber criminals.

Such type of software is available for purchase in the *Dark Web*, a term referring to the websites that deal in illegal activities, and it is not listed in the search engines. As for the mode of payment, cryptocurrencies are being used, thus, concealing both the seller and the buyer. According to the FBI, "... *earlier ransomware scams involved having victims pay ransom with pre-paid cards, victims are now increasingly asked to pay with Bitcoin,...*"*

Through ransomware, criminals access PCs with the ability to view the directories and to selectively damage, delete or encrypt files, or even change passwords. Often, such malware is installed and ransom is demanded for not activating it. However, there are ransomware scanning and ransomware removal tools that can provide defense in many ransomware cases.

Should one fall victim of such cyber extortion, always notify the cognizant authorities, who may possibly remove the criminal's lock over the data of the attacked PC. Either way, one should always record at least the cryptocurrency account number where the ransom is to be paid, for subsequent investigation by the cognizant authorities.

Besides anti-virus software that examine all access attempts to a PC and reject the illegal ones, there is a practice that can make ransomware less harmful. This is, backing up all files in write-only storage, that is, accessing only if disconnected from the Web.

Purchasing Cryptocurrencies

Cryptocurrencies are treated as commodities that are bought and sold in a variety of ways. Similar to the stock exchanges, there are

---

* https://www.fbi.gov/news/stories/ransomware-on-the-rise

cryptocurrency exchanges* where one may trade units of cryptocurrencies for other cryptocurrencies or for traditional currencies, dollars, euros, etc.

One may buy cryptocurrencies using one's own bank account, credit cards, ATMs, or using PayPal. However, such purchases are not totally anonymous, since such accounts have the customers' identity. The Swiss railroad system† has plans to "... *offer Bitcoin sales through its train ticket machines.*" It is not clear if these machines will accept cash. However, such purchases will require "... *a Switzerland-based phone number...*", a requirement that reveals the user's identity. Of course, one may purchase cryptocurrency from the wallet of an already cryptocurrency holder. Either way, while the identity of the cryptocurrency purchaser might be traceable, the use of the cryptocurrency is claimed to be untraceable.

Exercises

1. Visit the fbi.gov website, and summarize the type crimes committed in cryptocurrency.
2. Describe the cryptocurrency regulatory measures enforced in the European Union. Suggest possible improvements.
3. Define *Deep Web* and *Dark Web*, and describe their role in cybercrime.
4. Research Cyber Insurance, as it applies to the cryptocurrency industry.

---

* http://www.cryptocoincharts.info/markets/info
† https://news.bitcoin.com/switzerlands-sbb-railway-bitcoin-kiosks/

12

TRANSFORMATION OF TRADITIONAL CRIME INTO CYBERCRIME

A contribution of General Emmanuel Sfakianakis, Director of the Anti-Cybercrime Division of the Greek Police.

Introduction

The purpose of this chapter is to demonstrate how cyber and other electronic technologies are now in the service of criminals whose activities require investigators with advanced cyber skills.

Slowly and steadily we must realize that, in the coming century and through the Internet, our lives will become more beautiful, more enjoyable, more productive, and with unique experiences, in defiance of the increasingly sophisticated and growing cybercrime.

We must realize that the criminal elements—thieves, burglars, robbers, terrorists, etc.—are slowly abandoning their Stone Age tools, and entering into the high-tech era where, through electronic media, they will be able to invade our lives and reach their goals, this time online. To realize the gravity of possible cyberspace abuse, let's ask ourselves the following questions:

Fifteen years ago, would it have been possible for criminals

- To commit murders, or to blackmail and collect extortion money leaving no trace behind?
- To interfere with organizational operations (airplanes, trains, metro, banking institutions, etc.)?

Unfortunately, today via the Web, it is possible, and it is being done, daily.

The current online era has changed everything around us. The Internet gives us knowledge, information, communication, economic development, well-being and so much more. It can also give us pain through criminal acts.

Today, many people demonize the Internet, rather than accepting that it is like electricity. Electricity makes our lives easier, but it can also be fatal. If we do not follow the rules of Internet use, we may be the victims of criminal behavior, which varies in severity and danger.

People must understand that today crime has mutated from traditional to electronic. The sad part is that, worldwide, legislation has not caught up with this mutation. As a result, in the courts there are now thousands of cases, criminal and civil, that are purely electronic crimes, or contain some elements that demand cybercrime investigation. It should be pointed out that, little by little, every crime will require an electronic investigation.

All police investigations of major criminal offenses (terrorism, homicide, blackmail, abduction, suicide prevention, disappearances, etc.) include an electronic component. As a result, a new breed of police investigators is desperately needed. Consequently, everyone—probation officers, investigating magistrates, prosecutors, as well as judges—dealing with cases that have evidence of electronic components must be aware of the basic principles of electronic crime.

Since 1995, as a police cyber investigator, I have handled well over ten thousand cases out of my Department's total of about twenty-eight thousand cases. As I recall, in 1995, we had two to three cases per month. Today, in 2017, cyber-related complaints average eighty per day.

A typical cybercrime is *ransomware*, where a virus installs itself in a victim's computer. It locks all functions, displaying a message on the screen demanding ransom in exchange for unlocking the computer. Below are two typical ransomware cases authorities are facing repeatedly.

Case One: A ransomware virus hits victim-computers, locking all functions, displaying an extortion message. The message has the logo of the anti-cybercrime unit of the respective country's police department, claiming that this computer—the victim's computer—had visited websites of prohibited content and that it is being fined with X amount of euros.

The extortion message also includes instructions and links to websites where the victim may purchase e-cash and pay the ransom.

Case Two: A similar ransomware virus that has hit numerous computers encrypts all of the computer's files, displaying an extortion message demanding X amount of euros, to be payable in the BitCoin e-currency. Under the present circumstances, the BitCoin transactions are untraceable.

It is a fact that untraceable e-currencies have made it impossible for authorities, worldwide, to properly investigate and prosecute crimes.

It is worth reading white papers that project cyberspace into the future. One such paper is the *White Paper: Cisco VNI Forecast and Methodology, 2015-2020**, which predicts and analyzes the growth and trends of the Internet. Contrary to this exponential evolution taking place in cyberspace, the drafting of a new Legislative Framework on Electronic Crime is significantly lagging. The Cisco predictions are generally conservative, and extremely accurate, showing world's tendency for fast adoption to new technologies. The sad thing is that the availability of high technology increases the crime sophistication.

Electronic Crime

Let us first define what we mean by *Electronic Crime*, of which cybercrime is the major part. Basically, electronic crime is criminal offenses committed with the use of technology

- With stand-alone computers, counterfeiting currency or creating false documents. Or,
- With the exploitation of cyberspace insecurities, where there is a vast spectrum of crimes, ranging from intellectual property piracy to cyber bullying.

Case Three: Electronic criminals with high quality credit card producing equipment in cooperation with the cashier of a store "collected" the magnetic strip data of valid cards and embedded then in counterfeit cards bearing the name of users. Thus, the display of a valid photo

---

* http://www.cisco.com/c/en/us/solutions/collateral/service-provider/visual-networking
-index-vni/complete-white-paper-c11-481360.html

identification card was giving credibility to the credit card, since they both had the same name. However, an instant alert, on the use of the counterfeit card, led the police to the store where it was being used and to the arrest of the electronic criminal.

Cybercrime is quick, committed in milliseconds, and it is often not recognized by the victims. The speed and the ease with which cybercrime is being performed has attracted skilled cyber criminals, creating a major disadvantage and concern to the prosecuting authorities, worldwide. Reasons for the wide spread of cybercrime can be as follows:

- Specialized knowledge is not always required.
- Can be committed from a distance and anonymously.
- Allows criminals to communicate with like-minded people quickly and inexpensively, even in real time, without relocating.
- It is difficult to pinpoint the actual origin of a cyber criminal act.
- It is borderless. Very often, it requires multinational cooperation for its investigation and persecution.
- Investigated and prosecuted cybercrimes constitute the tip of the iceberg.
- Police investigation is relatively difficult and requires excellent training and specialized knowledge.

For those involved in electronic crime prosecution—police officers, district attorneys, judges, and lawyers—specialized knowledge, experience and skills are required. However, since they all follow the letter of the law, they cannot effectively perform their duties if they are not supported by an appropriate legal infrastructure.

Forms of Cybercrime

According to the survey* conducted by McConnell International in 52 countries, offenses committed in cyberspace are mostly as follows:

- Obstruction of (cyber) traffic
- Modification and theft of data

---

* IWS—The Information Warfare Site, McConnell International, December 2000
http://www.iwar.org.uk/law/resources/cybercrime/mcconnell/CyberCrime.pdf

- Invasion and sabotage in a network
- Unauthorized access
- Virus injections
- Treatment of offenses
- Plagiarism and fraud

The most common cybercrimes that keep anti-cybercrime authorities busy are the following:

- Scams through the Internet
- Crimes about morals
- Cracking and hacking
- Software hijacking and piracy
- Credit cards
- Drug trafficking
- Crimes through chat rooms
- Violation-Misrepresentation of Personal Data (Social media, etc.)

Investigating Electronic Crimes

In their cyberspace navigation, all Internet users leave unique traces of their electronic identity. Each electronic trace consists, as a minimum, of three parts that ensure the identity's uniqueness:

- The IP address (The address of the Internet connection granted for that particular communication)
- The date (Based on the geographical location of the used device)
- The time zone of the device location.
- Possibly the serial number of the connected device used (PC, phone, etc.)
- Possibly the serial number of the application used (browser, server, etc.)

In every online investigation, an attempt is made to locate the offender's electronic trail, which is unique to each data exchange, and it is very important evidence in any court process. In addition to using their real identity, one can access the Internet by posting and signing either as anonymous or even using a nickname.

This state of presumed anonymity on the Internet is what facilitates and motivates the perpetrators who think they will always remain anonymous to commit online criminal offenses. Anonymity makes it difficult to locate them, but when prosecuting authorities have the right tools and experience, the perpetrators will hardly be able to escape the law. If an anonymous person commits a cybercrime, the prosecuting authorities, through a court order, may be provided with the cyber trace by the Internet service provider (ISP). Often this process takes time, thus hindering the prosecution process.

To sum it up, there is no anonymity on the Internet, but there are cases where the online actor used various electronic tracing avoidance programs or free wireless networks. However, in such cases the crimes are investigated with special techniques leading to the identification of the offender.

> Case Four: A rejected lover anonymously posted photos of an ex-partner with a telephone number and erotic invitations. However, due to inexperience with the Web protocols, the lover left a lot of footprints that led to a successful prosecution.
>
> Case Five: Police investigators recognized the existence of a cyber criminal who was trading online illegal/immoral material operating out of Internet cafes that ensured anonymity of the user. However, using special programs, the police were able to recognize IP traces that led to the arrest of the suspect.

Hackers and Crackers

"The Assassins of the Cyberspace" can be distinguished in two categories, depending on their intentions, on how they penetrate, and on the desired result.

Hackers: Usually, hackers would "attack" one's computer without inflicting any damage or leaving any trace. Their motive can be pleasure or curiosity, without seeking any economic benefit. In some cases hackers would identify a cybersecurity weakness, and would report it to the computer owner in hope for recognition or other benefit.

Crackers: Usually, crackers would "attack" one's computer in an effort to identify a cybersecurity weakness and to capitalize on it. That is, they seek a financial benefit or cause a digital vandalism. In simple terms, crackers are cyber criminals who "invade" one's system to learn or to acquire something for subsequent commitment of an illegal act.

> Case Six: Financial mules. Owners of large sums of money wishing to move them from account to account anonymously solicit account holders who could "move" their money for a very high "fee". This way, such owners operate invisibly to the authorities.

Investigating Cybercrimes

The investigation of cybercrimes is a quite difficult and very time-consuming task. The investigators work on the principle that "*the criminal always leaves traces.*" Cybercrimes investigations mainly involve the identification of *electronic traces*. An investigation may take from a few minutes to years. It can be time consuming because cyber criminals benefit from the lack of legislation that gives investigators prompt access to cyber communications' historical data.

In every online survey, an attempt is made to identify the offender's *online footprints*, which are unique as each Internet user navigates the Web. Each *footprint* record may contain several parameters, such as date, time stamp, and serial numbers of associated applications (browser, word processor, image processor, etc.). The collection of such factual parameters serve as important and indisputable court evidence in the prosecution of the suspected crime.

Financial Cyber Scams

The basic principle of Internet fraud is to persuade the victim that by paying a small amount now, a much larger amount is awaiting. Web scams are increasing exponentially, with the fraudsters' sophistication equally increasing. The extent of financial cyber frauds has reached the point where such *categories* have been created, as described below.

The Nigerian Letter

This is an email that informs the potential victim that someone, presumably a "former high-ranking official" in the Nigerian government, needs help to transfer—under cover—a high amount of money (e.g.,

$30 million), and is willing to pay a "high" fee in exchange for such service. The receiver of this letter is being asked to help by acting as a "money mule" temporarily recieving that amount in his own account. In the letter, emphasis is placed on the confidentiality that should be respected. As a first step, the cyber criminals ask the candidate victim for his consent and and to provide information regarding his bank accounts and any information "deemed necessary" for the transaction. Numerous times and at the request of the unsuspecting victim, documents are presented, which appear authentic and official, in order to eliminate any doubts a naive victim may have had. Once the victim responds, an endless process of exchanging of mails, emails, and phone calls begins to make the potential victim believe that the process of receiving big money is near. Just before the presumed "final transfer of money", the cyber criminals inform the victim of an unexpected problem. Such problem may be the payment of a tax, an unexpected fee, or need for a bribe an bank employee who will authorize the money transfer. Here starts the "catch". The cyber criminals claim to be unable to pay this unexpected cost, because the big money is locked in the transfer, and they ask the victim-to-be to pay that amount, which, the victim is told, will be refunded upon completion of the transaction. Some of the victims are persuaded even to travel to Nigeria to pay the amount in order to "complete" the transaction. Furthermore, the victim is misled that they require no visa, ends up illegally in the country, falling deeper in the net of the Nigerian criminals. Such crimes are not new. They used to take place via letters and faxes. Today, they continue, with the only difference being that the Internet is the criminals' infrastructure.

> Case Seven. A lady of the highest level of education was persuaded to travel to a European capital in order to receive "awarded" funds. On arrival, she was treated lavishly while, presumably, awaiting for the funds transfer to take place. The lady was taken to a bank where she was met in a hallway by a, presumably, high "bank official" who assured her of her funds. The "official" pointed out that the bank will release the 12 million euros "award" immediately, as soon as the 0.5 million euro tax is being paid. The lady transferred her funds to the "bank official." The criminals were eventually caught, but the funds were lost forever.

The Spanish Lotto

This form of fraud is carried out by mass emailing to random Internet users. These messages inform them that in an Internet lotto they have earned a large amount of money, in the order of millions of dollars. However, the recipients have never participated in the lotto. The perpetrators, in order to be believed, use names from large companies (e.g., Microsoft, Yahoo, etc.) and accompanying the messages they send fake certificates regarding the alleged electronic draw. The fraud lies in the fact that they ask the presumed winners to pre-pay some taxes, usually amounting to a few thousand dollars. Surprisingly, this category of cyber fraud claims hundreds of victims.

Data Phishing

Phishing is usually carried out by sending bulk spam emails, which are supposed to be sent by an existing and legitimate corporation (bank, e-shop, e-payment service, etc.) in an attempt to mislead the recipient and to collect private personal and financial data. Subsequently, the perpetrators of this type of fraud use these data to commit criminal offenses. They usually ask for credit card numbers with a due date and a security number. With this information fake bank cards are made for fraudulent use.

Software Piracy

Software piracy refers to the unauthorized reproduction and/or disposal of computer programs that are protected by copyright laws. The distribution of the reproduced material began with the handling of CDs or diskettes. However, the spread of the Internet has opened the way to a new form of crime where material is being trafficked through e-mails, chat or peer-to-peer applications.

> Case Eight. A software package—intellectual property of the International Welding Corporation (IWC)—was illegally marketed and distributed in Europe via the Web, having resulted in a loss of many millions of euros to the software developers. The illegal advertising caught the attention of IWC, and in a matter of minutes, the criminals were located and taken to justice.

Credit Cards

Fraud phenomena with the use of credit cards in online markets are growing at a rapid pace. It is estimated that banks are counting millions of euros in losses from people who make counterfeit, intercept credit card numbers or others who make online purchases using card numbers found through, for example, phishing or manufactured with the help of analogous computer algorithms.

> Case Nine. A criminal advertizes the availability of a certain product at a very attractive price, asking for a small percent of the order to be paid— via a credit card—in advance, with the rest payable upon receipt of the product. Many fall for it, providing all of their card's data to pay the for the low "down payment." Based on this information, the criminals make fraudulent purchases, subsequently selling their purchases for cash.

Chat Rooms

Modern lifestyle does not allow parents to devote the necessary time for their children's supervision and guidance, leading to a gradual lack of communication. For their part, children love to send and receive messages and use chat rooms. In chat rooms, kids are looking to find the warmth, companionship and comfort they do not find within the family. However, there is no chat room without a *predator*, who will try to exploit the innocence of the youth. Unfortunately, *predators*, pretending to be teenagers, use chat rooms, social networking sites and other online communication sites to attract and abuse children.

Surprisingly, *predators* are usually people above suspicion, socially reputable, educated—scientists, teachers, entrepreneurs, and so on— often eminent, economically well-off, and usually with family of their own. Such individuals begin discussions with potential child-victims in order to develop a friendly relationship and to get as much information as possible about their personal lives—place of residence, interests, hobbies, etc. Discussions can take days, weeks, even months, until the *predator* gains the confidence of the child. Then, the predator slowly engages in conversations hoping that they lead into abusing the victim-child.

Trends in Cybercrime

Cyber Bullying

These are actions that take place over the Internet and are designed to intimidate and degrade a person from one or more individuals. Cyber bullying is usually found among minors, taking place through all modern online communications media—emails, social media, chat, instant messaging, etc.

Essentially, this is the mutation of traditional bullying. Sadly, the cyber version has been experiencing a worldwide upsurge in recent times, with incidents taking place mostly in school environments. Cyber bullying can take many forms, most of which are as follows:

- Sending of text, email, or instant messaging with offensive content (in instant messengers or chatrooms)
- Malicious photo posting on social networking sites, blogs or other websites for the sole purpose of harassment
- Dissemination of rumors and false facts for the purpose of defaming third parties in social media, blogs, websites, etc.
- Anonymous intimidating calls and messages.

Cyber bullying should not be viewed as an innocent joke among children, but as an act of severe adverse consequences on a child's life. Such consequences, which should alert parents and teachers include

- Absenteeism from school
- Abrupt drop in academic performance
- Performance of an act incompatible with prior behavior
- Commitment of illegal acts
- Desire of child to change own name
- Psychological depression
- Suicide thoughts or attempts.

Case Ten: In an elementary school a first-grade female student, A, was bullied by a classmate, B, who was threatening to post on the Web a naked picture of student A. The victim's academic performance was severely affected, attracting the attention of the school authorities, who investigated the incident and properly punished student B.

A survey carried out by the non-profit organization N.EO.I* in a sample of 422 children aged 13–18 (275 boys & 147 girls) found that:

- 16% of boys and 22% of girls aged 13–18 claimed that they have been victims of cyber bullying.
- 32% claimed that they had been intimidated by the publication of their personal photos on the Internet.
- 10% of boys responded positively to the question of whether they have been intimidated by a classmate, friend or acquaintance, through the Internet or other new technologies.
- 42% replied that they know or have heard about someone who has been the victim of bullying through the Internet and/or the new technologies.

Although the above statistics reflect the youth environment of Greece, where these data were available, the worldwide reality is far worse.

Suicides and Disappearances

A general concern about the role the Internet plays in the lives of its users stems from the suicide cases in which the Internet appears to have acted as a factor. Typical cases are suicides related to online gambling addictions.

> Case Eleven: In Greece, an 18-year-old student was found dead beside his computer, while the computer was online on a chat. On the screen there was a death recipe in an email from a person with a female name, giving him specific instructions as to what medicine to use to terminate his life.

Fortunately, there is a 24/7 online suicide prevention chat line that over the past years has apparently prevented well over a thousand possible suicides.

Worth mentioning is that, thanks to the Internet and the *footprints* left behind, numerous disappearance cases have been resolved.

---

* http://portal.kathimerini.gr/4Dcgi/4dcgi/_w_articles_kathworld_1_18/11/2009 _30864

Conclusion

In recent decades, technology has made large leaps, with new devices, new techniques, and new features. By now, computers and the Internet have become an integral part of our everyday life, have upgraded our life in infinite ways, and have made our activities much faster and easier. However, the same thing applies to criminal activities—they have become much faster and easier.

With the Internet having become a valuable and indispensable part of our everyday life, it would be wrong to demonize it on the pretense that it facilitates criminal activities. Through cybersecurity awareness training, we can protect ourselves from criminal traps and be extra suspicious toward *great offers*. It is a fact that we would avoid many Internet hackles if we knew some basic things about how to use it.

In closing, cybersecurity navigation is like navigating in the open seas, where specialized skills are required. Similarly, we all need to pursue some form of cybersecurity training, in order to have safe and pleasant Web navigation.

Exercises

1. Conduct Web research and write a four-page report on cyber-crime trends.
2. Conduct Web research and write a four-page report on recent legislation on cybercrime.
3. Conduct Web research and write a four-page report on child protection from Web predators.

Conclusion

References*

Chapter One

1. Making Security Measurable, http://measurablesecurity.mitre.org/.
2. One-Time-Password. Two Factor Authentication from Nordic Edge, http://www.nordicedge.se/en/products/one-time-password-server.
3. Weingart, Steve H., Using S'CAP to Detect Vulnerabilities, ATSEC Information Security Corp, http://www.atsec.com/downloads/pdf/UsingSCAP.pdf.
4. MITRE CVE List, http://cve.mitre.org/cve/index.html.
5. National Vulnerability Database, NVD, Version 2.2, http://web.nvd.nist.gov/view/ncp/repository.
6. Common Configuration Enumerator, CCE, http://cce.mitre.org/.
7. Common Platform Enumerator, CPE: Naming Example, http://cpe.mitre.org/images/naming.gif.
8. Common Vulnerability Scoring System, CVSS, http://nvd.nist.gov/cvss.cfm?version=2.
9. Common Vulnerability Scoring System, CVSS, Calculator, http://nvd.nist.gov/cvss.cfm?calculator&adv.
10. Specification for the Extensible Configuration Checklist Description Format, (XCCDF) Version 1.1.4, NIST, http://csrc.nist.gov/publications/nistir/ir7275r3/NISTIR-7275r3.pdf.
11. Open Vulnerability and Assessment Language, OVAL, http://oval.mitre.org/language/.

---

* All links accessible as of March 3, 2012.

12. Howard, Michael, and LeBlanc, David, *Writing Secure Code*, Microsoft Press ISBN-13: 978-0-7356-1722-3.

13. Shiralkar, Truptiand, and Grove, Brenda, Guidelines for Secure Coding, January 2009, http://www.atsec.com/downloads/pdf/secure-coding-guidelines.pdf.

14. Haugh, Eric, and Bishop, Matt, Testing C Programs for Buffer Overflow Vulnerabilities, http://www.isoc.org/isoc/conferences/ndss/03/proceedings/papers/8.pdf.

15. Wei, Tao et al., IntScope: Automatically Detecting Integer Overflow Vulnerability in X86 Binary Using Symbolic Execution, http://www.isoc.org/isoc/conferences/ndss/09/pdf/17.pdf.

16. Newsham, Tim. Guardent, Inc. Format String Attacks, September 2000, http://julianor.tripod.com/bc/tn-usfs.pdf.

17. Command Injection, https://www.owasp.org/index.php/Command_Injection.

18. Zuchlinski, Gavin, The Anatomy of Cross Site Scripting: Anatomy, Discovery, Attack, Exploitation, November 5, 2003, http://www.net-security.org/dl/articles/xss_anatomy.pdf.

19. SQL Injection Attacks by Example, Steve Friedl's Unixwiz.net Tech Tips, http://www.unixwiz.net/techtips/sql-injection.html.

20. Benoist, E., Insecure Direct Object Reference, Web Security, Summer Term 2008, http://electures.informatik.uni-freiburg.de/portal/download/111/6652/slidesInsecureDirectObjectReference.pdf.

21. Olzak, Tom, Improper Error Handling and Insecure Storage, Web Application Security, Part 8, August 2006, http://adventuresinsecurity.com/Papers/WebAppSecurity-ErrorsandStorage.pdf.

22. Schneier, Bruce, Security Pitfalls in Cryptography, http://www.schneier.com/essay-028.pdf.

23. Race Conditions and Mutual Exclusion, http://java.sun.com/developer/Books/performance2/chap3.pdf.

24. Hernan, Shawn et al., Microsoft, Uncover Security Design Flaws Using the STRIDE Approach, http://msdn.microsoft.com/en-us/magazine/cc163519.aspx.

25. Seacord, Robert, Secure Coding Initiative, Carnegie Mellon University, 2006, http://www.cert.org/secure-coding/content/seacord-secure-coding-initiative-cylab.pdf (p. 4).

26. Techniques and Tools for Software Analysis, Freescale Semiconductor, http://www.freescale.com/files/soft_dev_tools/doc/white_paper/CWTESTTECHCW.pdf.

27. Secure Coding Standard Development Guidelines, Software Engineering Institute, Carnegie Mellon University, https://www.securecoding.cert.org/confluence/display/sci/Secure+Coding+Standard+Development+Guidelines#.

28. Java Concurrency Guidelines, Software Engineering Institute, Carnegie Mellon University, http://www.sei.cmu.edu/reports/10tr015.pdf.

29. The CERT C Secure Coding Standard, Software Engineering Institute, Carnegie Mellon University, https://www.securecoding.cert.org/confluence /display/seccode/CERT+C+Secure+Coding+Standard.

30. The CERT C++ Secure Coding Standard, Software Engineering Institute, Carnegie Mellon University, https://www.securecoding.cert .org/confluence/pages/viewpage.action?pageId=637.

31. Vulnerability Notes Database, US-DHS-CERT, http://www.kb.cert .org/vuls/bypublished.

32. US-CERT Vulnerability Note VU#446012 on Microsoft Word, http:// www.kb.cert.org/vuls/id/446012.

33. Microsoft Security Bulletin MS06-027, http://www.microsoft.com /technet/security/Bulletin/MS06-027.mspx.

34. Vulnerability Notes Database, US-DHS-CERT, Sorted by severity metric, http://www.kb.cert.org/vuls/bymetric.

35. Dormann, W., and Rafail, J., Securing Your Web Browser, US-CERT CyLab Carnegie Mellon, http://www.cert.org/tech_tips /securing_browser/#why.

Chapter Two

1. Authentication in an Internet Banking Environment, FFIEC, http:// www.ffiec.gov/pdf/authentication_guidance.pdf.

2. PhoneFactor: Phone-Based Two-Factor Authentication, http://www .phonefactor.com/wp-content/pdfs/PhoneFactor-PhoneAuthentication .pdf.

3. One-Time-Password, OTP: Typically the OTP is sent to the user as an SMS via the user's mobile phone, http://www.nordicedge.se/en /products/one-time-password-server.

4. The Insider Threat to US Government Information Systems, http:// www.cnss.gov/Assets/pdf/nstissam_infosec_1-99.pdf.

5. Addressing the Insider Threat, Application Security, Inc., http://www .appsecinc.com/techdocs/whitepapers/Addressing-the-Insider-Threat -Fed.pdf.

6. The Insider Threat to Information Systems, http://www.pol-psych.com /sab.pdf.

7. National Training Standard for Designated Approving Authority (DAA), http://staff.washington.edu/dittrich/center/docs/nstissi_4012.pdf.

8. Global Positioning System, http://www.gps.gov/.

9. Warner, J., and Johnston, R., GPS Spoofing Countermeasures, http:// library.lanl.gov/cgi-bin/getfile?00852243.pdf.

10. 802.15 Working Group for Wireless—Personal Area Network, WPAN, http://standards.ieee.org/wireless/overview.html.

11. Bluetooth Security, ftp://wilbur.eng.auburn.edu/pub/avk0002/BE%20 Data/PAPERS/Ethical%20hacking/cybertrust_wp_bluetoothsecur.pdf.

12. Guide to Bluetooth Security, http://csrc.nist.gov/publications/nistpubs /800-121/SP800-121.pdf.

13. F-Secure First to Offer Full Protection to Smartphone S60, 3rd edition, http://www.f-secure.com/nl_BE/about-us/pressroom/news/2006 /fs_news_20061115_01_eng.html.

14. Bluetooth Networks: Risks & Defenses, http://www.airdefense.net /whitepapers/bluetooth_request.php.

15. Kostopoulos, George K., *Bluetooth in Mobile Telephony: Privacy and Security Issues*, Communications of the IBIMA (ISSN:978-0-9821489-1-4). 2009.

16. Wi-Fi: Wireless Fidelity, www.Wi-Fi.org.

17. 802.11 Working Group for Wireless Local Area Networks, http:// standards.ieee.org/wireless/overview.html.

18. Wi-Fi Alliance, WECA, http://www.weca.net/about_overview.php ?lang=en.

19. Wi-Fi Claims Lead in Wireless Standard Race, http://www.wireless newsfactor.com/perl/story/4805.html.

20. Category: 802.11n, http://wifinetnews.com/archives/cat_80211n.html.

21. Wi-Fi Glossary, http://www.wi-fi.org/glossary.php.

22. Quadrupling Wi-Fi Speeds with 802.11n, http://www.windowsfordevices .com/c/a/News/Quadrupling-WiFi-Speeds-with-80211n/.

23. Wireless Network Defense, http://www.windowsecurity.com/articles /WiFi-security-Part1.html.

24. WEP Cracking, http://cowifi.personalwireless.org/showthread.php?p=148.

25. Enable MAC Address Filtering on Wireless Access Points and Routers, http://compnetworking.about.com/cs/wirelessproducts/qt/macaddress .htm.

26. Free DLNA Analyzer, http://www.ethereal.com/introduction.html.

27. JiWire's Wi-Fi Hotspot Finder, http://v4.jiwire.com/search-hotspot -locations.htm.

28. JiWire's Wi-Fi Hotspot-Helper, http://hotspot-finder.ipass.com.

29. Using Windows Firewall, http://www.microsoft.com/windowsxp/using /networking/security/winfirewall.mspx.

30. Wi-Fi Watchdog Review, http://www.techworld.com/mobility/reviews /index.cfm?ReviewID=185.

31. 802.11w Fills Wireless Security Holes, http://www.networkworld.com /news/tech/2006/040306-80211w-wireless-security.html.

32. Toshiba Introduces New 4G WiMAX-Ready Laptops, http://us.toshiba .com/pressrelease/496206.

33. Intel WiMAX Adapters, http://www.intel.com/support/wireless/wmax /5350_5150/sb/CS-029552.htm.

34. Scarfone, K. et al., *Guide to Securing WiMAX Wireless Communications*, Special Publication 800-127, National Institute of Standards and Technology, US Department of Commerce.

35. Nazmus Sakib, A. K. M. et al., IEEE 802.16e Security Vulnerability: Analysis & Solution, *Global Journal of Computer Science and Technology*, Vol. 10, Issue 13, (Ver. 1.0), October 2010, http://globaljournals.org

/GJCST_Volume10/6-IEEE-802-16e-Security-Vulnerability-Analysis
-Solution.pdf.

36. Establishing Wireless Robust Security Networks: A Guide to IEEE
    802.11i, Special Publication 800-97, http://csrc.nist.gov/publications
    /nistpubs/800-97/SP800-97.pdf.

37. Guide to Securing Legacy IEEE 802.11 Wireless Networks, Special
    Publication 800-48 Revision 1, http://csrc.nist.gov/publications/nistpubs
    /800-48-rev1/SP800-48r1.pdf.

38. Guide to Securing WiMAX Wireless Communications, Special Publi-
    cation 800-127, http://csrc.nist.gov/publications/nistpubs/800-127/sp800
    -127.pdf.

39. Elastic Hosts. Cloud Computing Provider, http://www.elastichosts.com/.

40. Guidelines on Security and Privacy in Public Cloud Computing, http://
    csrc.nist.gov/publications/drafts/800-144/Draft-SP-800-144_cloud
    -computing.pdf.

Chapter Three

1. Defense in Depth, http://www.nsa.gov/ia/_files/support/defenseindepth
   .pdf.

2. Kelly Waters, Most IT Projects Fail. Will Yours? http://www.projectsmart
   .co.uk/pdf/most-it-projects-fail-will-yours.pdf.

3. Design of Complex Cyber Physical Systems with Formalized
   Architectural Patterns, https://agora.cs.illinois.edu/download/attachments
   /22843494/FormalizedArchitecture.pdf.

4. Managing Vulnerabilities in Networked Systems by Robert A. Martin,
   The MITRE Corp., http://cve.mitre.org/docs/docs-2001/CVEarticle
   IEEEcomputer.pdf.

5. National Vulnerability Database, http://nvd.nist.gov/home.cfm.

6. Tutorial on Defending Against SQL Injection Attacks, Oracle, http://
   download.oracle.com/oll/tutorials/SQLInjection/index.htm.

7. Privacy filters.
      http://www.secure-it.com/products/privacy_notebook.htm
      http://www.nextag.com/computer-monitor-privacy-screen/products
      -html

8. Laptop Tracking and Recovery.
      http://www.absolute.com/en/lojackforlaptops/home.aspx
      http://www.druva.com/safepoint/data-loss-prevention

9. Bluetooth Proximity Lock Solutions.
      http://www.coolest-gadgets.com/20090507/phonenix-technologies
      -unveil-bluetooth-proximity-lock-system/
      http://www.novell.com/coolsolutions/feature/18684.html

10. RFID Proximity Alarm.
      http://www.nonlethaldefense.com/proximityalarm.html
      http://www.thespyshop.com/product.sc?categoryId=10&product
      Id=222

11. File Encryption.
   http://www.file-encryption.net/
   http://www.encryptfiles.net/

12. Password Strength Testing.
   https://www.microsoft.com/security/pc-security/password-checker
   .aspx
   http://www.passwordmeter.com/
   http://www.securepasswords.net/site/TestPassword.html

13. Automatic Live Files Backup, http://www.atempo.com/products/live
   Backup/default.asp.

14. Best Practices for Keeping Your Home Network Secure, http://www
   .nsa.gov/ia/_files/factsheets/Best_Practices_Datasheets.pdf.

15. FISMA, Federal Information Security Management Act of 2002, csrc
   .nist.gov/drivers/documents/FISMA-final.pdf.

16. A Framework for Using Insurance for Cyber-Risk Management, http://
   www.mendeley.com/research/framework-using-insurance-cyberrisk
   -management/.

17. Cyber Risk Insurance, SANS Institute InfoSec Reading Room, http://
   www.sans.org/reading_room/whitepapers/legal/cyber-risk-insurance
   _1412.

18. Security and Privacy Insurance Application, http://www.axisins.com
   /docs/Cyber_Risk_App.pdf.

19. ISO/IEC 17799:2005 Information Technology—Security Techniques—
   Code of Practice for Information Security Management, http://www
   .iso.org/iso/catalogue_detail?csnumber=39612.

Chapter Four

1. Dalton, G. et al., Modeling Enterprise Security Architecture, Air
   Force Institute of Technology, http://www.dodccrp.org/events/11th
   _ICCRTS/html/presentations/020.pdf.

2. Cyber Defense Technology Networking and Evaluation, DETER, http://
   www.cs.berkeley.edu/~tygar/papers/Cyber_defense_tech_networking
   _and_eval.pdf.

3. DETER, cyber-DEfense Technology Experimental Research Laboratory Testbed, http://www.isi.edu/deter/.

4. Kostopoulos, G., *Denial of Service Countermeasures: Intelligence
   Development and Analysis at the Network Node Level*, Communications of
   the IBIMA (ISBN: 978-0-9821489-3-8), 2010.

5. ISO/IEC 17799:2005, http://www.iso.org/iso/catalogue_detail?csnumber
   =39612.

6. Electronic Data Shredding, http://www.datadomain.com/pdf/TechBrief
   -Electronic-Shredding.pdf.

7. Shred Deleted Files, http://www.pcmag.com/article2/0,2817,1159624,00
   .asp.

8. NIST Special Publication 800-88 Guidelines for Media Sanitization, http://csrc.nist.gov/publications/nistpubs/800-88/NISTSP800-88_rev1.pdf.

9. National Industrial Security Program—Operating Manual, http://www.dss.mil/documents/odaa/nispom2006-5220.pdf.

10. Encryption Methods. Finnish Communications Regulatory Authority, http://www.ficora.fi/en/index/palvelut/palvelutaiheittain/tietoturva/salausmenetelmat.html.

11. The Password Meter, http://www.passwordmeter.com/.

12. Password Tester, Safety & Security Center, Microsoft, https://www.microsoft.com/security/pc-security/password-checker.aspx.

13. Guide to Enterprise Password Management (Draft), NIST Special Publication 800-11, http://csrc.nist.gov/publications/drafts/800-118/draft-sp800-118.pdf.

14. Two Factor Authentication Features, http://nordicedge.com/products/one-time-password-server.

15. Ellison, R. J., and Woody, C., Survivability Analysis Framework, www.cert.org/archive/pdf/10tn013.pdf.

Chapter Five

1. Framework for the CIO Position, http://net.educause.edu/ir/library/pdf/ERM0465.pdf.

2. Five Skills You Need to Be CIO, http://www.zdnet.com/news/five-skills-you-need-to-be-cio/158281.

3. MBA in Information Systems, Georgia State University, http://www2.cis.gsu.edu/cis/program/mbacis.asp.

4. How to Become a CIO, http://blog.makingitclear.com/2005/12/13/howbecomecio.

5. Clinger-Cohen Act of 1996, http://www.cio.gov/Documents/it_management_reform_act_Feb_1996.html.

6. Why CIOs Should Clone Themselves, http://www.cio.com/article/688896/Why_CIOs_Should_Clone_Themselves.

7. Technology Professional Liability, http://www.baldwinandlyons.com/Root/Protective/ProtectiveSpecialty/technology_professional.aspx.

8. Identity and Access Management, http://www.onelogin.com/.

9. GSM Access Control, http://www.wireless-intercom.co.uk/gsmintercom.htm.

10. Cyber Awareness, http://www.wcboe.org/teachers/cmolnar/cyber_awareness.htm.

11. Cyber Security Awareness Online Training Course, DHS, http://www2.dir.state.tx.us/SiteCollectionDocuments/Security/Training/TEEX%20Cyber%20Awareness%20Flier.pdf.

12. Cyveillance Cyber Safety Awareness Training, http://www.cyveillance.com/web/solutions/cyber-safety-awareness-training.php.

13. NFPA 1600 Standard on Disaster/Emergency Management and Business Continuity Programs, http://www.nfpa.org/assets/files/pdf/nfpa1600.pdf.
14. SO/IEC 27002:2005 Information Technology—Security Techniques—Code of Practice for Information Security Management, http://www.iso27001security.com/html/27002.html.
15. Contingency Planning Guide for Information Technology Systems, NIST, http://www.drivesaversdatarecovery.com/images/pdf/sp800-34-rev1.pdf.
16. CIO 2.0, http://content.spencerstuart.com/sswebsite/pdf/lib/CIORoute09.pdf.

Chapter Six

1. ISO 17799 World, http://17799.macassistant.com/def.htm.
2. Business Continuity Planning, A White Paper, Upper Mohawk, Inc., http://www.uppermohawkinc.com/docs/business%20continuity.pdf.
3. Hackers Follow Microsoft Patches with Malware, http://www.computerworld.com/s/article/108825/Hackers_follow_Microsoft_patches_with_malware.
4. Cisco—Disaster Recovery: Best Practices White Paper, http://www.cisco.com/warp/public/63/disrec.pdf.
5. Disaster Recovery Planning—EDUCAUSE, http://net.educause.edu/ir/library/pdf/DEC0301.pdf.
6. Disaster Recovery Planning—Process & Options, http://www.comp-soln.com/DRP2_whitepaper.pdf.
7. Disaster Recovery Strategies, http://www.redbooks.ibm.com/redbooks/pdfs/sg246844.pdf.
8. Biometrics in Access Control, http://www.visualaccesssolutions.co.uk/accesscontrol.htm.
9. Mobile Telephony Access Control Technologies.
   http://www.mars-commerce.com
   http://www.text-lock.com/
10. ISO/IEC 27002:2005 Information Technology—Security Techniques—Code of Practice for Information Security Management, http://www.iso27001security.com/html/27002.html#Section6.
11. ISO 17799: What Is It?, http://www.computersecuritynow.com/what.htm.
    http://www.computersecuritynow.com/what.htm.

Chapter Seven

1. Guide to Intrusion Detection and Prevention Systems, NIST, http://csrc.nist.gov/publications/nistpubs/800-94/SP800-94.pdf.
2. García-Teodoro, P. et al., Anomaly-Based Network Intrusion Detection: Techniques, Systems and Challenges, http://ceres.ugr.es/~gmacia/papers/COMSEC09_AnidsPublishedVersion.pdf.

3. Kostopoulos, G. K. et al., Denial of Service Countermeasures: Intelligence Development and Analysis at the Network Node Level, http://www.kostopoulos.us/website/articles/cybersecurity-01.htm.

4. Gong, F., Deciphering Detection Techniques: Part II Anomaly-Based Intrusion Detection, McAfee Network Security Technologies Group, https://secure.mcafee.com/japan/products/pdf/Deciphering_Detection_Techniques-Anomaly-Based_Detection_WP_en.pdf.

5. Guide to Intrusion Detection and Prevention Systems, NIST, http://csrc.nist.gov/publications/nistpubs/800-94/SP800-94.pdf.

6. Frederick, Karen Kent, Network Intrusion Detection Signatures, Part Five, http://www.symantec.com/connect/articles/network-intrusion-detection-signatures-part-five.

7. Enterasys Dragon Network IDS Appliance (Fast Ethernet), http://www.enterasys.com/company/literature/dragon-idsips-ds.pdf.

8. IDPS Administrator's Console, Juniper Networks, http://www.juniper.net/techpubs/images/s036695.gif.

9. Kostopoulos, George K., Wi-Fi Security Precautions, http://www.kostopoulos.us/website/articles/wi-fi.htm.

Chapter Eight

1. File Transfer Protocol, http://filezilla-project.org.

2. Files Back Up, http://www.secondcopy.com/.

3. Disk Imaging Tools.
   http://www.drive-image.com/
   http://www.dubaron.com/diskimage/
   http://www.acronis.com
   http://www.laplink.com/
   http://www.seagate.com/support/discwizard/dw_ug.en.pdf
   http://www.thefreecountry.com/utilities/backupandimage.shtml

4. Files Backup and Disaster Recovery, http://technology.inc.com/2008/10/01/data-deduplication-for-disaster-recovery/.

5. Typical Disaster Recovery Configuration, http://www.intrapower.com.au/uploads/images/DisasterRecoveryv2.0.720.jpg.

6. Disaster Recovery Issues and Solutions, http://www.hds.com/assets/pdf/wp_117_02_disaster_recovery.pdf.

7. Shredding Algorithms, http://www.fileshredderpro.com/shredding-algorithms.html.

8. Disk Wipe, http://www.diskwipe.org.

9. File Undelete Tools.
   http://www.snapfiles.com/downloads/recuva/dlrecuva.html
   http://ntfsundelete.com/http://undelete-360.en.softonic.com/

10. MEO Encryption Application, http://www.nchsoftware.com/encrypt/index.html.

11. TRUECRYPT Virtual Encrypted Drive, http://www.snapfiles.com/get/TrueCrypt.html.

12. Data Manager, http://www.drpupcdatamanager.com/.
13. SPECTOR PRO, http://www.spectorsoft.com/products/SpectorPro_Windows/index.asp.
14. Registry Repair Wizard, http://www.registryrepair.net.
15. Key Scrambler by QFX Software Corporation, http://www.qfxsoftware.com/download/whats-new.htm?ver=2.8.2.0.
16. AVG Anti-Virus FREE 2012, http://www.avg.com/eu-en/free-antivirus-download.
17. Rootkit Scanning, Detection, and Removal, http://www.sophos.com/en-us/products/free-tools/sophos-anti-rootkit.aspx.
18. Hard Disk Fragmentation, IBM, http://www-10.lotus.com/ldd/dominowiki.nsf/dx/01152009062114PMWEBVDT.htm.
19. Junk Files Cleaner, http://www.digeus.com/products/junkcleaner/index.html.
20. Microsoft Baseline Security Analyzer 2.2 (for IT Professionals), http://www.microsoft.com/download/en/details.aspx?id=7558.
21. Password Meters.
    http://www.passwordmeter.com/
    http://www.yetanotherpasswordmeter.com/
    http://www.geekwisdom.com/dyn/passwdmeter
22. Password Storage Locations For Popular Windows Applications, http://www.nirsoft.net/articles/saved_password_location.html.
23. Cain and Abel, http://www.oxid.it.
24. Benefits of a Firewall, Intrapower, http://www.intrapower.com.au/Firewall.html.
25. SaaS Email Security Suites, https://www.mcafeeasap.com/MarketingContent/Products/SaaSEmailSecurity.aspx.
26. Email Protection Vicomsoft, http://www.vicomsoft.com/services/email-security/features-benefits/.
27. Email Protection, http://www.compcenter.com/businessedge_Email.cfm.

Chapter Nine

1. Draft Convention on Cybercrime, Council of Europe, http://assembly.coe.int//Mainf.asp?link=http://assembly.coe.int/Documents/AdoptedText/ta01/eopi226.htm#_ftn1.
2. Convention on Cybercrime, Council of Europe, Budapest, Hungary, 2001, http://conventions.coe.int/Treaty/en/Treaties/Html/185.htm.
3. Signatories to the Convention on Cybercrime, Council of Europe, http://conventions.coe.int/Treaty/Commun/ChercheSig.asp?NT=185&CL=ENG.
4. Additional Protocol to the Convention on Cybercrime, Council of Europe, Strasbourg, France, 2006, http://conventions.coe.int/Treaty/en/Treaties/Html/189.htm.

5. Convention on Cybercrime: The Treaty Document—A Proposal. Twelfth United Nations Congress on Crime Prevention and Criminal Justice, Salvador, Brazil, 2010, http://www.cybercrimelaw.net/documents /UN_12th_Crime_Congress.pdf.

6. International Criminal Court, http://www.icc-cpi.int/Menus/ICC.

7. Europol, https://www.europol.europa.eu.

8. The North Atlantic Treaty Organization, http://www.nato.int.

9. Tikk, Eneken, Global Cyber Security—Thinking about the Niche for NATO, http://www.ccdcoe.org/articles/2010/Tikk_GlobalCyberSecurity .pdf.

10. Active Engagement, Modern Defence, http://www.nato.int/cps/en/natolive /official_texts_68580.htm#cyber.

11. NATO Cooperative Cyber Defence Centre of Excellence, Tallinn, Estonia, http://www.ccdcoe.org/.

12. Tikk, Eneken, Ten Rules for Cyber Security, http://www.ccdcoe.org /articles/2011/Tikk_TenRulesForCyberSecurity.pdf.

13. INTERPOL, International Police Departments Association, http:// www.interpol.int.

14. Cyber Security Threats, INTERPOL Seminar, https://www.interpol .int/Public/ICPO/PressReleases/PR2011/News20110707.asp.

15. The Commercial Privacy Bill of Rights Act of 2011, http://kerry.senate .gov/imo/media/doc/Commercial%20Privacy%20Bill%20of%20Rights %20Text.pdf.

16. The Cybersecurity Act of 2010, http://frwebgate.access.gpo.gov/cgi-bin /getdoc.cgi?dbname=111_cong_bills&docid=f:s773rs.txt.pdf.

17. The Federal Information Security Management Act of 2002, http:// www.marcorsys-com.usmc.mil/sites/pmia%20documents/documents /Federal%20Information%20Security%20Management%20Act%20 (FISMA).htm.

18. FISMA Purposes, Legal Information Institute, Cornell University Law School, http://www.law.cornell.edu/uscode/44/3541.html.

19. SEC 2011 FISMA Report, http://www.sec-oig.gov/Reports/Audits Inspections/2011/489.pdf.

20. The Patriot Act of 2002, http://epic.org/privacy/terrorism/hr3162.html.

21. USA Patriot Act, http://www.aclu.org/national-security/usa-patriot-act.

22. Communications Assistance for Law Enforcement Act.
    http://transition.fcc.gov/calea/
    http://www.askcalea.net/calea/103.html
    http://www.askcalea.net/docs/calea.pdf

23. CALEA Concern by the ACLU, http://www.aclu.org/technology-and -liberty/calea-feature-page.

24. Computer Security Act of 1987, http://www.nist.gov/cfo/legislation /Public%20 Law%20100-235.pdf.

25. The Federal Information Security Management Act (FISMA), http:// csrc.nist.gov/groups/SMA/fisma/index.html.

26. The Privacy Act of 1974, http://www.justice.gov/opcl/privstat.htm.

27. FBI 2009 Cybercrime Statistics, ScamFraudAlert Blog, http://scam fraudalert.wordpress.com/2010/03/13/fbi-2009-cybercrime-statistics/.

28. Cyber Crime: A Clear and Present Danger, Deloitte, http://www .deloitte.com/view/en_GX/global/insights/thought-leadership /c2ac85e761e58210VgnVCM100000ba-42f00aRCRD.htm.

29. Investigations on a Cybercrime Hub in Estonia, http://blog.trendmicro .com/investigations-on-a-cybercrime-hub-in-Estonia.

30. Best Practices for Designing Mobile Touch Screen Applications, User Centric News, http://www.usercentric.com/news/2011/06/15/best-practices -designing-mobile-touch-screen-applications.

31. Mobile Application Design and Development, http://www.slideshare .net/ronnieliew/mobile-application-design-development-5465097.

32. Towards a Handbook for User-Centred Mobile Application Design, http://drops.dagstuhl.de/opus/volltexte/2005/166/pdf/04441.SWM3 .Paper.166.pdf.

33. Cybercriminals Target Online Banking Customers, M86 Security Lab, http://www.m86security.com/documents/pdfs/security_labs/cybercriminals _target_online_banking.pdf.

34. Brightmail Product Family, Symantec, http://www.symantec.com/business /products/family.jsp?familyid=brightmail.

35. One-Time-Passwords, OTP, Nordic Edge, Inc., http://www.nordicedge .se.

36. BullGuard Mobile Security 10, http://www.bullguard.com/products /bullguard-mobile-security-10.aspx.

37. A Good Decade for Cybercrime, McAfee, http://www.mcafee.com/us /resources/reports/rp-good-decade-for-cybercrime.pdf.

38. Cyber Crime Protection, http://www.safechecks.com/products/pdf/cyber _crime.pdf.

Chapter Ten

1. Enabling Distributed Security in Cyberspace, Department of Homeland Security, http://www.dhs.gov/xlibrary/assets/nppd-cyber-ecosystem-white -paper-03-23-2011.pdf.

2. Denial of Service Countermeasures: Intelligence Development and Analysis at the Network Node Level, http://www.kostopoulos.us/website /articles/cybersecurity-01.htm.

3. Cornish, P. et al., On Cyber Warfare, Chatham House, http://www .chathamhouse.org/sites/default/files/public/Research/International %20Security/r1110_cyberwarfare.pdf.

4. Jane's DS Forecast on Cybersecurity, http://www.janes.com/images /JDSF_Cyber_Operations_Market.pdf.

5. Cyberwarfare, CRS Report for Congress, http://www.fas.org/irp/crs /RL30735.pdf.

6. Tsymbal, V. I., "Kontseptsiya 'Informatsionnoy voyny,'" (Concept of Information Warfare), speech given at the Russian–US conference on "Evolving post Cold War National Security Issues," Moscow, 12–14 Sept. 1995, p. 7, Cited in Col. Timothy Thomas, "Russian Views on Information-Based Warfare." paper published in a special issue of *Airpower Journal*, July 1996.

7. China Confirms Deployment of Online Army, http://www.chinadaily.com.cn/china/2011-05/26/content_12583698.htm.

8. Siberian Pipeline Sabotage, Video, http://wn.com/Siberian_pipeline_sabotage.

9. Dickman, Frank, Hacking the Industrial SCADA Network, November 2009, Vol. 236, No. 11, http://www.pipelineandgasjournal.com/hacking-industrial-scada-network.

10. Russel, Alec, CIA Plot Led to Huge Blast in Siberian Gas Pipeline, 28 Feb. 2004, http://www.telegraph.co.uk/news/worldnews/northamerica/usa/1455559/CIA-plot-led-to-huge-blast-in-Siberian-gas-pipeline.html.

11. Raised Doubts. Moscow Times, http://en.wikipedia.org/wiki/Siberian_pipeline_sabotage#Raised_doubts.

12. Pipeline SCADA, http://images.ookaboo.com/photo/m/Pipeline_Scada_m.jpg.

13. Geers, Kenneth, Cyber Weapons Convention, http://www.ccdcoe.org/articles/2010/Geers_CyberWeaponsConvention.pdf.

14. Gordon, Sarah, Cyberterrorism? Symantec, http://www.symantec.com/avcenter/reference/cyberterrorism.pdf.

15. Distributed Internet-Based Load Altering Attacks Against Smart Power Grids, http://www.webpages.ttu.edu/amohseni/MRLGjTSG11.pdf.

16. Staged Cyber Attack Reveals Vulnerability in Power Grid, http://www.youtube.com/watch?v=fJyWngDco3g.

17. Mouse Click Could Plunge City into Darkness, Experts Say, http://www.cnn.com/2007/US/09/27/power.at.risk/index.html.

18. Richard Clarke: Disconnect Electrical Grid from Internet, http://www.youtube.com/watch?v=78wIaRL89Zk&feature=related.

19. Cyberterrorism: The Next Arena of Confrontation, http://www.kostopoulos.us/website/articles/cyberterrorism.htm.

20. New Cyber Attacks Will Target Power Grids and Major Public Works, http://crisisboom.com/2011/09/15/new-cyber-attacks-will-target-power-grids-and-major-public-works/.

21. Exclusive: Operation Shady RAT—Unprecedented Cyber-Espionage Campaign and Intellectual-Property Bonanza, http://www.vanityfair.com/culture/features/2011/09/operation-shady-rat-201109.

22. Messmer, Ellen, Cyber Espionage Seen as Growing Threat to Business, Government, Network World, http://www.networkworld.com/news/2008/011708-cyberespionage.html.

23. Homeland Security Act of 2002, http://www.dhs.gov/xabout/laws/law_regulation_rule_0011.shtm.

24. DHS. Who Became Part of the Department? http://www.dhs.gov/xabout/history/editorial_0133.shtm.
25. DHS Organizational Chart, http://www.dhs.gov/xabout/structure/editorial_0644.shtm.
26. Ministry of Homeland Security, http://www.ministryofhomelandsecurity.us/index.shtml.
27. DHS National Cyber Security Division, http://www.dhs.gov/xabout/structure/editorial_0839.shtm.
28. United States Computer Emergency Readiness Team, US-CERT, Reporting a Cyber Incident, https://forms.us-cert.gov/report/.
29. Ballentstedt, Britanny, Nextgov. Tougher Standards for Cyber Training?, http://wired-workplace.nextgov.com/2010/06/tougher_standards_for_cyber_training.php.
30. US-CERT Sign Up to Cybersecurity Alerts, http://www.us-cert.gov/cas/signup.html.
31. Privacy Impact Assessment, Department of Homeland Security, December 11, 2008, http://www.dhs.gov/xlibrary/assets/privacy/privacy_pia_ia_slrfci.pdf.
32. Measuring Cyber Security and Information Assurance State-of-the-Art Report (SOAR), http://iac.dtic.mil/iatac/download/cybersecurity.pdf.
33. Using Security Metrics to Assess Risk Management Capabilities, http://csrc.gov/nissc/1999/proceeding/papers/p29.pdf.
34. Payne, Shirley C., A Guide to Security Metrics, SANS Security Essentials, http://www.sans.org/reading_room/whitepapers/auditing/guide-security-metrics_55.
35. Enabling Distributed Security in Cyberspace, Department of Homeland Security, http://www.dhs.gov/xlibrary/assets/nppd-cyber-ecosystem-white-paper-03-23-2011.pdf.
36. Cyber Warfare Simulation and Firewall Testing, BreakingPoint Systems, Inc., http://www.breakingpointsystems.com/cyber-tomography-products/breakingpoint-firestorm-ctm/.
37. Cyber Warfare, http://www.scalable-networks.com/content/solutions/cyber-warfare.
38. Cyber Endeavour, http://cyberendeavour.com/.
39. Fact Sheet: Cyber Storm Exercise, http://www.dhs.gov/xnews/releases/pr_1158340980371.shtm.
40. Pan-European Cyber Security Exercise, 'CYBER EUROPE 2010,' http://www.enisa.europa.eu/media/news-items/faqs-cyber-europe-2010-final.

Index